HIGHER THAN EVEREST

HIGHER THAN EVEREST

MEMOIRS OF A MOUNTAINEER

Major HPS Ahluwalia

NIYOGI BOOKS

Published by
NIYOGI BOOKS
D-78, Okhla Industrial Area, Phase-I
New Delhi-110 020, INDIA
Tel: 91-11-26816301, 49327000
Fax: 91-11-26810483, 26813830
email: niyogibooks@gmail.com
website: www.niyogibooksindia.com

Editor: Gita Rajan
Design: Shashi Bhushan Prasad
Cover Design: Bhanu Pratap

ISBN: 978-93-85285-26-4
Publication: 2016

Printed at: Niyogi Offset Pvt. Ltd., New Delhi, India

Contents

Foreword

Although I was born on one of the flattest plains of the world, I have always regarded myself as a child of the mountains. Not merely because that is where my ancestors belonged, but because I feel more at home there and they seem to fulfil an emotional need, if I may borrow Justice G.D. Khosla's phrase.

It is difficult to pinpoint the reason underlying any emotion. What do I see in the mountains – beauty of landscape, purity of air, solitude or the greater challenge to one's endurance and resourcefulness? Perhaps all these and something more. On the plains one is surrounded by the works of man and consequently full of the importance of human beings. The heights give another perspective – man is but an insignificant speck, dwarfed by the giant forces of nature.

Whatever the reason, I love all mountains. What fun it is to run up and down the hills. How soothing to the eye is the cool green of the higher, forest-clothed ones, heady with scents of pine and a myriad other trees and plants, where one must make one's own path. No less attractive are the many and ever-changing hues of the barren rocks, so stark and strong. And, of course, there are the majestic snow-covered peaks, glistening gold and silver in the sunshine or coyly veiled with wisps of cloud. I never cease to be

FACING PAGE: Lhotse Face, Mount Everest

astonished and delighted at the sight of wild flowers in the high mountains, their tiny colourful heads peering out of unlikely nooks and crevices, tenaciously defying the most inhospitable elements.

Major Ahluwalia has the distinction of belonging to a select band of men – the few who have stood atop the highest peak in the world – Mount Everest. He has distinguished himself equally on the field of battle in defence of our country. Courage has many faces. The manner in which Major Ahluwalia faced his long and dreary treatment and convalescence called for the same grit and perseverance.

Major Ahluwalia now shares with us the hardships and the pain, the exhilaration of success and the understandable periods of depression. To his other accomplishments he adds that of authorship. I especially enjoyed his description of the Everest expedition.

New Delhi
12 March 1973

(Indira Gandhi)

Preface to the First Edition

This book is not an official account of the Indian Everest Expedition of 1965, which has already appeared in *Nine Atop Everest*. It is an autobiography with a somewhat detailed description of my own role in the expedition.

Let me clarify at the outset that I have no pretensions to being a writer and when someone suggested that I should write such a book I was inclined to treat the suggestion lightly. But later, at the insistence of friends and relations, I began to put my experience on paper and about four years labour resulted in this book. I am conscious that not all facets of my life will be of equal interest to the reader but I hope he or she will find the narrative interesting as a whole and perhaps not lacking in inspiration.

I take this opportunity to express my deep debt to HC Sarin. He has been my friend, guide and mentor throughout. He has helped me greatly in my rehabilitation and it would not have been possible for me to undertake this project without his active interest and assistance. He has gone through every word of the manuscript and has made innumerable improvements.

There are several other friends who have helped me in numerous ways. Frank Moraes, Dom Moraes and Marilyn Silverstone made many useful suggestions regarding the writing, titling and layout of the book. Lt Gen. Har Prasad was kind enough to scrutinise the chapters relating to military affairs. Dr JJ Walsh and Maureen Pouyoucas made a similar scrutiny of the chapters relating to Stoke Mandeville Hospital. Captain Vijay Kumar made various useful suggestions which have improved the book. Barbara Farr compiled the history of Wendover for me. Dolly Ahluwalia, my sister-in-law, gave up much of her leisure to take down and type my notes from time to time.

I am thankful to Melville de Mellow for allowing me to use his radio script, 'The Concept of Courage,' and Derek Standen of Stoke Mandeville, Lt Col GS Pablay, PRS Pillay and KS Kulkarni for supplying me the necessary photographs, Cdr MS Kohli, AVSM, and Air India International facilitated my trip to the UK and back. My rehabilitation has been eased by the valuable assistance of RM Mazumdar, Director General Ordnance Factories, and R Srinivasan. Lt Gen. C Sundara Rao, DEME, and the officers and men of the Corps of Electrical and Mechanical Engineering were a constant support to me.

I am also grateful to VS Nanda, former Managing Editor of *Span* magazine, who edited the entire manuscript.

To these and many other friends I am indebted for any merits the book may possess. For any errors, drawbacks or deficiencies, the responsibility is solely mine.

New Delhi
1973

(HPS Ahluwalia)

Preface

There has been an inexplicable gap between the last edition of the book and the present one. I feel happy that many children and adults including some from overseas corresponded with the publishers and with me to share with us the inspiration they drew after reading *Higher Than Everest.* The book ran into several reprints, was translated into major Indian languages and was adapted for a children's book for compulsory reading in classes V, VI and VII. Most of all was the success of the Russian translation which sold out fifty thousand copies within seven days. Then for reasons of change in publishing rights and my involvement with various activities that constitute daily living, there was a gap. I feel very happy that I have the chance now to share the joys of living with all my friends.

It is forty years since I wrote *Higher Than Everest.* Life goes on and does not end, no matter what the distress or the disability. This is what I have learnt from climbing Mt. Everest and then negotiating the route down to the base camp. These years have been as much packed with adventure and drama as any person's who decides to live life to its fullest.

It is not as if these years have been a constant saga of success and achievement. Like every person's life there are ups and downs, successes and failures and joys and despair. My job

View of Everest North Face

as Deputy Director General in the Ordnance Factories Board, Ministry of Defence kept me occupied and busy. I have been able to always keep myself involved in adventure activities which I feel is the best and noblest way to stay young at heart and fresh in the mind.

The notable feature was my determination to start a rehabilitation centre for the spinal injured in India. This dream became a vision and reality when the Prime Minister Shri Rajiv Gandhi laid the foundation of the Indian Spinal Injuries Centre on 30th March 1989. The work of the Hospital began in full swing. I have given a detailed account on this in Chapter 10 titled, 'A Long-Cherished Dream Fulfilled.'

Meanwhile, there was a restlessness in me. I wanted to know what lay on the other side of the mountain. What were the people like, the flora and the fauna. I am fortunate that I got the opportunity to go to the other side and be on the northern side of Mt. Everest. How I did it is the story of the *Silk Route Expedition*, which you can read about in Chapter 9.

I wish to extend my gratitude to Sunita Khosla, Ishika Ahluwalia and Col N.K. Bhimwal for editing and placement of the photographs in the chapter 'A Long Cherished Dream Fulfilled.' I also wish to thank Bhanu Pratap for designing the cover of the book.

I am thankful to Deepa Bisht for her excellent secretarial service and last but not the least Bikash Niyogi for his effort in the production of the book and supporting me throughout this endeavour.

Indian Spinal Injuries centre
Sector 'C', Vasant Kunj,
New Delhi-110070
10 April 2016

HPS Ahluwalia

End of a Long Dream

I woke to darkness in a strange room. Consciousness returned slowly and fitfully. The present and the past mixed together in an unreal kaleidoscope. I dreamt of Gulmarg in Kashmir and its snowy mountain slopes where I skied and laughed the hours away. Then the summit of Mount Everest which I scaled a few months earlier. Was it only a few months ago? It seemed an age away. The scene changed quickly yet again, to my detachment in some lonely picket where I was briefing my boys for a night patrol or ambush. Then I saw myself in a jeep, bumping down a lonely, endless road swallowed by darkness and distance.

Always there would be the darkness and the mist, like coils of smoke in a room, and they would blot out the scene, leaving only a deep, meaningless void. When finally the mists cleared and I opened my eyes on 15 October 1965 – that was the date as I discovered later – there were three people at my bedside. There was my mother who was in tears, HC Sarin who was closely connected with the Everest expedition and Narinder Kumar who had been the deputy leader of the expedition.

I was puzzled to see my mother crying. Not yet aware of my own serious condition, I wondered if there had been some tragedy in the family. Sarin, his chin cupped in his palm was looking at

FACING PAGE: The road across the Himalayan range connecting Nyalmo with Zhangmu at the border of Tibet and Nepal

me thoughtfully. I could not understand why he did not speak to me. When I tried to speak to them, I found that I could not utter a word. I then tried to signal to them but discovered I could not lift my right arm. Terribly frustrated and not knowing how to communicate with my mother and friends, I closed my eyes to black out everything around me and to give myself time to think.

When I reopened my eyes a few minutes later, my visitors had gone but a nurse stood above me. Soon I realised that there was a tube fastened to my nose and that the nurse was pouring a liquid into it with a syringe. I could feel the liquid pouring through my nose into my throat, and as I swallowed it I had a feeling of renewed energy. But I could not understand why I was being fed in this novel fashion.

A full awareness of the situation slowly dawned on me. The nurse had left but another group of friends and relatives were in the room. I dimly recognised them but could not recall everyone's name or relationship with me. I did recognise my two sisters and my fiancée who was wearing a white sari and sobbing quietly. I had a strong desire to hold my fiancée's hands but all I could do was to nod my head in a vain attempt to reassure her that I was all right. More visitors now came into my room. They talked to one another in whispers. Now and then some people would ask me how I felt. This was rather a pointless question since I could not reply.

During the night I attempted once more to recall what had happened to me. The events of the last few months when I had climbed the Everest were still clear in my memory. I could see the faces of the friends who had climbed with me and I vividly recalled the view from the summit of Everest and the sense of exhilaration and achievement which filled them. But nothing more recent came to my mind. It was only during the long and lonely days of slow and painful recovery which followed that I was able to recall what had happened to me since that fateful evening of 30 September 1965, when I had stood on that dark road in Kashmir.

The Indo-Pakistan was had just ended and a cease-fire had been declared. I was on the battlefront in the Sonamarg area with other officers. Captain Jal Master from the Parachute Regiment was the first face that flashed before me in those drowsy days. He had a very pleasant personality. Although I came to know him only when I joined the school, his cheerful disposition was always a welcome diversion in those gloomy days.

Major Surat Singh, Captain Jal Master and I were returning to our base late one afternoon. Suddenly there was the crack of a bullet and I fell down. As I discovered later, the bullet had hit me in the neck. Following my collapse, I was put on a stretcher and taken by ambulance to the Base Hospital in Srinagar. I recalled that the journey to Srinagar was a nightmare. Dr Roy, Major Vasudev and my batman, Sher Singh, rode with me in the ambulance. I kept lapsing into unconsciousness from time to time, and, whenever I was conscious, I felt my body burning with fever and a great thirst. I shouted in Punjabi, 'Pani! Pani!' (water) and Dr Roy or Sher Singh would dip a piece of cotton-wool into water and press it into my mouth. During the bumpy ride in the ambulance and in my semi-conscious state, I would also occasionally shout a warning against enemy infiltrators into the area.

During the five-hour journey to Srinagar I had lost an immense amount of blood. Dr Roy and Major Vasudev said later it was a miracle that I survived. When I regained consciousness in the Srinagar hospital, blood and glucose were being pumped into my veins. I was breathing hard and the bed rocked to and fro with my laboured breathing. Among my visitors was an aunt of mine who produced a picture of Guru Nanak which she placed under my pillow. 'The Guru will look after you,' she said, as she burst into tears. At this time I may have been able to speak a little but the effort was painful and the doctor warned me not to speak. I was in the Srinagar hospital for two days although it seemed to me at the time that I had been there for only a few hours.

I had now to be flown to a hospital in Delhi, and was taken on a stretcher to the airport where an Air Force plane awaited me.

While waiting on the runway for the plane to take off, I had one of my brief spells of consciousness and overheard snatches of conversation between the pilot and one of the medical officers. 'Because of the bad weather conditions it might not be possible to take off,' said the pilot. But the doctor said, 'It is essential that Major Ahluwalia be flown to Delhi today. Otherwise it might be too late.' Before I could grasp the importance of this conversation I had lost consciousness again. When I revived we were in the air as the pilot had taken advantage of a momentary gap in the clouds. I felt extremely sick and when the doctor in charge tried to put an oxygen mask on me, I could not control my nausea and vomited on his clothes. I tried to show that I was sorry by shaking my head. However, the doctor did not seem to mind and said, 'Don't worry, please.' He wiped my face with his handkerchief.

Now I was in a hospital in Delhi. I recalled the period of great heat during which my temperature rose to 105 degrees, and the periods of cold and semi-consciousness. I was given water through wet cotton pressed into my mouth and sponged constantly with cold water by a nurse. For some reason this attention from the nurse annoyed me and I felt she was trying to shatter a dream from which I did not wish to awake. Sometimes I thought I must have had an accident when descending from the summit. I wondered why Rawat and Phu Dorji, who had climbed with me, were not trying to help me. But vaguely I hoped that I would recover very soon and would be on the mountains once more in the coming summer.

The doctors decided that I should have an operation. The operation, a tracheotomy – making an opening in the windpipe – was performed by General Joseph, an eminent surgeon and head of the surgical department at Military Hospital, who was assisted by a team of able doctors. After this operation I felt a little more comfortable and could move my arms, though with great difficulty. But I realised the seriousness of my condition and knew that complete recovery would never be possible. An essential part of my treatment from now on was a course of injections. I had an injection every two or three hours. Slowly sensation came back to my arms, but this caused acute pain in my fingers and wrists. I still had to spend all my time lying in bed and felt quite frustrated and helpless. My chest was full of blood clots which made it difficult for me to breathe. The doctors solved this problem by inserting a tube into the trachea and attaching the other end of the tube to a jar equipped with a small motor.

When the motor started, the blood clots were sucked out from the windpipe into the jar. This was an extremely unpleasant process and I disliked it intensely. In addition to the 'sucker,' as it was called, the doctors also gave me hot steam treatment. A steam jacket was fitted onto my chest and face twice a day so that the blood clots could be softened and sucked more easily out of my windpipe. During the treatment my temperature rose to an uncomfortable 105 degrees but afterwards I was given a cold sponge bath and the temperature decreased. This process continued for ten days and my chest was cleared of the blood clots. My breathing improved.

Another step forward in my progress was my ability to swallow fruit juices through the mouth instead of being fed by tube. I tried to take in as much fluid as possible but evidently my initial attempts were not up to the mark as the nurse wished to use the tube once more. I hated tube-feeding and wished to avoid it at any cost, so I redoubled my efforts at swallowing by mouth and was apparently able to satisfy the doctors since the tube was not brought again.

There were other things I could not achieve. For example, much as I wanted to speak, I could not make myself intelligible to those near me. The opening in my windpipe distorted all the words I uttered. On one occasion, feeling the need for a softer pillow, I tried to ask for a Dunlopillo cushion, but nobody could understand me. It was a small request but important to me and I wept with anger and frustration when no one could make out what I wanted. Eventually after nearly two hours I succeeded in communicating my message by a peculiar speech-cum-gesture code. Somi, my younger brother, repeated the letters of the alphabet one after the other and I nodded my head each time he uttered the correct letter, till we had spelt out the words I was trying to say.

This communication problem did not last very long as the tracheotomy was taken out and the wound was dressed. It healed quickly and I was soon able to speak. I was overjoyed but even now I could not talk for very long since I was weak and would faint with the exertion.

My diet had hitherto consisted of fluids only, but I was slowly put on solid foods. Difficult to digest at first, my system gradually got used to it. But a new complication set in when I developed a urine infection accompanied by high fever. To combat this I had to take some fifty tablets of various drugs a day, and also two pethidine tablets to make me sleep. The sleep inducing tablets were effective at first but I soon got inured to them and the doses had to be increased. Pethidine injections were substituted for tablets but these too worked only for a time and I began to pass sleepless, restless nights. The insomnia was a problem for the doctors but it was even more a problem for me. I wondered if I had become addicted to drugs and would I ever be able to give them up. One day my mother brought in a homoeopathic doctor. He produced a vial of colourless liquid and said, 'Please take twelve drops – neither more nor less – this will make you sleep.' I took the nightly dose as prescribed and after taking it for two nights I found that I was sleeping even better than I had done with the drugs. When I met the homeopathic doctor two years later, I complimented him on the efficacy of the marvellous medicine he had prescribed for me. To my amazement he said, 'The phial I had given you contained nothing but water.'

The routine of my days in hospital followed a fixed pattern of treatment and visits from my family, my fiancée and my friends. My mother would be the first to arrive, at about 7:00 am. Since she lived quite a long way from the hospital, it was inconvenient for her to come so early but whenever I remonstrated she refused to listen to me. Although I felt guilty for putting her to such inconvenience, it was always a comfort for me to see her. My fiancée would come in the late afternoon and spend four or five hours by my bedside. She would read to me from a book or magazine or she would describe the plot of a film she had recently seen. But often there would be long spells of silence between us, and I felt that this silent communication was as important as our conversation in revealing to me new facets of her personality.

Among my other visitors was Narinder Kumar who brought a friend of his to see me. The friend said he had been very sorry to hear about my accident and asked Kumar if my faculty of speech had been restored. This irritated me and wishing to avoid further questions I merely smiled and kept quiet. When Kumar said that I could speak, the friend enquired if my brain was damaged. This annoyed me even more and I felt inclined to ask the inquisitive gentleman if he had any mathematical problem for me to solve. It has always seemed to me that to bestow sympathy and pity indiscriminately on those who do not want it does more harm rather than good. Such sentimental platitudes carry very little sincerity or conviction and are often counter-productive.

In contrast, there was my batman, Sher Singh. He is not educated and I expected him to utter the usual trite phrases of sympathy. But he did nothing of the kind. 'You have not lost anything,' he told me. 'A Sikh is alive even after his head has been cut off.' He narrated to me the story of Baba Deep Singh, one of our Gurus, whose head was cut off during a battle. Undeterred, he took his severed head in one hand and fought on with the other. He won the battle and returned to Amritsar where he fell at last in the Golden Temple. This story left an indelible impression on my mind and provided inspiration in the difficult days that lay ahead.

One of my visitors was my relative Major Kulvinder Singh, a patient in the same hospital. He had been wounded too but was recovering rapidly. He brought me some information about new

Indian Army rules. He told me that the Army had agreed to pay us full salary during our treatment and convalescence and had plans to rehabilitate us. I was regularly visited by Sarin's son Guppy. He was studying in college and would make it a point to give me all the interesting news of the town, particularly of the movies being shown at the time.

Republic Day, 26 January, is an important day in the history of independent India. On that day Delhi is the venue of an impressive parade in which Army and civil units take part. This time the successful Indian Everest team was also invited to participate. I longed to see my team mates in the parade and asked for a television set to be installed in my room. Unfortunately this was not possible and I was not well enough to be moved to one of the larger wards. So I missed seeing my comrades in the parade, going past the saluting base where the President of India acknowledged their achievements, past India Gate, the memorial to war heroes, past Connaught Place, Delhi's well-known business centre, and on to the Red Fort which enshrines so much of Indian history.

But there was a wonderful surprise in store for me. In the afternoon I heard the sound of cars being parked outside my room, and a moment later my Everest friends came crowding around my bedside. The parade was over and they had made my hospital their first port of call after the event. Among them were Rawat and Phu Dorji with whom I had shared a rope to the summit. There was also Commander Kohli, the leader, who embraced me affectionately as he did when I returned from the summit. But the affectionate gesture reminded me of the tragic difference between my former and present condition. While I would always be one of the small band of the Everest brotherhood I would never be able to climb the slopes of the mountain again. This gloomy thought, which I did not reveal to my friends, was, however, short-lived. I told myself that even if I could not climb again, I was extremely lucky to have scaled the summit. My friends left soon to fulfil other engagements. I was touched by Phu Dorji's parting words. 'I will go to Thyangboche monastery and request the head Lama to conduct special prayers for you,' he said. I vividly remembered the monastery, with its red roof prominent against the eternal snows and the plumed cap of Everest.

When I was a child I was brought up within sight of the mountains. A part of my childhood was spent in Simla, in the foothills of the Himalayas. In winter the lawn in front of our house was covered with snow. We children made sledges from wood around the house and used to slide on the snow. Little did I know at the time that I would visit places where the snow never melted.

The ambition to unravel the mystery of the mountains was born in me as a boy in Simla. Ahead lay years of discipline, hard work and effort besides that inner core of ambition. After all it is ambition which drives a man onward – whether he is a scientist intent on discovering something new in his field, or a poet striving to express the ineffable, or a mountaineer like myself trying to reach the actual physical summit.

My condition killed any further mountaineering ambitions I may have entertained. But I had to face the future and I was suddenly reminded that circumstances had created another Everest for me to surmount. I had been seeing my fiancée every day. She was undoubtedly in distress at my condition but she never gave me an inkling of her anxiety or despondency. She assisted the doctors and nurses in their daily chores, and was constantly cheering me up. She had a wonderful way of raising my spirits and in her presence I almost forgot my illness. There was a quality in our relationship which seemed perfect at the moment. But how long could our relationship last? I felt it right and proper to try and discourage her. And yet, at the same time, as time passed I began to need her more and more and a new and beautiful relationship was growing between us which at times I did not have the courage to disrupt or bring to an end. All along when she used to be with me we would hardly speak to each other but at the same time we had started understanding what was in the other's mind through the long silences. Even otherwise she never spoke much. But silence always revealed her innermost mind. I used to like this in her because it made me feel secure and wanted.

It was hard to think of a way out but I had to do it. One day I gently hinted that I could not hold her to any pledge she might have made before my injury and that the time had come to part as friends. She burst into tears. I immediately felt guilty and choked the tears welling in me. Walking over to me, she put her fingers on my lips and whispered, 'Please promise me, Hari, that you will never repeat this.'

I did not want to hurt her. But as the days grew into weeks and months and I knew I would never be a whole man again, I simply had to summon up courage to talk to her seriously. However cruel the parting, the time for it had come. As she sat in my room one day, I looked out of the window. In the garden the roses were in bloom, the bees hummed and all seemed right with the world on that beautiful day, though darkness was about to descend on my own little world. The nurses left in the afternoon and my fiancée and I were alone in the room. She was sitting on my bed talking to me. Taking her hands in mine, I said, 'This cannot go on. You know my disability is serious. As a husband I would be a burden. You must forget me and go and live your own life.' She did not take me seriously. With a sparkle in her eyes she said, 'Hari, you are forgetting your promise!'

I decided I had to be ruthless, even cruel. Tightening my grip of her hands, I said in a hard, hollow voice, 'Do you want to marry a man who will be dead in eight months? Don't you know this is the most that the doctors, promise?'

The smile froze on her lips and she seemed stunned. She then burst into tears and said, 'Hari, please don't utter such words!' At that moment I longed above all to say something which would wipe out the harshness of the words I had just spoken. But I had to go through with it and my resolve remained unshaken. There was a long silence. My hand passed over the engagement ring on her finger. I well remembered that ring and where I had bought it. Shortly before the expedition left for Everest, my mother and I visited Agra where the Taj Mahal stands like a silver butterfly against the hot, tropical sky. The Taj was built by the Mughal Emperor Shahjahan in memory of his queen Mumtaz Mahal, and I thought it appropriate to buy the engagement ring in that city whose greatest monument is dedicated to human love. It was a Sunday, I recalled, and all the shops were closed. I had to get a jeweller to open his shop to buy the ring which, so many months and events later, I now felt on her finger.

I could not bear to look at her any longer and felt miserable myself. There was a long silence in which none of us spoke to each other. I closed my eyes in sheer exhaustion and mental agony. When I opened them, she had disengaged her hand from mine and was no longer in the room.

I never saw her again.

Childhood and Youth

My earliest recollection is that of Simla when I was four or five years old. Our family lived there in a small, rented cottage in Phagli valley, about an hour's walk from the city's main shopping centre. My father was employed as a civil engineer in the Central Public Works Department and was responsible for the maintenance of the Viceregal Lodge. I was fond of walking up the steep climb to the shopping centre with him and enjoyed running down to the cottage on the way back. When he was busy or too tired after a hard day's work, I accompanied my mother on her shopping expeditions. She would buy vegetables and fruit or other household stores and would sometimes engage a porter to carry them. We used to call them coolies. In the days of the British, it became a somewhat contemptuous term for a native load carrier. We now avoid that name, though for those on whom old habits hang heavy, he is still a coolie. My offer to assist her was usually turned down. But when I was a little older, I would take a small knapsack whenever we went shopping and brought it back filled with fruits or other eats. I felt proud that I was strong enough to help.

I looked forward to Sundays and other holidays as those were the days when we visited our relations in other parts of Simla. Two

FACING PAGE: As a youngster

Maternal Grand Father, Capt. Sampuran Singh and Great Grand Father, Sardar Bahadur Singh

places which I remember were my maternal grandfather's house near the shopping centre and the Mall, and the house of my mother's aunt in Kaithu, at the other end of Simla. My grandfather lived on the upper floor of a double-storeyed house. All the rooms opened onto a veranda and had no connecting doors. The sitting room and dining room were closed to children and it was in the spare room that we usually met our grandfather.

As I look back on the days of my childhood, the towering personality of my grandfather stands out clearly and most impressively. One of the first Indians to be commissioned in the Indian Army, the Royal medical Corps, he held the rank of Captain, which was a rare distinction for an Indian those days. A devout Sikh, he was as proud of his religion as he was of his profession. His day began at four in the morning when he bathed in cold water even though it might be mid-winter and Simla in the grip of a snowstorm. The bath would be followed by prayers lasting about an hour and he would then go out for a brisk walk. By 7:30 am he was ready to leave the house on horseback to call on his patients before reporting at the hospital. The horse was a noble, gentle animal, of a rich golden colour. My grandfather also had at the time a golden cocker spaniel which followed him almost everywhere. The rider, horse, and dog made an unforgettable spectacle as they travelled from one part of the city to another. My grandfather was a familiar figure in Simla and the local people respected and admired him. He treated everyone with kindness. He seemed to know everyone's problems. What fascinated me was his army uniform and the baton which he always carried. One of my most enjoyable experiences was the occasional ride he permitted me on his horse accompanied by the syce. I felt very elated when the shopkeepers recognised me and greeted me and said, 'Here is Captain Sahib's grandson!'

With his other qualities, my grandfather combined a quick temper and all of us, including my grandmother, were scared of him when he was in a bad mood. The only member of the family who escaped his wrath was my mother. I never heard him scold her for he was very fond of her and treated her with great consideration. But with us children he could be very firm and ruthless. I recall one of our Sunday visits to him when he decided that all the children – my two sisters, younger brother and myself, besides my maternal uncle's children who were living with grandfather – should be inoculated against typhoid. Terribly afraid of the needle, we tried to hide ourselves and sought places of refuge in the house. But when grandfather gave the order to queue up, there was no escape. One after another we all trooped up before him and our cries went unheeded as the syringe was inexorably pushed into each child's arm. For me that day was no holiday. My arm started paining soon after and in the afternoon I felt feverish and uncomfortable. I had to miss my horse ride.

The military tradition has been strong in our family. My great-grandfather served in the Cavalry. At the time I am writing this he had retired and was living in our ancestral village Mehlowal in Sialkot district. My grandfather was awarded the Order of the British Empire (OBE) and Membership of the British Empire (MBE) for his service in the Army. My grandfather fought in the First World War and received a number of decorations from the British. These awards were accompanied by large grants of land in the village.

My grandfather from my father's side was an engineer – the same profession my father was to take. A man of principles, he dominated his large family. Though he was offered promotions, he did not take them as he did not want to leave Delhi. With two of his brothers (together known as the 'Big Three' of the family) he stayed in Delhi and remains a continual source of inspiration to the family.

Although our house in Phagli (Simla) was quite comfortable, my father, with his growing family, looked for more spacious accommodation and we shifted to Hishnaki Cottage, very near the Mall and not far from my grandfather's residence. The house had a large compound and everyone liked it, although I missed the excitement of the daily climb from and descent to the valley.

In our new compound were a couple of apple trees, then laden with fruit although the apples were not yet ripe. Our parents warned us not to pluck or eat the raw apples but the temptation was too great for my younger sister, Guddi, and myself. We helped ourselves to the fruit whenever no one was looking and found it delicious taken with a dash of salt. But our apple plucking spree did not last very long. One morning my mother noticed that one of the large branches on the tree had been completely denuded of apples. We tried to pretend innocence and turning to my mother my elder sister Gurmit said, 'Biji, I am sure the dhobi boys have plucked the fruit.' Not suspecting that we were the culprits, my mother said she would have to scold the dhobi boys. Our relief proved short-lived, however, as on our return from school, mother was in a bad temper, very unusual for her. She had found some apples which we had hidden in our room and also salt in a wrapper. 'Now, tell me the truth!' she said menacingly. 'Who plucked those apples?' Further excuses proved futile and both of us received a thrashing.

This incident upset my mother who is very religious minded and expected her children to be truthful and good at all times. At the evening prayers that day, which we all had to attend, she ended the session with a special invocation, 'O, God,' she said, 'if you have given me children, let them be true and noble minded so that they do good deeds of which I can be proud.' After the prayers she again warned us to speak the truth and ask God to forgive us. As an admission of our guilt, and our resolve not to steal again, we had to bow low and touch the ground with our foreheads. While I was careful enough not to let my nose rub the ground, Guddi observed no such caution and bruised her nose. When my grandfather noticed the injured nose, the whole incident had to be narrated to him by mother who received a scolding in turn as my grandfather did not believe in such punishment for small children.

That winter Simla had, so we were told, its heaviest snowfall in many years. My mother had been busy knitting pullovers, gloves and stockings for the family. This was an yearly chore since garments knitted for children during the previous season became too tight for use the following year. One of our favourite winter pastimes was sledging on the snow-covered ground in front of our house. The ground sloped gently below the house and was ideal. We made sledges out of wooden cases and crates and a carpenter in the neighbourhood improved them by fixing sheeting to the bottom of the sledge which would make it run smoother and faster. It was great fun rolling down the slope in our sledges and we fancied ourselves as young Eskimos in their snow-bound land. But we had our share of accidents as well. Once, after a heavy snowfall, I glided down the slope with Guddi sitting at the back of the sledge. The sledge gathered speed and overturned and both of us were thrown out. Although we were not injured, Guddi was scared and would never sit with me in the sledge again. But with constant practice I became somewhat of an expert. I learnt to use my feet properly to get a good braking

With a leopard cub

effect and sledge riding became safe and enjoyable. While not objecting to the sport, my mother sometimes got annoyed after our outing in the snow when we came into the house making it wet and dirty. She would not allow us to enter the house unless we changed our shoes. Every night she would wash our feet before we went to bed.

Winter in Simla had its compensations. The trees in the distance, their branches decked in snow, made a wonderful spectacle and reflected a myriad colours in the light of the rising or setting sun. Our visits to our grandfather's house continued. A particularly memorable one was when I had my first glimpse of a maharaja. My grandfather had arranged a big dinner party in honour of the Maharaja of Patiala who was then on a visit to Simla. Elaborate arrangements were made and the elite of Simla were invited. Although children were, of course, excluded from the dinner, my curiosity was aroused. I imagined a maharaja to be splendidly attired in a golden sherwani and *chooridar* pyjamas, wearing necklaces of diamond and other precious stones and a large shining diamond of the Kohinoor variety on his turban. I had once asked my father what a maharaja looked like but his reply was evasive and failed to satisfy me. My grandfather often told us stories about the Maharaja of Bharatpur whom he had served for many years as personal physician. The dinner party was a unique opportunity of seeing a maharaja in flesh and blood and I induced my cousin Jagmohan, who was older than me, to let me have a stealthy look at the exalted personage. My grandfather somehow had confidence in Jagmohan who would help him in organising drinks at parties and at times even supervise the preparation of food.

When the guests all arrived and were seated in the room, Jagmohan took me to an adjoining room from where I could have a peep. 'Where is the Maharaja?' I asked him in an excited whisper.

'There, in the centre, sitting next to grandfather,' he replied.

'Do you mean the one wearing a black suit?' I enquired again, hardly believing what I saw. As he nodded his head in confirmation,

I had one of the greatest disappointments of my childhood. The glamorous, resplendent figure I had conjured was only a prosaic, ordinary looking, middle-aged man.

A somewhat painful incident lingering long in my memory concerned the sad end of my grandfather's horse. One morning while going to school I noticed that the horse was still in his stable. This was unusual as my grandfather was out on duty and he never went without the horse. Noticing my grandmother near the entrance, I enquired how the horse happened to be there. She said, 'The horse is ill and your grandfather has had to go walking.' The news worried me and at school I kept thinking of the horse. After school I rushed to the house and the stable. I came upon a strange sight. The horse was lying down and by his side were my grandfather, a doctor with a long tube in his hand, the syce and the dog Tommy. My grandfather said, 'You'd better go home. The horse is very sick.' On reaching home I passed on the news to my mother and we were all greatly worried about the fate of the horse. Soon a servant from my grandfather's house brought the sad tidings that the horse had been killed. Why killed, I wondered, and I was in tears. When we went to the stable, we found it deserted. Tommy did not greet us with his usual bark and wagging tail. He was crouching in a corner of the veranda and looked awfully depressed. My grandfather said, 'I am sorry we had to shoot the mare to relieve her of the misery. She had taken some poisonous weeds with the grass and would never have recovered.' I had lost a dear friend. I could hardly bear to pass by the stable after this tragedy.

My grandfather was now about to retire from government service and planned to settle in Lahore. After dispatching surplus household goods to our village Mehlowal, he came to Lahore, where we now lived, and rented a separate house, some distance away from our residence on Nisbet Road. When our schools closed for the summer vacation it was decided that rather than go to Simla or Delhi, we should spend our holidays in Mehlowal and get some experience of village life and farming. My great-grandfather who lived in the village was informed and he confirmed telegraphically that he would be delighted to have us and to make all arrangements for our visit to our ancestral home.

Our journey to Mehlowal was unlike any journey I had ever undertaken. Leaving Lahore by train, my aunt, two sisters and I reached Narowal in the late afternoon. Narowal was the railhead and the remaining distance had to be covered by road. We were met at the railway station by some of our relatives who lived in Rab village where we had to halt for the night. My great-grandfather had also sent a servant to escort us to Mehlowal. We proceeded to Rab by tongas. The rains had started and all around us were pools and ponds overflowing with water. After a fairly comfortable night's rest at Rab we were ready but I was somewhat dismayed to find that the journey had to be done by mules. Since the road was kutcha and wet and at many places had been washed away by the rain, mules were considered safe transport. I had never ridden a mule and it was not without some trepidation that I now mounted one. After riding a little distance and just as I was feeling somewhat reassured and we were crossing a shallow pond, the mule sat down in the water and no amount of coaxing or cursing would make it get up. I was completely wet and loudly blamed my aunt for making me ride such an animal. She promptly offered to exchange her mule with mine. But I had enough of mule-riding and preferred to walk the rest of the distance with the servants. We had been riding through an unending vista of cultivated fields; maize stood five to six feet higher than any other crop. We made a brief halt for lunch which was brought to us from Mehlowal by a servant.

My first impression of Mehlowal was that of peace and quiet and an all-pervading freshness. My aunt, who had been to the village before, pointed to our ancestral home. It was a very large house with a big compound and a well. Sitting in an easy chair near the well was my great-grandfather who had then reached the ripe age of ninety-four. Despite his years he appeared remarkably well preserved. He was smartly dressed in a white kurta and pyjama, both well starched. When we arrived on the scene, we were surprised to see that he was helping himself to roasted gram. 'How wonderful!' Gurmit said. 'He must have a strong set of teeth.'

'And they are his own!' my aunt remarked, with pride in her voice. My great-grandfather greeted us warmly and hugged each of us. As headman (Lambardar) of Mehlowal, he was its leading citizen. We were introduced to other prominent people of Mehlowal and neighbouring villages who had been invited to meet us.

In the afternoon we were treated to a sumptuous tea. And then our aunt took us to the citrus and mango orchards which were part of the family estate. They stretched over a wide area and made a pleasant and refreshing sight. We revelled in the greenery and verdant glory of the orchards. The following morning we had the opportunity of exploring the house and were especially interested in my great-grandfather's collection of antiques and weapons. There were guns and rifles, pistols and bayonets, and old china and other crockery, huge brass pieces shaped as animals and various types of flower vases. I was fascinated by a horse fashioned out of clay or porcelain. My grandfather's room too had many articles of unusual interest. He had served the Maharaja of Bharatpur as his personal physician and had been given a number of presents on various occasions. These were neatly arranged in the room. There was a sword with a golden handle encrusted with rare stones. I was told that this sword belonged to a chief in Maharaja Ranjit Singh's days. There was also an *achkan* made of *zari* or gold thread. My grandfather wore it whenever he attended the Maharaja's durbar.

My aunt, who was familiar with the house, proved a good guide. On rainy days when we could not go out, we sat with our great-grandfather and listened to his reminiscences of the 'good old days.' For his service in the army he had won many awards including the title of Sardar Bahadur. He liked good food and before dinner had two pegs of whisky. Everyone frowned on the drinking of alcohol but for an Army man it was all right. The accompanying snacks were onions soaked in vinegar. In his younger days my great-grandfather had been a well-known *shikari*. He said that shikar provided him with at least two kinds of meat for his dinner. The area around Mehlowal abounded with *titar* and pheasant and sometimes one came across deer too. My great-grandfather had, however, given up hunting and shooting long ago. His main occupation now was that of Lambardar, in which capacity he was responsible for collecting revenue from the zamindars and settling any minor disputes which might arise in the village.

Our fortnight's holiday in the village passed all too quickly and the morning of our departure had already arrived. We bade goodbye to great-grandfather who appeared to have enjoyed our company and like us was looking a little depressed. He deputed servants to accompany us, and in view of my unhappy experience with mules, provided a horse to take me up to Rab village. The return journey was uneventful. My father and mother received us at Lahore railway station. Soon we were back at school and to the normal routine of life in the city.

My father being a busy official, it was not often that he had time to accompany us for an outing. One weekend, however, he took us in his car to Amritsar to see the Golden Temple. The distance from Lahore to Amritsar is barely thirty-five miles but my father being a slow and careful driver, it took us over two hours to cover this distance. My mother showed us around the Golden Temple. She narrated to us the history of the temple in great detail and I was as deeply impressed by her religious fervour as by her profound knowledge of Sikh history and the life of the Sikh Gurus. We listened for some time to the *kirtan* (religious songs) and sipped the holy water from the temple.

By 1947 the situation in Lahore deteriorated rapidly. On many occasions the schools were closed either for the whole day or part of the day because of disturbances in the locality. My grandfather had hired a *tonga* on a monthly basis to take us to the school in the morning and bring us back home in the afternoon. The *tonga* driver, whom we called Miyan, was an old Muslim who loved children and kept his horse and *tonga* in tip-top condition. He had named his horse Bijli (lightning). I never saw Miyan using a whip or stick to drive his horse. The animal seemed to follow his master's speech and would run or slow down at his bidding; a gentle tap on the back was all that was needed to make him run really fast. Miyan told us that the horse had been born to a mare he owned earlier and he had bred Bijli with much care.

One morning as we were ready for school and waiting for the *tonga*, Miyan turned up without the vehicle. He told my grandfather, 'The situation is worsening. There has been a murder in the locality. I shall not be able to take the children in my *tonga* for some days. I advise you not to let them go out of the house.' My grandfather became anxious about our safety since the neighbourhood was a predominantly Muslim one. We were literally locked up in the house and were not even allowed to go up to the terrace. I could not get in touch with my sisters in Kinnaird School which was some distance away from our house.

Tension in the city continued to mount and there were many incidents of murder and stabbing. The fiery speeches delivered by leaders of various communities merely added to the communal frenzy. The fate of Lahore hung in the balance. The Boundary Commission was then holding its meetings in the city and hearing arguments by the representatives of Hindus, Muslims and Sikhs to decide whether Lahore would belong to India or to Pakistan Soon it became increasingly obvious that Lahore would be part of the new state of Pakistan, and the minority communities – Hindus and Sikhs – became extremely panicky. The burning of the well-known Hindu shopping centre of Shahalmi Gate was the final blow which broke the back of the Hindu mercantile community. Thousands of shopkeepers and others left the city daily by train or bus, taking with them whatever moveable property they could.

My father, posted in Dehradun, was greatly worried about our safety. He sent an attendant to escort us to Dehradun but the attendant was a Sikh and thus conspicuous by his beard, long hair and turban. Sikhs on the city roads and streets had become easy targets of Muslim fanatical fury. We sent the attendant back to Dehradun and it was decided that my sisters and I should travel by an evening train to Amritsar. But my sisters were at Kinnaird School and had to be fetched from there. In those turbulent days, buses and *tongas* had ceased plying and it was difficult to get any kind of reliable conveyance, and it was of course dangerous to walk any distance. We sent for our old friend Miyan and asked for his assistance. He promptly agreed to take me to the school and advised me not to wear a turban as it might attract the attention of passersby. I arranged my hair into a long plait and hurriedly bade goodbye to my grandparents and cousins.

And now began the first part of a journey which was not without some harrowing experiences and provided my first insight into the tragic consequences of Partition. I sat in the front of the *tonga* with Miyan, who was driving fast while keeping a vigilant eye for any hostile elements on the road. We had not proceeded far when a small crowd of Muslims rushed towards the tonga. Perhaps they had noticed that it carried a Sikh. In fact I recall someone shouting, 'Catch that Sikh boy!' Miyan knew that to stop the tonga would be fatal, so he kept driving recklessly. When someone tried to grasp the back rail of the tonga, he beat him off with his whip. I was very frightened but joined Miyan in goading the horse to run faster. And Bijli proved true to his name; I had never seen him show such a spurt of speed. We managed to shake off our pursuers and did not stop till we reached Kinnaird School. On the way I had seen many bodies with stab wounds lying in pools of blood. I was scared out of my wits and felt helpless.

We found the college guarded by sentries. I met the Principal and my sisters. Many of the girls had already moved out and the others were ready to leave. Since Miyan thought it would be too risky for him to take us to the railway station, the Principal promised to arrange for our transport.

Miyan hugged me and said, 'Allah will look after you. I must leave immediately.' In the evening a covered military truck was sent for and we had a safe journey to the railway station. The scene on the platform was one of great confusion. Besides people from Lahore, a number of refugees had arrived from places as far north as Peshawar. The train was packed like a tin of sardines. The ladies' compartment which we managed to enter had about fifty passengers against a scheduled capacity of fifteen. We did not know when the train would leave; someone said it might not leave at all. Everyone was in a state of great suspense and anxiety. Some of the women in the compartment were scared by the sight of a Sikh boy who might endanger their lives. I felt very miserable but there was nothing I could do to help myself or the others. At last the train began to move and we all heaved a sigh of relief. But hardly fifteen minutes had passed when it slowed down to a grinding halt. Apparently it had been stopped by some Muslim hooligans. We heard much shouting and sound of firing. The ladies in the compartment became very nervous. One of them said, 'Hide this boy. They are after Sikhs and will probably search every compartment!' Gurmit was in a panic and did not know what to do. She tried to push me into the toilet but an elderly lady thought it would not be a safe place. I was then pushed under the seat and crouched behind the sari of this old lady who was sitting next to my sister.

The entire journey to Amritsar, although it covered a distance of only about thirty-five miles, was a nightmare. The train halted frequently and at each halt we heard blood-curdling cries. Some passengers must have been dragged out of the train and attacked. The lateness of the hour – it was about midnight – and the surrounding darkness added to our terror. The lights in the train had been switched off, probably as a safeguard against attack. Before long the train seemed to be entering a railway yard. It halted again and someone said, 'This is Amritsar. Thank God we have arrived safely!' But we did not move out until we were absolutely sure that it was Amritsar and not some wayside station with its lurking dangers. On the platform we were met by a man who had brought a message from my father in Dehradun. I was at last able to relax and as I rested my aching body on a seat near the window, I pondered over the tragedy of the Partition of India and the ordeal we had gone through.

Our parents were at Dehradun railway station to receive us and the reunion was surcharged with a good deal of emotion. After our departure from Lahore my grandfather left for village Mehlowal which he thought would continue to be included in India after Partition. This proved a vain hope and he was eventually forced to flee the village with my grandmother. It took them four weeks of arduous travel by foot, bus and rail to reach Dehradun. They were forced to spend many days in hiding – in fields and deserted houses – often unable to get any food or even clean drinking water. When they reached Dehradun they were weary and exhausted and their clothes were in tatters. But my grandmother had managed to salvage her jewellery which she had sewn into a belt and tied round her waist. That grand old man, my great-grandfather, also managed to reach Dehradun safely, but unfortunately did not survive more than a week after his arrival. His ambition had been to live up to a hundred. But the shock of Partition and its aftermath, with the accompanying loss of so much he held dear, proved too great for him. He died at the age of ninety-six.

By now my cousins also arrived in Dehradun. My grandfather, grandmother and my cousins shifted to another house which was close to ours. It was big and spacious and had a huge compound in front which we used as a playground. In the compound grew fruit trees – guavas, mangoes, pears, *litchis*, papayas – and some vegetables. In comparison, our house was not as big and it did not have fruit trees. My grandfather's daily routine had changed somewhat. Partition had sobered him a great deal. He seldom lost his temper now. He had become very religious minded, a teetotaller and a vegetarian. My mother was very happy as her parents were now living close to her. It was decided that all the

Walking down from Picture Palace, Mussoorie

boys would be enrolled in St. Joseph's Academy. I was admitted to fourth standard and my cousin DP to the third. Both my younger brothers along with my sisters attended the convent school. We were provided bicycles and it was fun going to school. My school, St. Joseph's Academy, was on Rajpur Road which was part of the highway leading to Mussoorie, a favourite hill station. St. Joseph's was, like any other public school, much bigger than the school I attended in Lahore, and was spread over a vast area with playing fields on either side of the building. The school was run by some Irish priests who were strict disciplinarians. Games were compulsory and we had a number of outings, which I used to look forward to greatly. I took up hockey and football and was also keenly interested in athletics.

Dehradun is located in a valley at an altitude of 1,000 metres. It is a very pretty valley and has a number of easily accessible picnic spots. There were the Shivalik Hills, with the towns of Rishikesh, Chakrata and Mussoorie. Dehradun is not very hot. The climate is healthy and it is usually sunny throughout the year. I liked this place which, unlike Simla, was not severely cold in winter or, like Lahore, intolerably hot in summer.

During one weekend we all got together and decided to walk up to Mussoorie from Rajpur. 'We'll go on bicycles up to Rajpur and from there walk to Mussoorie,' said DP. The idea was appreciated but unfortunately we had only two bicycles which meant that we had to double ride seven or eight miles up to Rajpur. Also, the journey involved quite a climb as Rajpur is at the base of the hills from where the actual steep climb to Mussoorie begins. We were all very excited about this trip to Mussoorie. I was particularly happy as this would be the first time I would do some climbing since I left Simla.

There were Bhim and Puran whom we came to know, and also Ruskin Bond, who was not studying with us but lived in Dehradun with his mother. DP and I got ready at five in the morning. We had to pick up Bhim and Ruskin Bond from Ashley Hall, a place close to our school where they lived. I took Bhim as my passenger while Ruskin sat on DP's bicycle, and we started our journey to Rajpur. Since it was going uphill it was very hard work. Bhim would get down at difficult places and would push the cycle and then jump

Major Ahluwalia and family with Ruskin Bond in Mussoorie, 2004

on to the carrier. Bhim then got a novel idea. 'Let me also put my feet on the pedals and we could then both apply pressure and get the wheels to move faster,' he said. I found this helped us a great deal. Often while pedalling, Bhim's feet would slip off the pedals but somehow we kept our position on the cycle and kept it on the move. DP who was stronger than me kept a sturdy pace with Ruskin on his carrier. It took us almost an hour to reach Rajpur and it was almost 6:30 am when we finally left that town for Mussoorie. 'What a lovely day,' said Ruskin. Ruskin was fond of writing. He had begun writing short stories quite early and was especially good at describing the countryside. Bhim was in my class and was one of the brighter students. Whenever I had any problem, especially in mathematics, I would take his help. DP who was in a class junior to ours was doing extremely well. He was at the top of his class and maintained this position throughout the year. He was not very good at hockey or football and was more interested in athletics. He was at his best in short races.

As we began our climb on the mule track, the ascent was steep and the path lay along a ridge with a lovely view of the forests, springs and waterfalls. But we did not enjoy the scenery much as the initial climb was hard and tiring. Before tackling the next part of our climb, we had tea at a small tea shop owned by a Pahari. There was a fresh-water spring by the side of the shop where the shopkeeper had cleverly fitted a tap. 'I wonder how he lives here with his family in this wilderness.' I remarked. 'Oh, Paharis are quite used to such surroundings,' said Ruskin. The shopkeeper had a goat and a cow and a small dog. 'I suppose the dog does all the watch-keeping for him,' I said. 'He can at least look after the goat and the cow,' said Bhim.

The next part of the climb was not steep and was more enjoyable as it was through a thick growth of trees. Looking down one could see the zigzag metalled road from Rajpur leading to Mussoorie. It takes hardly an hour and a quarter to get to Mussoorie from Dehradun by car. But we were expecting at least a two-hour climb from Rajpur to Mussoorie on this mule track. We were making the journey leisurely and it was already eight when we left the shop. We passed by Oak Grove, a boarding school sponsored by the Indian Railways. After that was a sturdy climb to a place called Barlow Ganj where St. George's College is located. We could see the college from a distance as it is the only building on that particular hill, and its huge clock tower is something of a landmark. Our school in Dehradun was in fact a branch of this institution. As we did not know anyone in the college, we passed it by. Mussoorie, like other hill stations, has a number of public schools where children come from far and wide.

It was almost lunch-time when we reached Landaur Bazar in Mussoorie. Since it was only the end of March, the busy season had not yet begun and there were not many people on the roads. Most of the shops were closed as it was a holiday. After walking for half an hour or so, we settled down for some lunch in one of the shops in the bazaar. We had hot *puri* and *chana*. It was a simple meal but we enjoyed it as we were very hungry. We had strict instructions from our parents to be back home before dark. It was now time for us to make a move. It was almost three. We had to rush down. At times we ran and occasionally slipped on the slope. Ruskin was reluctant to run but we managed to make him do it. We were in Rajpur before 5:00 pm. We were no longer worried as the cycling would be all downhill. We rode rather fast and by about 5:30 pm we were all back in our homes. This was our first trip to Mussoorie, and we were all very tired with blistered feet and aching muscles. This trip had created a new interest in me and I wanted to make more such trips. My companions agreed and we went on similar excursions almost once every four weeks. We explored all the neighbouring areas on our bicycles. We visited Rishikesh, Chakrata, Raipur and many other beautiful spots.

The Indian Military Academy was in Dehradun. Its passing out parade and the cadets walking about in their impressive uniforms in Dehradun fascinated both DP and me. We made up our minds to join the Army. We were of course aware of the hard competition for admission to the Academy and that only very few boys come up to the Academy's strict standards. Possibly my preference for an Army career was also influenced by my grandfather and great-grandfather who had talked to us a great deal about it. My father, however, was extremely keen that I should become an engineer.

In 1952, my father was posted to Calcutta and the family moved there. All my brothers and sisters went with my parents and joined various schools there, but I stayed on with my grandparents in Dehradun for a few months till the final examination. After my examination was over I too left for Kolkata to spend my vacation.

This was my first visit to Kolkata. My father had rented a flat on the third floor of a residential building. Kolkata overwhelmed me. Not used to such large crowds, I felt quite excited going round the city. The vast Howrah Bridge over the Hooghly river with ships and motor vessels plying under it was very impressive. Life seemed to be moving at a fast pace. Although my parents, brothers and sisters had adjusted to it rather well, I was quite unhappy. I found the city too full of people, dirty and suffocating. Not knowing what Kolkata would be like, I had carried my bicycle with me but my parents were not willing to let me use it there. I would sometimes carry it down the stairs and go to the nearby park on the road running along the Hooghly river and do a little cycling. People thought I was crazy. But this was the only exercise I could get.

Major Ahluwalia (R) at Inter-School Boxing Championship, St. George's College, Mussoorie, 1952

The vacation ended and I obtained admission to St. George's College, Mussoorie.

This made me happy as I longed to be back in the hills. The college is spread over a vast area. Our football field could also be used for hockey. Unlike the green playing fields in Dehradun, the playing fields here were laid out on hard ground. I took science subjects and lived in the boarding house. The college had a hiking society. Since I was interested in photography, I also joined the photography club. I tried my skill at rock climbing too. At times it was wonderful standing outside the college and looking down at the tiny zigzag road to Dehradun on which buses looked like so many toys slowly moving up or down.

We had a physical Training Instructor, Greenwood, who was interested in mountaineering and boxing and gave us lessons in both. He often stressed the importance of these sports in making a man tough and hardy. In order not to displease him I started boxing although I was not enthusiastic about it. But finally I gave it up because I did not like to have my nose bashed up.

I made a number of friends in the college. One who was very close to me was Satpal, the son of our mathematics teacher, Munshiji, whom we all respected at lot. Munshiji had a very likable way of teaching mathematics and treated us with great kindness.

I had not given up my habit of walking down to Rajpur on the mule track but it was not easy to get permission to go down. Sometimes I would slip away from the college on a Saturday afternoon. If my absence was noticed, Satpal would come to my rescue and would say that I was around somewhere in the college or at the camera club. On such occasions, I would spend the night with my grandparents in Dehradun and return to Mussoorie on Sunday evening. These trips were tiring but I enjoyed them.

My studies were progressing well, and so were my hobbies – trekking, hiking and photography. Once I met a team of climbers returning from the hills. I found their experiences on the mountains very exciting. They had done some climbing in snow-clad areas and were in their mountaineering outfits, with ice axes in their hands, wearing climbing boots and carrying rucksacks. I was so excited that I literally went around touching their boots and rucksacks and took one of the ice axes in my hand to get its feel! I did not know at that time how important this item of equipment was for a mountaineer. Soon after those boys left, I went to Greenwood. I said, 'Mr Greenwood, would it be possible for me to join these boys in one of their climbing expeditions?' His reply disappointed me. He said, 'That would

(L to R) Principal Bro. Carroll, Bro. Gannon, Bro. Tunne and Lt Gen. Menezes at the Centenary Celebrations of St George's College

not be possible as you do not have enough experience or time. Nor can we arrange an expedition of St. George's College students as it would cost a lot.' Only rich institutions such as Doon School could afford such expeditions.

I was involved in a good deal of extracurricular activities, but my most enduring interest proved to be mountaineering. I would go to the library and pick up books on rock climbing and on basic techniques of mountaineering. I constantly looked for opportunities to try out these techniques and acquire practical experience of climbing.

Back in Kolkata, after passing my Intermediate examination, I was at a loose end again. There was nothing much for me to do. I used to go out on my bicycle early in the morning towards the Hooghly river when the traffic was not much. That was all the outing I could give myself. I found the big city tolerable only during the early hours of the morning. There was then a certain amount of freshness, but as the day advanced it would get too crowded, hot and dirty.

My future became something of a problem for my parents as we did not know what I should do for a career. There were many suggestions from friends and relatives. Some said that I should join the Navy as sea life is good and healthy. I had two friends who were then on a ship which used to touch Kolkata harbour once every three months. Although their stories of the countries they visited were interesting, somehow a naval career, which meant being cooped up in a ship, did not attract me much. However, on the bidding of my parents and others, I sat for a competitive examination for admission to the Navy. I passed the written examination and then went to Bombay (now Mumbai) for an interview. When the merit list of selected candidates was published, my name did not figure in it and thus ended all talk of my joining the Navy. I now joined a local college to complete my course for a science degree, and took up mathematics, physics and chemistry as my main subjects.

After joining the college, my days in Kolkata were crammed with activity. Besides my studies, I devoted a good deal of time to photography. One of my friends, knowing my interest in photography, bought a Rolleicord camera for me and I discarded the old bellows-type camera belonging to my father which I had been using for a number of years. With the new camera my hobby acquired a new dimension. I could now take more sophisticated pictures. I had already learnt how to develop my own films and print and enlarge the pictures. I did all my developing and printing at home and converted one of the rooms into a dark room. Photography became one of my obsessions.

One of our neighbours in Kolkata with whom we became quite friendly was Mr Dhyan Singh who also had a large family. His eldest daughter, Surjit, was very friendly with Gurmit and they were always making some plan or the other for an outing or a picnic or a small party in the house, or even a film show – anything to get together. We would sometimes go boating to Eden Gardens and other places. I soon purchased a movie camera and started making amateur movies. I would take shots of the Hooghly river with the fishing boats setting out for the sea in the early hours of the morning. I once took a trip with a fisherman and photographed the entire operation of throwing the net, waiting for the fish to be caught, and then taking the net out with live fish. This gave me an insight into the daily life of a fisherman. It made an interesting story on an 8 mm cine camera. With this maiden effort, I got into the field of movie making and produced a number of short documentaries.

In spite of these diversions, I missed the hills and longed to be back where I could feel the freshness of the mountain air and hear the chirping of the birds. I had already sat for the Indian Military Academy examination. Having passed it and having got through the Services Selection Board, I obtained admission to the Academy in Dehradun for two years' training for a permanent commission in the Army. I was happy at the prospect of being in Dehradun again. It would be nice meeting old friends and visiting the old places. But when I reached Dehradun and joined the Academy, I found a cadet's life entirely different from what I had imagined.

It was a busy, hard and tough life and I knew it would be so throughout my two-year stay. There was hardly time to meet old friends or to have any outings. The schedule of studies and drill was full and the discipline very strict. I could not go out and in fact life there was so hard in the beginning that many a time I felt like leaving the Academy. The ragging by the senior boys was severe. Ironically most of the ragging was by boys whom I had known at Dehradun but who happened to get to the Academy earlier. We busied ourselves with classes and extracurricular activity as any time in between was utilised by the seniors for ragging. Once I was called away from my company to another company by a few senior cadets whom I knew quite well. One of them took me to his room, where two other seniors joined him and I knew I was about to be ragged. 'You need a bath,' said one of them. They made me take off my coat and trousers and pushed me into the bathroom where two buckets of cold water were lying. One of them picked up a bucket and threw the cold water on me. Since it was February and very cold in Dehradun, the cold water made me shiver. 'One is not enough,' said another cadet and took up the other bucket and emptied it over my head. It was very unpleasant but I could not say a thing. In the course of ragging one was subjected to all kinds of whims and irritations. Finally, they asked me to pick-up a large box and put it on my head. I tried to lift it, but it was too heavy. Two of them then picked it up and placed it on my head. They knew it was heavy and I could not hold it for long but they refused to help me put it down. This annoyed me and in my anger I threw the box on to their feet, exclaiming, 'To hell with you!' As the box was not closed properly when I threw it down, the lid came off and there was a shattering noise of broken glass and crockery. The damage included a broken time-piece. The senior cadets started shouting at me together. The one who I knew said, 'I will see that you are punished for this rude behaviour.' While they were still shouting at me, I left them and came back to my own company. This incident seemed to have sobered them, and there was no more ragging for

Indian Military Academy, Dehradun

me. Later, I discovered that if ragging is done within certain limits, it does help an individual to adapt more quickly to a tough life.

The Indian Military Academy is four to five miles from the city. There were few opportunities of cycling down to the town. In fact during the first term of six months, freshers were not allowed much freedom and were hardly allowed to visit the town. Fortunately, most of the time was spent outdoors but there were classroom studies also. I did not find the academic course difficult as I had already studied most of the science subjects. The real emphasis was on activities such as drill, physical training, weapon training tactics and map reading.

The Academy is divided into various companies named after famous battles fought in World War II. I was in Sangro Company which had about 150 cadets. The cadets were addressed as 'Gentlemen Cadets' and popularly known as GCs. The Commanding Officer of our company was Major Bhagat Singh, a tall Sikh officer from the Infantry. He loved the profession. He was very particular about the turnout of Sikh cadets. He insisted that we keep our beards properly dressed and tie our turbans properly and well. He would not hesitate to give punishment if he found any slackness on our part in this respect. He used to say that if a Sikh did not keep his beard well and tie his turban properly, he would never look smart. He also took special interest in developing our physique.

Our Assessing Officer, Captain Chopra from Armoured Corps, was also very strict and we were all quite scared of him. He watched us even during the off hours. 'As long as you are in the Academy, whether it is day or night, you are always on parade. Remember that,' he said. I never saw him smile. He was forever taking down notes in a small book which he carried with him. I was quite surprised when one day captain Chopra called me to his office and said, 'I am afraid you are weak in outdoor activities and I have to give you a 'warning.'

This was a shock for me but I did not protest as he disliked any argument. All I could say was 'Yes, Sir.'

'If you do not improve by the end of this term, I am going to relegate you and you will lose six months,' said Captain Chopra.

I found myself saying again, 'Yes, Sir.'

'March him out,' said Captain Chopra.

I tried to find out where I was weak in outdoors. I intensified my practice in physical training in the evening and when we did not have anything on, I would come to the fields and practise various tests which were laid down in the physical training programme. The Physical Training Instructor was very considerate and agreed to give me extra coaching on holidays. I started taking greater part in games like hockey and football. There were some cadets in my course with whom I had become quite friendly. There was Sudershan who was very good at tennis and who had become the vice-captain of the Academy tennis team. He insisted that I take tennis also as this would get me extra credit for outdoor marks.

It was now the middle of the term and we were all kept very busy. A number of extra drills were awarded to several cadets during the course of the week. Invariably on weekends I found myself doing these extra drills. My Assessing Officer liked prescribing extra drills particularly on weekends to make certain that we did not get into the habit of going to the town too often.

Once I had planned to go out with Sudershan, but in the morning there was rifle inspection. While the inspection was on, Captain Chopra came up to me and wanted to look through the barrel of my rifle. To check the barrel, the other end is placed against a black background. The normal practice is that you hold the rifle close to your boot which provides a shining background and the rifle can then be looked through and checked for cleanliness. While Captain Chopra was looking through the barrel of my rifle, he shouted, 'One extra drill GC Ahluwalia, for wearing dirty shoes!' It surprised me how Captain Chopra could have detected this by looking through the barrel of the rifle. Given the extra drill, my entire programme for going to town was shattered.

Sudershan had to go alone. In the evening he came to my room and brought some eatables and also two bottles of beer. Another cadet, Narinder Singh, happened to be in my room. 'I have brought some beer for you people to drink,' said Sudershan. He had been drinking beer frequently although drinking is strictly against the rules of the Academy. I was scared when he placed the bottles in front of me. 'I am not going to have it,' I said. And Narinder Singh was equally reluctant to touch the stuff. 'Look, after joining the Army you have to drink sooner or later, so why not start now,' said Sudershan. Much against our wishes, he eventually succeeded in persuading us to have half a glass of beer. Neither of us had tasted any alcoholic drink before. The moment I took a sip, I said in disgust, 'Oh, this is bitter and undrinkable!'

'I knew you would not like the taste of beer the first time,' he said. 'I've brought some lemonade to mix with it. This will improve the taste and you'll like it,' said Sudershan. The lemonade did make

Major Ahluwalia and his fellow cadets at the Indian Military Academy, Dehradun

some difference and we gulped a glass of beer each, and somehow escaped getting caught.

I sincerely felt that my outdoor performance did not call for a 'warning' but I was determined to remove my Assessing Officer's doubts about my ability in this respect. I made sure that I was in the fields when my Assessing Officer was on a round in that area.

It was an extra effort to show him how keen I was on outdoors. My efforts were rewarded. Towards the end of the term I was called by Captain Chopra. I was not too sure what my Assessing Officer had to tell me and when I presented myself before him, it was in great suspense. 'You have shown progress,' said Captain Chopra.

'Yes, Sir,' I said.

'I am taking you out of the warning category but this does not mean that you will cease to improve. Should I find any slackening on your part, I will not hesitate to put you up for a warning again,' he continued.

'Yes, Sir,' I said. In the Academy I learnt that to avoid unnecessary trouble your dialogue with your superiors should be confined to two words: 'Yes, Sir.'

'March him out,' said Captain Chopra, ending the interview, and my feeling was one of tremendous relief. The term was coming to an end soon with a break of a month's vacation. After spending the vacation with my people in Kolkata, I was back in the Academy. We took our studies and outdoor activities even more seriously for the final commissioning.

In a way, my Assessing Officer's warning had done a lot of good. Even though I was no more on warning, my interest in outdoor activities had grown tremendously. I would now take part in all the games. I also picked up a good bit of tennis from Sudershan. In the third term, we were sent out to a camp in which we were trained to live off the land and adapt our living to conditions of war. This camp was completely outdoors and although we had a tough time it was an interesting experience. During the last term break I accompanied a team from my Academy to Poona (Pune) where they played matches in hockey, football, and athletics with teams of the National Defence Academy, Khadakvasla, near Pune. This gave me an opportunity to meet my cousin DP, who had by now joined the National Defence Academy.

In our final term we had to attend another camp which was of a longer duration than the earlier one. My Assessing Officer now seemed quite happy with me. The final term proved rewarding in every way, and in December 1958 I was commissioned in the Corps of Electrical and Mechanical Engineering.

A number of my relatives and friends gathered to attend the passing-out parade which is a big social event in Dehradun. Unfortunately my parents could not come, but my sister's friend Surjit, who was now married to a tea planter, attended the parade. After I was commissioned I had two months' vacation before taking up my new appointment.

Lure of the Mountains

I left for Secunderabad where I had to attend a twelve-month course on basic automobile engineering. I found Secunderabad a congenial place. A relaxed atmosphere prevailed at the Military College of Electrical and Mechanical Engineering compared to the strict discipline of the Academy. The automobile studies were not very demanding. There was emphasis on practical work. We acquired knowledge of various automobile engines and their parts. There was plenty of opportunity for extracurricular activity. Secunderabad had beautiful rocks and one could go for small rock-climbing trips. We used to get together and bicycle to Hyderabad which is about ten miles away. In fact, Hyderabad and Secunderabad are twin cities and there is only a bridge and a lake separating them. I found the people of this area cultured and well-mannered. They observed the traffic rules, which is unusual in our country.

The Nizam of Hyderabad had the reputation of being the richest person in the world. I was quite fascinated when I saw his palace in Hyderabad. A number of old palaces in Hyderabad are now rented by the Army. In fact, the EME Centre Officers' Mess was also housed in one of the smaller palaces. Hyderabad also has a number of other palaces of historical interest.

FACING PAGE: With Vasudev and Bahuguna at High Altitude Warfare School, Gulmarg

Apart from the regular instruction imparted to us in the classroom, we used to have lectures by prominent people and specialists visiting Hyderabad and Secunderabad. One occasion I vividly remember is the visit of Brigadier Gyan Singh. He had come to talk to us on mountaineering. It was January 1960, just a month before the first Indian Everest Expedition led by him was to leave for the mountain. A large gathering had collected to hear the Brigadier on the eve of his departure. He was the Principal of the Himalayan Mountaineering Institute, Darjeeling. He illustrated his talk with slides and a film titled *Call of the Mountains*. This talk was by far the most exciting event for me during my year's stay at Secunderabad. After the talk I went up to the Brigadier to find out how I should proceed for a course at the Mountaineering Institute, Darjeeling. He gave me every encouragement and also an application form for admission to the basic course. I wasted no time in filling up the application, attached a medical report and had it forwarded through the School.

After completing my year's training at Secunderabad, I was posted to a workshop in the Jammu and Kashmir area. My new unit was located in the hills and I felt quite happy as it offered many opportunities for small climbs, although there were no high ranges. At the beginning of 1961, I was informed that I could join the basic course for mountaineering. Meanwhile, Colonel Kapoor, under whom I was serving then, thought that I would only be wasting my time doing a course in mountaineering. I was a technical man, and technical people could not be spared for courses which had no direct correlation to their career. But I was very keen on the course and explained to him that the duration of the course was only forty-two days. 'A course of forty-two days means an absence of almost two months from the unit,' said the Colonel.

'Yes, Sir,' I replied. Colonel Kapoor kept explaining to me that I would be making a mistake by going on a course like this and that he would prefer that I should go for a technical course. But in the end he said, 'Since you are so keen, I have no objection if you forgo your annual leave.'

'Yes, Sir,' I repeated. And thus I obtained the necessary clearance and left for Darjeeling.

To go to Darjeeling by train you have to tranship from the broad gauge to the meter gauge at Lucknow. The train for Siliguri, the railhead for Darjeeling, leaves Lucknow early in the morning. When I boarded it, the weather was quite chilly. One of the other passengers in my compartment was Colonel Jaiswal, looking smart and rather young for his years in a blue blazer and grey trousers. I introduced myself and told him that I was going to Darjeeling for the basic course in mountaineering. I was pleasantly surprised to learn that he too was going to attend the course.

Colonel Jaiswal was Commandant of the Army Physical Training School in Pune and appeared to be quite keen on mountaineering. He had read a number of books on the subject. Among those he was carrying with him, I noticed one titled *Tiger of the Snows*. It was a biography of Tenzing and I thought it would make interesting reading. When the Colonel was retiring for the night, I borrowed the book from him and was so absorbed in it that it was almost dawn before I had finished reading the last chapter. I eagerly looked forward to meeting Tenzing at the Institute.

From Siliguri, where we arrived in the afternoon, we drove by taxi to Darjeeling. A tiny hill railway connects the two stations, but it is too slow. It is much quicker by car. The two-hour drive was through typical hill scenery and the journey was not unlike those I had often undertaken between Rajpur and Mussoorie. Near Darjeeling, in the distance loomed the mighty Kanchenjunga, its colour changing from light blue to a light pink as the rays of the setting sun illuminated the peak. Against the background of clouds and snow, it looked like a large painting. I had no idea how far the mountain was from Darjeeling; it looked quite near but I found out later that it was some forty miles away as the crow flies.

After a number of turns, the road led to the Institute. Passing through the main entrance, what immediately arrested our attention was the carved figure of a man climbing a rock and bearing the inscription, 'May you climb from peak to peak' – obviously the motto of the Institute.

There were thirty students for the basic course in mountaineering, hailing from various parts of India and drawn from many walks of life. Among them were several officers of the armed forces. A Sherpa instructor received us on arrival and led us to the hostel. Colonel Jaiswal and I were accommodated in the same room and thus became constant companions for the duration of the course. A third room-mate was Surinder, an officer from the Merchant Navy.

The next morning our course commenced with an opening talk by Brigadier Gyan Singh, the Principal of the Institute, whom I had already met. He outlined our programme briefly. We could spend a week in Darjeeling visiting various places on foot as a preliminary toughening-up. We would then begin our march to the base camp where we would remain for another week. This would be followed by special training in ice craft and rock climbing. We were glad to learn from the Principal that the prime Minister, Pandit Jawaharlal Nehru, had agreed to preside over the graduation ceremony which would be held on completion of the course.

On the first day, besides the Principal's address, there were a number of talks by various instructors. These were followed for the next few days by visits to places of interest in Darjeeling. The visits involved a good deal of walking on steep roads and tracks and were quite tiring, but they were a necessary part of our training. Each of us had also to take a medical test of fitness. Before we started for the base camp we were given our quota of mountaineering equipment, including an ice axe, a jacket, a sleeping bag and gloves.

The march commenced with a descent from a height of 7,140 feet to Naya Bazar at an altitude of 1,000 feet. Going through fields along the Ranjit river, we came to our next halt at Rishi. From here our third day's march took us to a place called Legship in Sikkim. We were not allowed to use transport and had to walk the entire distance. Unfortunately after walking for three days I had an acute pain in my left knee-cap and found it difficult to keep pace with the team. Beyond the point we had reached there was a steady climb and each further step I took involved much exertion. I was left behind and sat down trying to decide whether I should drop out or keep marching in spite of the pain. Just then a jeep drove up and in the vehicle was Tenzing.

'How are you feeling?' enquired Tenzing.

'I have a terrible pain in my left knee-cap,' I said.

He looked at the swollen knee and asked, 'Is the pain acute?'

'Yes, when I move,' I answered.

He appeared to be lost in thought for a while, and then asked, 'Have you ever had this pain before?'

'No, never.'

The Sherpa accompanying Tenzing said, 'This jeep will return to the Institute after dropping Tenzing. There is another student who cannot go up and has to be sent back to Darjeeling. Why don't you go back in the jeep?'

This was one of the most depressing moments for me. If I went back, it would mean the end of my mountaineering career and the shattering of all hopes I had entertained.

'No, I don't wish to go back,' I said.

Tenzing pointed to a hill and said, 'Look at that hill. You'll have to climb it, and it's almost a 3,000-feet climb. Do you think you'd be able to do it?'

I did not know what to say. Tenzing then took out a small tin of some balm and asked me to apply it on my knee. 'Walk up slowly after a few minutes and if the pain does not disappear, you should go back.' He then drove away in the jeep but left the Sherpa behind with me.

I applied the balm, covered up the knee-cap with a piece of lint, and resumed walking but at a slow pace. To my surprise and delight, the pain was not acute now, and with the Sherpa's help I was able to keep climbing and we reached Tashiding. This was a small place on top of a hill, and it had a school and a little market. We stayed for the night in the veranda of the school which was unoccupied at the time. Before going to bed I applied a little more balm. By next morning the pain had vanished. This was a crucial day in my career. It was to make all the difference to my future as a mountaineer.

I caught up with my companions, Colonel Jaiswal, Manohar Gill and Surinder, the next morning and we resumed our march together. It was the beginning of spring and the hillside was covered with foliage. Flowers, especially orchids and rhododendrons, were in full bloom. The morning walk in these surroundings was very pleasant and I took a number of pictures. We soon came across some orange orchards. We went into one and started plucking the fruit. The sherpa who was following us said, 'This house belongs to a Lama and you must pay for what you eat.'

'There does not seem to be anyone about. Who should we pay?' asked the Colonel.

The Sherpa went inside and returned with the Lama's son. Manohar paid him a rupee and said we had eaten about twenty oranges. The boy asked us to wait while he went in to check the cost. He soon came back with a basket of oranges and said, 'You may have another thirty oranges as they are fifty for a rupee.' We were greatly impressed. The Colonel offered him another rupee but he would not accept it.

After walking for about three hours, the path became narrower and the climb stiffer. The breeze was cool and crisp as we reached the last habitation, Yoksam village. Situated at a height of 5,500 feet, the village was at one time the capital of Sikkim. '*Yoksam*' means a meeting place. According to tradition, it was the point where three Lamas, travelling from three different directions, met and so this was chosen as the site of the State's capital. Later the capital was shifted to Gangtok.

At the graduation ceremony at HMI, Darjeeling

Yoksam is a pretty village with a large camping area. The local inhabitants have Mongoloid features. Their main occupations are agriculture and dairying, piggery and poultry farming. The village has an ancient monastery which the Colonel and I visited. Our schedule allowed a day for rest and we took the opportunity to see a lake nearby. The march was resumed the next day. Our path now lay through a dense forest-like area. There were many bamboo trees and we had to walk through a thick growth of vegetation. Our progress was slow and difficult. The next halting place, Bakkim, was hardly a suitable place for camping. The camp here is usually crowded and unpopular as the place is infested with leeches and is always wet. We were glad to leave Bakkim and the next day's march was a steep climb, through a growth of bamboos at the start, but as we proceeded the tree line gradually disappeared and we entered an area almost without any vegetation.

It was snowing when we reached D'zongri, a pass in the mountains. It kept snowing the whole day and throughout the night but we woke up to find the sun shining brightly. The next stage of the march was across a fairly level area with a steep stretch towards the end. With increasing height the climb was becoming more and more laborious. In the afternoon we reached our base camp Chaurikhang at a height of 14,500 feet. The camp is in the south-west of Kanchenjunga, at the base of the Kanchenjunga massif. All around it are snow-clad mountains – the Kokthang, Kabru, Rahthong and many others. Sleeping in tents at this height was difficult during the first night as it takes some time for a person to adjust himself to the altitude.

We had another day's rest before the training programme was resumed. The trainees were now divided into 'ropes,' each rope consisting of six members. My instructor Ang Temba was a very sturdy man and exceptionally good at rock climbing. There were some good rocks, though not very high, near the base camp. Ang Temba taught us the basic elements of rock climbing. When two of the members of my rope fell ill, Ang Temba had to go down with them and the remaining boys were distributed among other instructors. I was allotted Tenzing's rope and took lessons from him every day. I watched carefully every step that he took so that I could emulate him and learn the correct way of using the equipment. He was cool-headed and never lost his temper. It is to him that I owe much of my knowledge of snow craft, crevasse rescue, belaying and other techniques involved in mountaineering.

Coming from the plains, it was an unforgettable experience for me to be in a region where the snow perhaps never melts and to see for the first time glaciers, avalanches, crevasses and moraines. This was truly nature as I had visualised it and which I had longed for. But our week's course at the camp was over very soon and we were already on our way back to Darjeeling. Those of us who had successfully completed the course were proud of our achievement and looked forward to the graduation ceremony. The short training course had given me a real feel of the snow-covered mountains and a powerful impetus to my enthusiasm for mountaineering. I earnestly hoped that I would make the highest grade to qualify for the advanced course.

The arrival of Prime Minister Nehru was a great occasion for the Institute. BC Roy, Chief Minister of West Bengal, and HC Sarin were also there. Nehru was taken around by Brigadier Gyan Singh and introduced to the instructors. The graduation ceremony had all the colour and dignity of such ceremonials and we were all extremely proud when the Prime Minister pinned the coveted silver axes to our jackets. I had after all qualified for the advanced course.

Back in my Army unit in May 1961, I was glad to find that my course mate Vishnu had been posted to the same unit and that my father's younger brother, Captain Kulvinder, who was about my age, was stationed nearby. The three of us got together on weekends and holidays and had enjoyable outings including visits to remote places in the hills. By now Colonel Kapoor had come to realise that I was genuinely interested in climbing and he invited me to join him whenever he went out on an excursion to the hills. During one of these outings he asked me when I intended to take the advanced course at the Institute. Since I had to go to Pune early next year for my degree course in Electrical and Mechanical Engineering, it would suit me if I could take the mountaineering course this year in September or November. I explained this to Colonel Kapoor who understood my problem and promised to help me. A vacancy was allotted to me for the November course at the Institute.

In November I was again in Darjeeling. This time there were only thirteen of us for the advanced course and in the group was my old companion Colonel Jaiswal. Brigadier Gyan Singh told me that a film team from the Films Division, Bombay, had arrived and would be photographing some of the areas covered by our course. Since I had some knowledge of photography, he asked me to assist the team, and I was introduced to NS Thapa, leader of the team. Thapa said that the projected film, *Songs of the Snow*, would not be directly concerned with our training as he was primarily interested in shooting some high-altitude scenes. I was also glad to meet Lt

Kohli who was then an Equipment Officer in the Institute and had done extremely well as a member of the first Indian Everest Expedition of 1960.

I had the opportunity of getting better acquainted with Thapa and his camera team on our way to the base camp at Chaurikhang. While I had made some 8mm movies, I now had a chance to work with Thapa and his 35 mm cameras. These were huge professional cameras but the basic principles of using them were the same. Thapa was extremely helpful and willing to explain to me the finer points of 35 mm film making. The new film was being made at the instance of Prime Minister Nehru whose love for mountains was well known. Thapa was himself a man from the hills and had made a number of good documentaries. He was anxious that the project he had now undertaken should be completely successful.

Unfortunately all the members of Thapa's team, except himself, fell ill at the base camp. This posed a problem for him but he did not wish to waste any time and decided to go up himself. Some of the mountaineer trainees had fallen ill too and had to be left behind. A small group consisting of Colonel Jaiswal, Thapa, some trainees and myself eventually left for the advance base camp which was very close to Frey Peak, a rocky peak rising to a height of about 19,000 feet. The advance base camp itself was at an altitude of 16,000 feet and the tough climb to Frey Peak was included in the advanced training course. Lt Kohli had told me in Darjeeling that this year, owing to bad weather and other difficulties, none of the trainees had been able to reach the peak. He had also remarked that if anyone from our group managed to climb Frey Peak, he would have a good chance of being included in the Second Indian Everest Expedition which was scheduled to leave in February 1962.

With this conversation in my mind, I became deeply engrossed both in climbing and in photography. Apart from the pictures I took myself, I also helped Thapa. We traversed the area near the advance base camp and photographed the glaciers, crevasses and the many icicles which glittered like diamonds against the deep blue sky. We then pitched camp at the base of Frey Peak from where we would make the final attempt on the peak. The peak is named after Frey who had gone up with Tenzing in 1952 but unfortunately slipped and died while he was half way up the peak. He had fallen close to the spot where we had pitched our camp. Tenzing, who had buried him there, showed us the exact place, and we could see the dead mountaineer's boots and ice axe protruding from under the snow and ice.

We left for the summit early in the morning. Besides Colonel Jaiswal, Thapa and myself, there were the Sherpa instructors. On the first day we had only climbed about half way up when Colonel Jaiswal slipped. Fortunately the rope between him and myself was well secured and he sustained only some minor injuries on his arms and knees. After this accident we could not go any farther and had to come down. This setback was very discouraging but with the Colonel's approval, Thapa, some Sherpas and I decided to make another attempt the next morning.

Profiting from our previous day's experience, we made good progress in the earlier part of the ascent, but as we climbed higher we found that the rocks were very loosely held together and there was a constant danger of crampons slipping on the loose stones or the stones falling and hitting us from above. In fact a stone did fall on Thapa's rucksack but fortunately did not cause much damage.

We, however, kept going and reached the summit by noon. There was snow on the top. Thapa was greatly excited as he moved his camera in all directions from the summit and took some rare shots. He had never had the opportunity of taking photographs from such a height before. I was elated at scaling the peak and was filled with a sense of achievement and self-confidence. In the afternoon we made the descent to the camp and were completely exhausted when we rejoined Colonel Jaiswal and our other companions. Tenzing, who was with the boys at the main camp, had seen us hoisting the national flag on the peak. He sent us a message of congratulations and a cake baked at Chaurikhang.

We returned to Darjeeling after the completion of our outdoor training. Brigadier Gyan Singh and Lt Kohli were quite pleased with our performance and the latter indicated that there might be some chance of my being included in the 1962 Indian Everest Expedition. The report on my advanced course, which came a little later, also recommended that I was suitable for a high altitude expedition.

When the selection of the Everest team was announced in January 1962, my name did not figure in it. But a little later the Army authorities planned to send an all-Army team to scale the 20,000 feet high Mount Kokthang which had not been climbed till then, and I was happy to find that I was selected for this team.

During my advanced course I had done some reconnaissance of Mount Kokthang which was adjacent to Frey Peak and looked like a long ridge. The Army team consisted of Major Rana the leader, Major Ravinder Singh, Captain T Ao, who was a medical officer as well as a climber, Captain Chaudhury and myself. We left Darjeeling on 11 April with eight porters and about two tonnes

Preparing for the All Army Expedition 1962

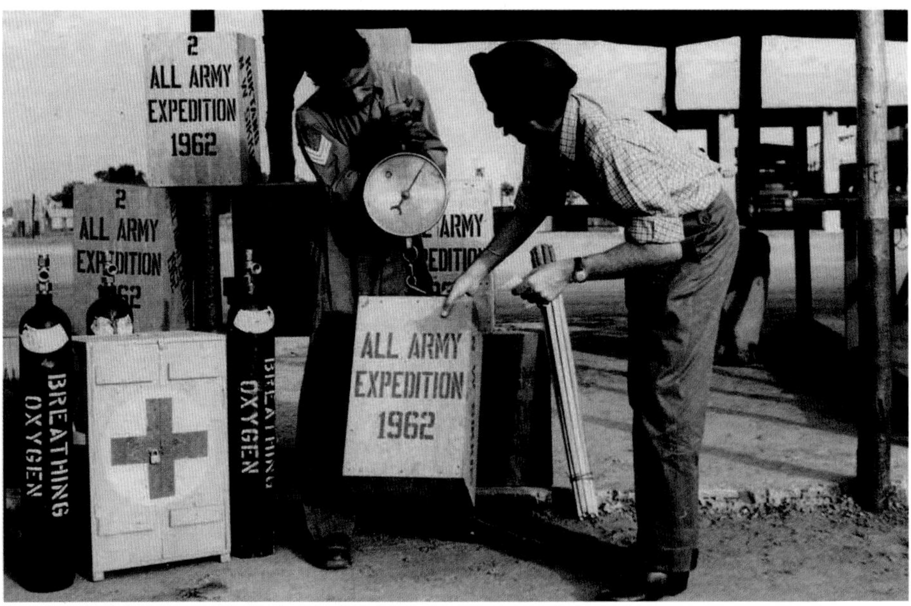

of equipment and stores. Since I was the Quarter Master of the expedition, most of the packing was done under my supervision at the station workshop at Siliguri, where I was posted.

From Darjeeling we followed the same route we had taken for the basic and advanced courses. We spent a day in Yoksam repacking and also had useful discussions with Tenzing about our projected climb to Kokthang. From D'zongri we followed a different route and came through a valley to the site of our proposed base camp at an altitude of 15,550 feet. This place was slightly south-west of the peak, but the peak itself was not visible from there because of a high ridge in between. It was snowing when we reached the site of the base camp.

The weather was very bad and we had to reduce the period of our acclimatisation at the base camp. In spite of the heavy snowfall we succeeded in establishing Camp I at a height of 17,000 feet. Camp II was established at a height of 18,000 feet. The route beyond Camp II was very difficult and we had to cross some crevasses before we put up Camp III at a height of 19,500 feet. The camp was pitched on a broad stretch of hillside with a gentle slope. Sherpa instructor Gombu thought it would make an excellent skiing area.

We left for the summit at 3:00 am on 26 April. I was roped with Sherpa Gombu and Dorji, and we were followed by the leader and another Sherpa in the second rope. In spite of poor visibility and the difficulty of the climb, we made steady progress. Approach from the left was very risky because of the avalanches. Approach from the right would be very long and involve a lot of ice work. We decided that our best course was to follow a lane in the middle of the hill. It started snowing heavily but we kept moving and reached the summit after seven hours of strenuous climbing.

It was a tremendous feeling to stand where no one had stepped before. The weather had cleared by now and we took some photographs from the summit. I could see the other mountains – Janu, Kanchenjunga, Rathong and Kabru. I would have liked to feast my eyes much longer on the panorama of lofty peaks around me but it was getting late and we had to make our way back to the camp. In fact it was quite dark when we did reach the camp and with only one torch between us we had some difficulty in locating it. We had almost decided to make an ice cave and spend the night there, when one of us spotted the camp and we staggered into it.

We had been listening to All India Radio for news on the progress of the Second Indian Everest Expedition led by Major John Dias. While descending to the camp we also heard the broadcast about the success of our own expedition. It was a thrilling experience. The Everest Expedition had eventually to be abandoned owing to bad weather. Commander Kohli, Sonam Gyatso and Hari Dang, who constituted the summit party, had succeeded in climbing to within about 400 feet of the summit, and this was indeed a remarkable achievement. But they could not reach the top, and owing to the early break of the monsoon that year, the expedition had to return without scaling the peak. With this ended our two unsuccessful attempts to scale Mount Everest. Would there be a third Indian attempt, I wondered, and would it succeed? I hoped if there was a third attempt it would not be during the next two years when I would be in the College of Military Engineering.

While we were climbing Mount Kokthang, a French team was trying hard to scale Mount Janu nearby. This is a difficult mountain and the French had been at it for a couple of years and failed several times. But despite repeated failures, they kept trying and succeeded that year in reaching the summit. I thought if Indians showed the same persistence there was no reason why they should not be able to reach Everest.

It was now the beginning of June and time for me to join the College of Military Engineering, Pune, where I would have to study for the next two years for my degree in engineering. It was a prospect I did not look forward to as I would not be able to do any mountaineering for some time.

June is hot and dusty in the plains of northern India but Pune in the west is comparatively cool. Its climate is not unlike that of Secunderabad. The college is located in Kirkee, a suburb of Pune, on the Mumbai-Pune road. Its impressive blocks of buildings are visible from a distance and are spread over a large area. Divided into various wings – administrative, mechanical, engineering and electrical – the college had a large auditorium and an open air theatre. Near the playing fields is a club with a swimming pool and golf links. The training facilities include a narrow-gauge rail track, locomotives and wagons. Located as it is near a river, boating is a favourite pastime for the students, and the college maintains a good boating club. The annual May Queen Ball or river dance held on a huge float on the river is a popular event.

Our course had twenty officers. We were a well-knit, friendly group as we were all previously together in Secunderabad and knew one another quite well. We were comfortably accommodated in a two-storeyed building near the mess. My old companion Vishnu occupied a room next to nine. The atmosphere in the college and hostel was congenial and not different from that of an academic institution except that there was greater emphasis on physical training and we had to wear uniforms.

Our day began with half an hour of physical training at 7:15 am. Class-work continued till 1:30 pm, with a fifteen-minute break in between. There were no classes in the afternoon but we were expected to play games. Thereafter, we could go out to the town if we liked. We were all mobile as most of us had scooters. One or two even owned cars. Studies were not arduous, and unless one aimed at a very high grade, apart from the classes an hour's work at night was adequate. So far as Vishnu and I were concerned, we were not too ambitious and the time we devoted to studies left us with enough leisure to visit our friends in the town. But nearer the examinations, we reduced our outings and took to studies more seriously. I liked the college system of periodical examinations at the end of each three-month term and new subjects being taken up in each term. This system allowed for a good deal of extracurricular activity. I took full advantage of the college camera club to pursue my interest in photography and also occasionally played golf or went boating or sailing. The college had an excellent sailing team and participated in a number of competitions in India.

In Rajouri, Kashmir with Vishnu Sharma

Meanwhile, my interest in mountaineering remained as keen as ever. The second Indian Everest team had returned to Delhi and though the team missed the peak due to very bad weather, there were reports of their experiences which were full of adventure. It was also announced that the third Indian expedition to Everest was scheduled for 1965. This was welcome news to me. By then I would have completed my engineering course and could join the expedition if selected. Of course, my inclusion in the expedition was yet only a hope and a dream, but it was a dream I cherished. I started reading whatever literature on Everest was available in the college library. The books ranged from accounts of the earliest explorations to the Swiss Expedition of 1956. They made fascinating reading, although the names of places in the Everest region and such terms as Western

Cwm and Geneva Spur were then quite unfamiliar to me. Apart from this reading, the nearest I could get to mountaineering during my course at Pune was the cross-country trek organised by the college during the monsoon. There is hilly terrain around Pune with quite a few rocks but not very high. We were transported on vehicles in the morning to a point from where the cross-country trek began through such terrain. The four or five hour walk, with lunch awaiting us at the other end was enjoyable, even though rain sometimes made us quite wet and soggy.

About this time there was a certain amount of pressure from members of my family that I should get married and settle down. Had I succumbed to this pressure, it might possibly have meant goodbye to my mountaineering ambitions. Although several of my course mates had got married and were now living in family quarters outside the college, I was not keen on such a venture and had ignored the matrimonial offers I received through relations and friends. But one particular proposal brought me rather close to matrimony. One of my uncles accompanied a marriage party to Pune and I was also invited to join the party. When we sat down to lunch, facing me was a very charming, young Punjabi girl and I soon guessed that my relations had arranged the seating at the lunch so that I could meet her. With her fair complexion and sharp Aryan features, I was greatly drawn to her. She looked bright and intelligent. In the course of the lunch I often looked at her and could hardly conceal my feelings towards her. But all the time a mental conflict was going on within me and I could not rid myself of the fear that marriage would thwart my ambition of scaling Everest. Even if my future wife did not object to my mountaineering activities, I was sure that my mother would not let me expose myself to the risks of high altitude climbing after my marriage.

Following this meeting, the girl's parents were anxious that I should come to an early decision. It was an embarrassing situation for me as I could not very well tell them that I had to choose between Everest and their daughter. Eventually I sought the help of Major Surinder Singh, an uncle of mine in Pune, and frankly explained my problem to him. He appreciated my feelings and said, 'The chance of anyone's climbing Everest occurs only once in a lifetime. If you do get such a chance, you should not miss it by going for an early marriage.' He was good enough to explain the position tactfully to the girl's family. But when the proposal was dropped, for a time I was filled with remorse.

With the passing of each term in the college, we had to give increasingly serious attention to our studies. The first term covered mainly revision of basic knowledge of mathematics, physics and chemistry but in subsequent terms we had to delve into higher mathematics and engineering. I was interested in electrical engineering but found the theory of machines quite a bore and often enlisted the help of Vishnu or some other course mate in solving the problems.

After the completion of our fourth term we had a month's vacation and I went to Dehradun to attend my sister Guddi's marriage with DP. After the marriage, which was a simple affair, I stayed in Dehradun for a couple of days and then went hiking up to Mussoorie. I did trekking and cycling and met my old officers in the Military Academy. In Dehradun, there was a reunion with many members of the family, which included my younger brother Chotu. He had opted for a naval career and had just passed an examination for admission to the Marine Engineering College in Kolkata.

The month in Dehradun passed all too quickly and I was back in Pune to continue my studies. It was the beginning of 1964 and three mountaineering expeditions had been scheduled for the coming summer. Every mountaineer believed that the team for the 1965 Everest would be selected from among the members of the 1964 expeditions on the basis of their individual performance. Unfortunately, I could not join any of these expeditions as the dates clashed with my final examinations which had been advanced by six weeks. This meant harder work.

After the graduation ceremony at the beginning of June, we dispersed and were posted to different stations. I was glad to be back in Kashmir, this time as an instructor in the high altitude warfare school. Sonamarg, where the school was then in summer camp, was a new area for me. Located in a little valley and surrounded by high hills, it is near an easily accessible glacier and the undulating landscape, with its thick growth of pine and birch trees, provided a magnificent view.

I now had the opportunity of indulging in my favourite hobby again but not having done any climbing for two years, I had some difficulty in adapting myself to it. I got tired quickly and obviously needed to build my stamina again. I decided that if I was to be a successful mountaineer I must take up a fresh training course and revise my lessons in ice craft and rock climbing. This I did and found the training routine both interesting and worthwhile.

The Sponsoring Committee of the Indian Mountaineering Foundation decided to hold all-India trials for selection of the Everest team in October. The selection had to be made from a list of thirty climbers who would participate in the trials. Among those selected where three officers from our school, and I was one of them. Since I had not done many climbs, I guessed that I must be somewhere at the bottom of the list. I would have to compete at the trials with mountaineers who had gone with many previous expeditions and some who had been to Everest twice before. We also feared that all three of us might not be spared from the school as there was a shortage of instructors. But these fears proved unfounded as our Commandant, Lt Col Chadha, not only agreed to let us go but insisted that we put in some more mountaineering practice before we left for Darjeeling.

We assembled in Darjeeling in the first week of October. I was glad to meet Colonel Jaiswal again. He was now living with his family in the Principal's house in the Institute. The Colonel, his wife, and their four children made delightful company and we felt quite at home with them. I met the Sherpa instructors too. Among them was Gombu who had become famous after climbing Everest with the Americans in 1963.

Eventually twenty-eight climbers participated in the trials. Most of them had accompanied expeditions during the year to Nanda Devi, Trisuli, Nanda Devi East and Panchuli. One of the participants was Dr DV Talang, a medical practitioner from Ohio, USA. Mount Rathong (21,911 feet), a virgin peak, had been selected for the trial ascent. The peak had defied previous attempts to climb it. It had been chosen for the trials of Brigadier Gyan Singh's Everest Expedition of 1960 but could not be reached owing to bad weather. A group of mountaineers from West Bengal had also recently failed to scale it.

We left Darjeeling on 15 October, 1964, on a bright, sunny morning. Up to Chaurikhang we followed the usual route taken by the Institute's basic and advanced course trainees and beyond that point we hit Rathong La pass and entered Nepal. The first camp in Nepal was pitched on the moraine of East Rathong La pass. In this region the moraines and glaciers looked quite different from those in Sikkim. They were barren and rugged, with many big boulders, and had a frightening look.

On 20 October, we established our base camp at a height of 15,500 feet on the moraine of Yalong glacier. We then divided into three groups and work began on opening other camps higher up on the hill. But this was the time of the Dussehra festival and we had a lot of trouble with the porters who often got drunk and lingered on in the villages. This interrupted transport of supplies to the base camp and at one stage the situation became so acute that we had no rations left except a tin of condensed milk and some rice and dal. We feared that the progress of the expedition would be hampered and wondered if we could emulate the example of an earlier German expedition.

The Germans had camped at the same site in April that year to climb another peak. When their food supplies had been completely exhausted, they resorted to taking yak blood. Not far from the camp was a herd of hundred yaks, the herd men having migrated from Tibet. The Germans bought yak blood from them at ₹ 5 per litre. (I understood that a large artery in the neck of the animal is pierced to draw the required amount of blood and the wound is then patched up. The Mongols are said to have adopted the same technique with their horses in earlier days). The blood was thickened by boiling and made into small rolls which the Germans were reported to have relished. We preferred, however, to collect some yak milk and cheese instead and fortunately did not have to subsist on these products for long as the porters finally arrived with our stock of provisions.

We set up Camp I at a height of over 17,400 feet, which was almost a four-hour ascent over the glacier. A peculiarity of the glacier was that, although we went over it a number of times, on each occasion we lost our way to the camp. Once it took me over two hours to find my way to Camp I. The next three days were spent in reconnaissance of the peak and a likely approach to it. We took our route to Camp II through crevasses. The route was initially very difficult and later became very tiring as it never seemed to end. Progress was also hampered by some members of the team who fell sick and had to be evacuated. The first summit party of ten members, including Lt Commander Kohli, Colonel Jaiswal and myself, had left for Camp II on 28 October. The distance between the two camps was quite long and it was almost dark when we reached Camp II. We felt that another camp should have been set up in between. Having arrived at the site after a weary climb, it took us a long time to pitch tents and spread our sleeping bags. It was not only dark but the temperature had also dropped considerably after sunset. My fingers and toes became numb. One of us accidentally hit the kettle and the tent was flooded with hot water. This was a minor disaster as we could not prepare any tea and spent a very uncomfortable night.

On the morning of 20 October, we left for the summit. The ascent was extremely arduous as the snow was soft and knee-deep right up to the Col at a height of 20,200 feet. When we reached the Col, we could see the north-western part of Sikkim and the sun slowly coming up the horizon. Beyond this point we had to make our ascent along the main ridge to Rathong. We had walked for about two hours when we realised that to proceed further on the ridge would be dangerous as it was full of cornices. To add to our troubles we had no water and were almost completely dehydrated. We were affected by glacial lassitude and felt drowsy and sleepy. Time too was running short, and we could not discover any easier or safer route.

But the peak was now only 700 feet away and it looked gorgeous and very tempting. Gombu and I roped together and started climbing the ridge again. Another pair, Dorji and Ang Kami, followed us. But the rest did not wish to climb any further and started going down. It was tough going. To overcome dehydration I picked up some icicles and kept sucking them. This helped me a great deal although I had a terrible sore throat later. The four of us kept climbing. The peak looked deceptively close and often we thought we had reached it, only to find that we had come to another hump. It was at about 1:15 pm that we reached the last hump. This was the summit.

The view from the summit was breathtaking. The entire mountain range looked magnificent. The Kokthang appeared a small ridge-like peak; the Frey, rocky and formidable. Opposite was Janu, which the French climbed in 1962. Gombu, Dorji and Tashi looked at Janu and prayed. The Sherpas regard this as one of the most difficult mountains in the region and believe that to climb Janu one must be able to touch one's feet with one's head. Interpreted, it means that the climb to the summit being very tricky, with overhanging snow, the climber may often have to lift his feet so high that they touch his head.

Our success in scaling Mount Rathong gave us an exhilarating sense of fulfilment. The last part of any climb to the summit is the toughest and there is always the feeling of suspense and uncertainty about being able to make it. When you do reach the top you are thoroughly exhausted both physically and mentally. But so great is the joy that your state of exhaustion does not last long. You suddenly feel relaxed and infused with fresh energy for the descent.

I now began to feel confident of being included in the Everest team although of course there was always the proverbial slip between the cup and the lip. We spent about thirty minutes on Rathong peak, resting and taking photographs and then started moving down. The remaining members of our party were making the descent too and we soon caught up with them. The Colonel greeted us and we had some fruit juice. We reached Camp II at about 4:00 pm where the second summit party had already arrived, and spent the night there. The next morning we left for the base camp while the second party consisting of seven resumed the climb to the summit. They too succeeded in reaching the top.

Our return march to Darjeeling began on 1 November and we decided to come down through eastern Nepal which at that time of the year looked quite picturesque. We passed through four or five villages in a day. Dr Telang was very popular with the villagers. They would gather to consult him about some ailment or the other. He supplied them medicines and they offered us chickens, eggs and fruits which were welcome additions to our stock of provisions. It was Diwali time and the villages wore a festive look. We reached Darjeeling on 9 November. Two members of the Indian Mountaineering Foundation, Khera and Sarin, had already arrived there. A few days later, in consultation with Commander Kohli and Colonel Jaiswal and after having detailed discussions on every climber, the selection of the Everest team was finalised and the names were announced the next day. Nine of the participants in the recent trials were selected and I was one of them.

Thus my dream of going up to Everest was nearer fulfilment. Preparations for the Everest Expedition began almost immediately. Major Kumar, who had been put in charge of equipment, wasted no time in taking our measurements for the outfits we would need for the expedition. The clothing would be made in Indian ordnance factories, except for some woollen garments from Ludhiana, while special boots would be ordered from Italy. Those selected for Everest were given various preparatory assignments. I was assigned photography and the task of assisting the Quarter Master. I left for Kashmir with the satisfaction of having achieved something and with hopes of greater achievements to follow.

Before returning to duty I took a month's leave. I thought it would be a good idea to have a holiday since I was quite tired after the trials and it would also refresh me before I left for Everest. To spend my leave I went to Amritsar where my father was posted. The last I had visited Amritsar was when I was a child and had come from Lahore. Amritsar is a big town and is also famous for the Golden Temple. I went with my mother early in the morning to the Golden Temple. It was indeed very soothing listening to the prayers and the *kirtan* there.

My mother had decided to visit her mother who was staying in Agra. Since I was on holiday, she asked me to accompany her. My grandmother was very pleased to meet me. She knew about my going to Everest which she did not mind at all and this really surprised me. In Agra were also staying the in-laws of my cousin Gurjit. They came over to see my mother and with them also came their daughter Mohini who had just finished college.

While I had come to Agra for a holiday, it turned out to be the venue of a marriage proposal. Mohini's parents knew my family rather well and were very keen to arrange her marriage with me. They had already discussed the matter with my grandmother who in turn discussed it with my mother and one fine morning I found myself confronted with this problem. I do not remember how, but the whole thing got decided extremely fast and there was a little ceremony in which I gave her a ring. My only condition was that there could be no marriage till I returned from Everest which was promptly agreed upon. So at last I was fixed (matrimonially speaking) but I did not mind it as long as I was free to go to

Everest. Mohini was very charming and fresh from college. She was intelligent too and my cousin often talked about her. She had taken keen interest in my activities in mountaineering and she was quite excited about my going to Everest.

As my stay in Agra was extremely short I could only go out with her once when we went around Agra. She took me to Taj Mahal. This was the first time I was visiting this famous monument. Although it was a hurried trip, I enjoyed it. The architectural work was unparalleled; I had not seen any monument of this kind before. My fiancée had been to this place a number of times and she acted as a good guide and very briefly narrated the entire history of Taj Mahal. While we were inside the dome, she remarked, 'Isn't it beautiful?' Looking at her I nodded. Her face with its sharp features and her long hair made into a straight plait left an impression of ineffable charm and grace.

I met her again the same day in the evening just before I was to leave for Amritsar with my mother. I was on the terrace of my grandmother's house taking photographs of Taj Mahal and the surrounding tombs when all of a sudden I saw her coming up to me. It was late evening and the sun had just set behind the mighty monument. As the sun dipped lower and lower, the white marble of Taj Mahal turned slowly from light scarlet to pink. It almost matched the colour of her sari. I felt her eyes on me and as I turned to her I saw a dramatic spectacle while the sun was going down. I again noticed her gaze on me. There was a look of faithfulness and belonging in her eyes. There was a long silence. I somehow did not want to break it. She leaned closer, placed her hands in mine and whispered, 'Hari, I wish you the very best of luck in your climb to Everest. I know you will make it.'

After a few long seconds I said, 'Thank you. Will you write to me on Everest?'

'Of course,' she replied.

I was getting late so I finally broke the spell by holding her close to me and wished her goodbye. We left the terrace but the memory of the scene lingered in my mind for a long time after we departed. I left for Amritsar with my mother. It was the end of December when I reported for duty. I could not even stay for a day in Kashmir as I had to move out on a special assignment which involved my training young officers in basic mountaineering and to make them accustomed to high altitude effects. I was given five instructors and led the team to the Eastern Himalayas. This was a fascinating trip which took me to the Assam-Sikkim Himalayas right up to the Indo-Burma border.

Among the places I visited in NEFA during my special mission of showing young officers how to get acclimatised to high altitude conditions and teaching them the basic elements of mountaineering was Seal pass. Situated at a height of approximately 16,000 feet, the pass connects Tezpur with Twang and Bum La on the Indo-Tibet border. The road to Sela passes through a beautiful valley which was one of the battlefields during the Chinese invasion of India in 1962, and at the time of my visit was still littered with grim remnants of the war. As we drove along, we came across a number of wrecked tanks – some precariously balanced on the edge of the road – as also mortars, rockets and grenades, many possibly unexploded.

As we stayed for the night at the top of Sela pass, I had plenty of time to explore the surrounding area. The two lakes on the pass were frozen as it was mid-winter. Nearby was a plateau which, I was warned, might be heavily mined. Luckily I had in my group some young officers who were knowledgeable about mines. We saw heaps of empty cartridges and a number of unexploded bombs and rockets. One site had obviously been an officers' mess at the time of the invasion, I picked up a torn mess register and helmets riddled with bullets. What had been the fate of the wearers of those helmets, I wondered. While coming up I also saw the spot where the Chinese ambushed and killed Brigadier Hoshiar Singh who commanded the Indian brigade in the area. On the other side towards the end of this road somewhere near Bum La, my uncle

Colonel Ahluwalia, who was commanding a battalion there, had fought the Chinese. Overwhelmed by a much larger force and the enemy's superior fire power, he had fought gallantly but was severely wounded and taken prisoner. He was treated well by the Chinese and released after the end of the war. The Chinese had taken him to Tibet where he visited the Potala Palace.

As is well known, the Chinese invasion had taken our troops by surprise. Untrained for fighting at high altitudes and without the proper equipment and clothing for such fighting, they were unable to resist the Chinese onslaught. Much of the fighting took place at altitudes ranging from 14,000 to 17,000 feet. At this level it takes a person more than fifteen days to get to breathe normally. But Indian soldiers had to be rushed to the sites of the battle from places more or less at sea level and had to go into combat in some cases within a few hours of their arrival. The enemy also had the advantage of vastly superior numbers and adopted their well-known 'human wave' tactics with a callous disregard for casualties. They operated from a more favourable terrain and many of their soldiers hailed from the mountainous regions of Manchuria and were experienced in mountain warfare. The network of strategic roads which they had been building in the preceding years and the Tibetan labour force which they were able to press into service were important factors in the logistic support of their army. They were able to bring essential stores and supplies by three-ton trucks to places within a day's march from the battlefield.

In spite of these very severe handicaps and being greatly outnumbered and out-weaponed by the Chinese, Indian troops offered stubborn and gallant resistance and fought many heroic actions. One of these was the battle at Razang La at an altitude of 17,000 feet. At this snow-covered height a single Indian rifle company of the Kumaon Regiment, assisted by a section of 3-inch mortars gallantly resisted massive attacks by a Chinese battalion which was supported by heavy artillery, mortars, rockets and heavy automatics. Ninety-six Indian soldiers perished in the action but

the Chinese casualties were much higher and ran into several hundred killed and wounded. A visit to the site after the battle showed it littered with Chinese field dressings and blood-splashed bits of Chinese clothing and head-gear. This battle will go down in history as an epic of undaunted courage and heroic resistance by a handful of Indian soldiers. It was fitting that the company's commander, Major Shaitan Singh, under whose gallant leadership the action was fought, should be awarded the PVC – the highest Indian military award for valour.

The role played by the Indian Air Force in this war was equally commendable and worthy of the highest traditions of the force. Indian pilots performed great feats of endurance, and skilful, determined flying under most unfavourable conditions. Aircraft landed on improvised strips at altitudes of 16,000 feet or higher, at times in the face of enemy fire. Airdrops in NEFA were made at places where normally flying a Dakota was considered extremely hazardous and prohibited in peace time. In the kind of terrain and the type of flying which the Indian Air force had to undertake during this war in NEFA the use of the autopilot was quite out of the question. Every minute of airborne time was thus manual flying and Indian pilots did an average of five and a half hours or more of manual flying every day through hazardous valleys and gorges. Helicopters, too, flying low and within easy range of the enemy's small army fire, undertook

FACING PAGE: With Mrs and Col Jaiswal, Principal, Himalayan Mountaineering Institute and Chogyal of Sikkim

gallant rescue operations for several hours every day. Some were shot down by enemy fire. As I lay in my tent at the Sela pass that night, I wondered why the Chinese, who had always professed to be friendly towards us, had launched this invasion. I recalled the slogan 'Hindi Chini Bhai Bhai' which was voiced by huge crowds at the time of the Chinese Premier Chou En-lai's visit to India.

What had happened to that goodwill and why had the Chinese so treacherously attached us?

It was now the beginning of February and my last assignment at the Indo-Sikkim border was coming to an end. Back in Gangtok, I met General Har Prasad popularly known as General HP. He was keenly interested in all kinds of outdoor activities and was now commanding a division there. He told me that he had a telephone call from Colonel Jaiswal and that the Colonel had invited me to spend a few days in Darjeeling before proceeding to Delhi. That suited me well and I left for Darjeeling the following afternoon.

It was the beginning of February and Darjeeling was still very cold. It was almost dark when I reached the Colonel's house. I went straight into the drawing room; there was nobody there. Perhaps they were all upstairs. Suddenly, I saw somebody coming down, wearing black jeans and a long coat. It was a girl. She came and stood in front of me. I had never seen her before. She looked good. 'I am Captain Ahluwalia,' I said. 'I am Rita, a guest here,' was her reply. 'I wonder if you know me.' She seemed to know a lot about me. Perhaps the Colonel and his family had been talking to her about me as they had become very friendly with me. There was a little fire burning in the fireplace. She picked up a few pieces of wood and threw them into the fire. 'It is very cold,' she said. 'Yes, it is,' I agreed, although I was in uniform and wore a greatcoat over it and did not feel very cold. 'I am sure the journey from Gangtok to Darjeeling must have been tiring in your jeep,' she remarked.

'It was rather pleasant driving up,' I said. She again looked at me, picked up a few pieces of wood lying in a basket and threw them into the fire. 'May I know where the Colonel and the children are?' I asked.

'The Colonel is away for some work but the children will be down in a minute. Do sit down please,' she said. In the meantime, she kept up the conversation. 'Colonel tells me that you did extremely well during your trials. Oh, I am sorry I did not ask you what you would like to have.'

In the meantime Mrs Jaiswal came in. She was very happy to see me and said, 'Hari, your room in the guest house is ready. The geyser is on; would you like to go and change?' 'That would be fine,' I said and left for my room.

There was another guest, Norman Dyhrenfurth, leader of the successful American expedition, who was also staying in one of the rooms in the guest house. For the few days that we were together I took every opportunity of getting from him as many details of Everest as possible. I was particularly curious about Hillary's Chimney. He told me that according to the accounts of the Chimney he got from his climbers, it was neither easy nor very difficult – it was a question of getting the correct hold to cross the hurdle. Norman was an expert in photography and he gave me valuable technical advice on how to get excellent pictures, both stills and movies. A number of receptions had been arranged for Norman. This kept me quite busy too, since I was staying in the guest house I would spend some time with Colonel Jaiswal and his family.

I boarded the plane at Siliguri and was in Delhi to join the rest of the members of the expedition. There was hectic activity and I did not have any time to think either of the future or of the past.

Upwards through Nepal

On the evening of 22 February we assembled at Delhi railway station. It was a cool wintry evening. The station appeared busier than usual. People moved hurriedly to and fro. Huge loads of mountaineering equipment moved slowly through the crowd. I followed one of the loads and reached the platform. A large crowd had gathered to say goodbye to us – our close relatives, friends and well-wishers. But there was an official touch too. A number of press reporters and photographers were there and their flashlights lit up the dusky evening. Everyone that I could think of, a friend or relative, was there and more people kept coming in a steady stream. The bogies allotted to the expedition were packed to capacity with stores and miscellaneous goods.

We had already dispatched most of our stores and equipment to Jaynagar or to Kathmandu. The bulk of our stores and equipment loads contained food, medicine and climbing gear. These were despatched by road earlier. Each load had been carefully packed weighing not more than sixty pounds. The cost of the entire expedition, with things bought at cost price and with some donations, was then between six to eight lakh rupees. Today the cost would be enormous. Foreign expeditions spend much more owing to the transportation of stores and members from the respective countries.

FACING PAGE:
On the way to
Camp III

Marking of loads in Jay Nagar

We had 800 porters who would carry the load from Jaynagar to the base camp. These porters had come from the Sherpa land which is close to the Everest camp. There were eighty Sherpas, who did not carry any load from Jaynagar but only helped porters in lifting the load across the Everest Camp. The loads were packed in such a manner that two boxes were opened every day to meet all our requirements for the day.

Some expeditions followed routes through Sikkim and Tibet prior to World War II but this was for the climb from the north side. For us it was easier and cheaper to start the journey from Jaynagar. We were satisfied with our allotment of equipment and commissariat goods. Almost everything that we required had been catered for. It is not easy to determine the exact needs of an Everest expedition; the more you go into minute details, the more items you wish to carry. In fact, there can be no end to your needs and one has to draw the line somewhere.

It was about 8:45 pm when the Lucknow Mail steamed out of the station. All of us waved a final goodbye to those who had come to see us off and went into our allotted compartments. Soon there was only the rhythmic noise of the moving train accentuated by the silent and contemplative mood of the members who sat thinking perhaps of the immediate past and probably of what the future might bring. Most of us doubtless felt a deep sense of separation – almost a wrench – from our friends, relatives and well-wishers who had been so close to us for the past few days in Delhi and many others who were at distant places and yet very close to us in spirit. Mentally and physically, we were all tired and needed some rest before starting our trek from Jaynagar.

We could not sleep as almost all the stations en route were full of people waiting to greet us. The hospitality and fellow feeling of our people is indeed commendable but sometimes it extends to a point where it becomes embarrassing. At one of the railway stations, past midnight, there was an old lady who could hardly walk but had taken the trouble to come to see us. She offered sweets to us and said, 'I may not be living when you return crowned with success, but I will remember you all in my prayers. You are going to a great mountain and I have no doubt that you will do great thing.' As she left, her eyes were moist.

We reached Lucknow in the morning, from where we switched over to the metre gauge railway and reached Jaynagar on the third day in the early hours of the morning. All of us were still asleep and had to be shaken awake. Since it happened to be a terminus some of us moved about on the platform in night clothes and dressing gowns. Our baggage was taken out and stacked neatly on the platform.

We were received by the officers of the Nepal Government and of the Indian Embassy in Kathmandu and also by the Sirdar and the Deputy Sirdar of the expedition. After the garlanding ceremony without which nothing is complete in India, the Sirdar and his Deputy greeted us in the Buddhist manner by draping our shoulders with silk scarves. After this ceremony we moved about on the platform. The colourful marigold garlands were still around our necks and the silk scarves around our shoulders. Some of the Sherpas who had climbed with us before and who would be very much a part of the expedition were also at the railway station. It was a happy reunion with them and there was much thumping of backs and shaking of hands. I was eager to see our Sirdar, Ang Tshering. He looked lean and very young. A lot would depend on how he controlled the porters and the Sherpas. There was also Phu Dorji, our Deputy Sirdar. He had an excellent record and we were proud to have him with us. He greeted us with a big Sherpa grin. I was meeting him for the first time and did not know that I would be teaming up with him for the climb. From our very first meeting I developed a tremendous liking for him. There was Nawang Hilla, too, who blushed like a woman and had his hair in pigtails. There were other Sherpas who had carried loads to great heights on Everest. I was delighted to be among these brave, happy people and looked forward to companionship with them.

We had booked a Dak Bungalow with a very large compound where the expedition would stay for the next two days to sort out the loads and allot them to various porters. The Dak Bungalow had five large rooms with a big veranda. In front of the veranda there was a huge mango grove under which we stacked our stores item-wise. In the backyard there was a well and a fairly large open area where fruit trees of guavas, bananas and papayas flourished. The well water was very sweet and, we were told, good for the stomach. It was to be drawn out with a bucket and rope.

The loads sent earlier had already arrived and were lying neatly stacked and the place was full of people – members, Sherpas, porters and many local enthusiasts. While some of the members were busy sorting out loads in the mango grove, others were busy getting their hair cropped by the barber in the hope of developing a new and plentiful growth in the mountains. At Jaynagar we had a very busy time checking and re-checking our food, medical and equipment loads. Some loads had to be opened and re-packed as many boxes had been damaged in transit. A medical check-up of the members and Sherpas was done by the expedition doctors. We were all inoculated and vaccinated against cholera, smallpox and typhoid.

On the 26th we had planned to leave this little town early in the morning but last minute hitches delayed our departure by two to three hours. We passed through the bazaar and the narrow streets of Jaynagar which were full of people. The womenfolk in their gaudy clothes looked as if they were going to a village fair. We looked different from the others because of our mountaineering apparel – marching boots, rucksacks in bright red and blue colours, bright coloured jerseys and trousers. For walking sticks, we used ice-axes. But we were by no means a strange sight to the local people. They had seen mountaineering expeditions passing through their streets before. Many small arches had been built to honour us. At a number of places we saw boards put up which read, 'Farewell to the Indian Everest Expedition,' both in Hindi and English. There was a group of schoolgirls who applied the traditional tika on the forehead of all the members and offered us sweets. At one end of Jaynagar town, a tea party had been arranged by the head of the town and prominent citizens. Some speeches were made, photographs were taken and we were again garlanded. We got so immersed in these delightful formalities that we had to be reminded that there was a long way ahead before we reached our next camping place. We also knew that we would have to go through different kinds of formalities with the Nepalese Customs authorities at the barrier. One of our hosts loaned the services of his truck to take us to our first camping ground. I thought it was a good idea to cover the first part of the journey on a truck as the sun was blazing hot. After all the lavish feasting we were in no mood to walk.

We soon reached the Customs barrier. There was a little hut by the side of the road and a long pole stretched across the road. Some Nepalese customs officials were on duty and they took quite a long time in clearing us. We had to fill in various forms and there were also some arguments between us and the officials. Eventually the pole was lifted and we were told that we could pass into Nepal. We resumed our journey by truck. The little road now turned into a bullock-cart track which was bumpy and very dusty and the journey became uncomfortable. Most of us preferred walking to getting the bumps in the truck. Reaching our first camping ground, we found that it was a beautiful place with a huge mango grove, well outside the village. The camp had been carefully set up. The mess could be seen from a distance with its colourful folding chairs and tables arranged outside the mess tent. The white mess tent used by the Sherpas also stood nearby. Indian film songs were blaring at full blast. This attracted the villagers who had already crowded round the record player. The Sherpas ate all their meals with the members, so the mess tent was mostly used for recreational purposes that is to say for gambling, a favourite Sherpa pastime. Often short of cash, the losers' slogan was, 'Debt payable when able.'

By late afternoon, all the loads had come in. A check was made and everything was in order. After having a little rest, we swung our towels across our shoulders and made a bee-line for a stream nearby to wash away the dust we had collected. Hereafter a set routine was followed. The day would begin rather early in the morning and we would be well on our march before sunrise. The porters were very prompt in collecting the loads. At times they were well ahead of us. It was pleasant walking early in the morning but as the sun rose on the horizon, it would get hot and on certain days the heat was unbearable. There was no greenery around. The fields were terraced and tidy, but the landscape was bare except for the sugarcane waving in the hot wind. We invariably stopped where sugarcane juice was being extracted. After having two to three glasses of fresh juice, we could resume our march. The juice was extracted in the same way as it is done in India. It is obtained by pushing the sugarcane through two rollers which turn on top of each other, power being provided by a moving ox who goes round and round in a circle. After the sugarcane has been crushed through the rollers, the juice would trickle down into a bucket.

We carried twenty-five tonnes of equipment and stores which were distributed among 800 porters to be carried up to the base camp. For higher camps, we had fifty Sherpas and most of them had come from the Solu Khumbu area. In fact most of the Sherpas and porters had walked all the way from their distant homes to join us at Jaynagar. Sherpas are the backbone of any expedition to the roof of the world. There were many Sherpas who had gone to Everest with previous expeditions. We had an excellent team of kitchen staff. Thandup was the chief cook, assisted by Danu and a team of ten other Sherpas. Thandup had been rising in honorary military rank with every successful expedition. He was 'Brigadier' when we left for Everest and on our return after the successful climb, we conferred on him the rank of 'Major General.'

By virtue of his experience in the mountains for the past twenty-five years, Thandup was a great asset. An excellent cook by any standards, clean, methodical and cheerful, he could bake anything from a bun to a large birthday cake. He was good at making steaks and could prepare European food, as well as Indian food. Since I was placed in charge of the kitchen as assistant to Mulk Raj, I was constantly in touch with him and I found that he was a moving encyclopaedia on mountaineering matters, particularly on the dates and details of all the previous expeditions to Everest. He was very frank in talking about the eating habits of members of previous expeditions – from roast yak and chips so loved by the English to the familiar Indian yak special curry of our group. He had been with almost every expedition that had gone to the region and knew all the camping spots used by the previous expeditions. We entrusted him with the selection of our camping places after each trek of four to six hours.

Our porters, both male and female, carried an equal amount of load. Each load was very carefully prepared and weighed sixty pounds. The deputy leader wanted to recruit more female porters than male as he said the women drank less and created less fuss in carrying the loads. They were indeed a hardy lot, strong and spirited. At times a woman porter would carry her husband's load a short distance in addition to her load, as he would be drinking or drunk. There were many female porters. In fact, of the 800 porters in the expedition, almost half were female. I remember an incident when a woman porter gave birth to a child. Just for a day or two after delivering the child she did not carry the load, but then resumed carrying the load. This is not unusual. She probably delivered the baby at a height of about 7,000 ft.

The loads were conspicuously marked with various colours, the idea being that one could make out from a distance whether it was food, equipment, medical stores or personal baggage. In every category each load was numbered. The expedition had made attractive badges which had been numbered and each porter was given a badge bearing the number of the load he was expected to carry. The porters are generally honest and there was no case of theft or any load being misplaced. Once a load had been allotted to a porter, one could rest assured that it would reach its destination. I remember we had about four to five loads of Nepalese currency. To ensure the safety of the precious cargo, we used to choose the prettiest Sherpanis to carry these loads. Most of the Sherpas and porters would constantly keep an eye on these charming belles. This made the precious cargo perfectly safe!

The leader was popularly known as Mohan by the members and Bara Sahib by the Sherpas and porters. Bara Sahib had an excellent record of service in the field of mountaineering. He had been to Everest with both the previous Indian expeditions. In the summit party in the second expedition in 1962 he had the unique experience of spending three consecutive nights at about 28,000 ft. Mulk Raj, who was known as Mulki, was the only vegetarian to go to such heights. It is always difficult to provide for the required amount of calories in the diet of a vegetarian, which is compensated by eggs, cheese, honey and chocolate. But since he was the 'housewife' of the expedition, he knew best how to tackle this problem. He had a reputation for strict supervision of the kitchen, whether he was out with an expedition or back in his own home. He was especially prone to making surprise checks on rapidly disappearing items of edible stores. One day when the consumption of eggs was excessive, I was asked to explain how this had happened and had to give details of the eggs consumed that day. We had consumed something like 120 eggs and it was quite a problem to account for each egg. However, with much effort, I accounted for all except ten. It took me quite a while to find out that Mulki himself had eaten ten eggs in lieu of our quota of meat. We were thankful to Mulki for such strict vigilance on the consumption of food which ensured that there was never a shortage of any kind of food right through the expedition and on its return journey.

On the approach march, our day used to begin at 5:30 a.m. and by noon we used to be well established in a new camp. Invariably we had hot lunch cooked by Thandup and his staff waiting for us. This routine continued for many days. Passing through streams, grassy slopes, terraced fields and forests, the march led on and on through the beautiful and picturesque countryside of Nepal. During the monsoon, the local bridges got weakened, and the lighter ones sometimes got washed away. We had, therefore, to construct several small bridges or strengthen the existing ones with logs which we bound together with ropes and cables from our stock. These logs were carried from one of the local villages and were sometimes as large as trees. To make a bridge two logs were bound together and put across a crevasse. We knew we had to do it the hard way or we would have to wade through the streams. Some of us had to make rough canoes from hollowed out tree trunks to ferry men, women porters and precious baggage across the fast moving small rivers. We went higher and higher towards the challenge of the eternal snows. Indians had faced this challenge twice before but both times had been forced back by bad weather while almost within reach of the summit. Would this be a case of being lucky the third time around?

The deputy leader of the expedition was Major Kumar who was popularly known as 'Bull.' He had been to Everest in 1960 and had reached a height of 28,300 ft. He had suffered heavy frost-bite on his feet in the expedition which he led to Mount Neelkantha in 1961. After Neelkantha, he had been in hospital for quite some time and had to lose bits of his toes from both feet. Extremes of temperature troubled him but he had equipped himself with battery-heated socks. During the early stages of the march, he had hired a pony which looked more like a donkey. It was quite a sight seeing Bull sitting on the animal with his feet dangling, almost touching the ground. He always used an umbrella to protect his head which had a growth far from luxuriant! He looked after his animal rather well. He used to share his breakfast with his pony and made sure that it had all the rest it needed. But in spite of all this, the animal failed to cope and Bull had finally to abandon the donkey ride and join us marching. He confessed that walking was much more comfortable. He had been given a most important assignment, namely, designing and procurement of equipment for the present expedition. The march now led us through the most remote villages of Nepal to its heavily wooded, magnificent countryside. We passed many paddy fields and maize plantations. We were all in the best of spirits and everyone seemed happy and optimistic.

The long approach march to the Everest provided a great opportunity to get to know one another and also to communicate with and appreciate the Sherpas, besides developing one's outdoor hobbies. The understanding that grows up among the members and the Sherpas is of great help later when the climb becomes difficult.

Members who are interested in photography, geology, flora and fauna and bird watching have ample time and opportunity to develop their hobby. My main hobby is photography and I got a rare opportunity to practise it. I took as many photographs from as many spots in the mountains as possible, once at the risk of my life. I had gone with Major Kumar to a place near the base camp. We had to walk two hours over rocks, snow, and at many places we slipped but we continued as we thought that farther up we would get a better view of the north face of Everest. It was after walking

Filming the expedition

almost three to four hours that we reached the spot and when I was about to take the photograph a thick cloud covered the Everest face. Our effort and hard labour was thus wasted. There were many occasions like this but at last I did get the picture I wanted. To me climbing a mountain and photographing it is like loving it. One inches up to the top and looks back, and then comes away and looks up. And all that you have with you is a feeling and a picture of the enchantment you have experienced. Photography is the eye with which you have a relook at the hidden past, the eye that makes the heart rejoice yet again and the mind recreate the glorious vision you had seen before. We had a number of cameras with the expedition ranging from the very simple and cheap ones to the most complex and expensive. For my personal use, I greatly depended on my Nikon camera which was very heavy. During the approach march there are many opportunities for making good movies – portraits, groups and landscapes. I was greatly helped by Cheema. We both shared the load of the movie camera. After the day's march, some

With Cheema and Bahuguna

of us used to visit the porters' camp and taste their *tsampa,* or their Tibetan tea. *Tsampa* and Tibetan tea are two important items of their diet. The tea taken with a little butter and salt is supposed to cure headaches, remove fatigue and make one feel fresh again. It is made from Chinese brick tea, and if well made, it leaves a delicate flavour in the mouth. I found that home-made beer and spirits called *chhang* or *rakshi* were very popular among the Sherpas. *Chhang*, the Tibetan version of beer, is brewed from barley and is an excellent drink. These drinks were also popular among children and the womenfolk. We also liked them but they were most popular with Gyatso and Cheema. They would be prepared to take on any of the locals in a drinking competition.

After five days of march, we reached a little river called Sunkosi which we crossed with the help of a craft made locally from thick logs hollowed from inside and fashioned into boats. Some of the members swam across this river which caused some excitement to the local population. Some of them followed the members into the river. Others kept giggling and laughing and making comments on our style of swimming. The river is fed by the melting snows of the high Himalayas and the water is extremely cold. I remember this as one of the prettiest camp sites before reaching Solu Khumbu. As the march was not very long we reached it before noon. Thandup, Danu and others had prepared a tasty meat curry and rice and there was chilled beer awaiting us. The beer had been kept in the river for refrigeration.

After a six-day march we reached an important place called Okhaldhunga. Okhaldhunga is perhaps the bigger village on this route to Everest. It has a college, a large post office and a good market place. It is also the headquarters of Bara Hakim. The village wore a festive look. People moved about in their best clothes, the women loaded with jewellery. One of the girls I photographed had a huge necklace with silver and gold coins more than forty of fifty years old.

We were met by the official of the Indian Embassy and prominent people of Okhaldhunga. I was delighted to meet Captain Jain of the Indian Embassy who was my course mate at the Military Academy. He had brought huge crates of tinned beer. 'There cannot be a more refreshing drink than beer after a long day's march,' said Captain Jain. I fully agreed and the beer started flowing like water. All you could hear was the gurgling of the liquid as it came out of tins and Jain saying, 'Oh, you are slow, have another one.' We met a few ex-servicemen who had served the British in World War II who proudly displayed their medals. I met two Gorkhas who had won the Victoria Cross, both very simple, dignified and very proud of their Army service.

We camped on ground close to the college. In the evening we played a volleyball match with the college team. I do not remember who won, but it was a good game. In the evening we celebrated the birthday of Dr Talang who was popularly known as Lala. Lala's interest in mountaineering brought him all the way from Cleveland, USA. He is a gynaecologist but served the expedition extremely well as a physician. Thandup had baked a huge birthday cake for him. In the evening the leader gave a dinner to the senior officials of Okhaldhunga and a few members of the American Peace Corps. Most of us sent heavy mail home to friends and relatives. Later I was to discover that some of my letters posted at Okhaldhunga reached India only after our return!

The next day happened to be a weekly market day. Gyatso, who was a local purchase officer, bought a few loads of dry rations including vegetables. Some of us sat down for a morning session of left-over beer. We took it leisurely as we were told that the next march was not lengthy, only up to a place called Lakhop, at a pass of 10,000 ft. We finally left Okhaldhunga around lunch time. The path slowly became steeper and there seemed to be no end to it. It was about 10:00 pm when we reached the new camp tired and exhausted as a number of times we had lost our way. In fact our leader was very worried and was about to send a search party when we arrived. The dawn next morning brought us a truly magnificent view of the mountains. The sun was just beginning to rise in the distance. The mountains started turning slowly from pink to scarlet and then to gold. There were Pumori, Gaurishanker, Tewache and many others, all clad in a soft, gold-coloured blanket.

Our march now took us to the districts of Solu and Khumbu. All the Sherpas hail from these two districts. One can see a distinct change in the countryside here. The meadows are bigger and the landscapes wider and more colourful. They are overgrown with pine trees, fir trees and rhododendrons. Plants and flowers in full bloom were all around us. All this added to the grandeur of the region. We soon reached a place called Phaplu where there was a little school and a monastery. We had a special audience with the Lama who looked very young. Beyond this point the path led on to high passes and for the first time we came across the Mani Walls and Chortens and the prayers carved on them. One would invariably see a Lama turning a prayer-wheel and chanting the mantra, 'Om Mani Padme Hum' (Hail, the jewel in the lotus).

The view of the changing landscape was often breathtaking and we seemed to be looking at a large painting hung on a wall.

There was increasing depth and colour. We also noticed a marked difference in the costumes of the villagers and their rituals. Those who lived at lower heights in Nepal were Nepalese of Hindu faith. The Hindu religion doubtless came to Nepal from northern India. In the higher regions are the Sherpas who have Mongol features and are Buddhists. It is said that Saint Padma Sambhava introduced Buddhism into Tibet around AD 750. It then spread to the upper regions of Nepal. In Tibet, the Indian saint is known as Lopen Rinpoche, Guru Rinpoche and Ugyan Rinpoche.

After a march of eleven days, we reached Dudhkosi (river of milk), a mighty stream gushing down the valley. This stream is fed by melting snow from the southern side of the Everest massif. We crossed the river with the help of a wooden bridge, a very primitive form of bridge which is joined with the end of tackles and is not very strong. It is quite dangerous to cross these bridges and we were careful to send parties of only two or three people at a time. Some of us who had reached the place early had a dip in the Dudhkosi and enjoyed the ice-cold bath. The next bath, we knew, would be after many weeks. We were beginning to tire of our daily marches. Suddenly we would come across a steep path taking us to a height of about 10,000 ft. or above, and then down into the valley only to find that the next march would also be through a high pass. It was not unlike a constant game of 'snakes and ladders.' Carved prayers on Mani Walls were quite common along the paths and also the Chortens. We found a lot of prayer flags tied to a tree at the highest point on the pass. The Buddhists believe that if the prayers are written on a piece of paper or cloth and made to flutter at a height, they spread the message farther and deeper. At times we would come across prayer flags on a long ring with its two ends tied on the sides forming an archway on the pass. The prayer flag can be of any colour – red, blue, yellow, green, orange or white. Prayer flags provided a very welcome sight to us as they often meant the end of a steep climb. After marching up and down endlessly for days, at last Namche Bazar was sighted. Just short of this point we passed the Lukla air strip which was built through the efforts of Sir Edmund Hillary. Only a small plane can land on this strip. It is mostly used by tourists who come to this area to visit Thyangboche. Although Namche Bazar is at a height of 12,400 ft., there was no snow when we reached it.

Just below Namche Bazar there is a steep gradient, so one is quite exhausted on reaching it. At the entrance to the village we found a huge arch like gate on which 'Welcome Indian Everest Team' was written. Unlike other villages, there was nobody at the gate to receive us. At first sight, the village seemed uninhabited except for a few villagers hurriedly moving about. Later we came to know that the villagers had gathered there but since we arrived late, they had all dispersed. Namche Bazar is the most modern village of Sherpa land. All the renowned Sherpas hail from this village. It lies on a bare slope of a steep hill with rows of houses made of stones, mud and wooden planks. It looked extremely dry and dusty, with hardly any trees around. Water was brought with the help of bamboo pipelines from the fresh streams above. Namche Bazar had about a hundred and fifty families. The people of Namche Bazar were more prosperous than those anywhere else in Sherpa land. The village sprung to prominence after the nineteen sixties when the route from Nepal to Everest through the south face was opened. The route from Tibet through the north face had already been closed by the Chinese.

Ever since the Chinese took over Tibet, the route from the north had been closed. Thus Namche Bazar became an important base for all expeditions going to Everest or to mountains close to it. The village also had a flourishing trade with Tibet. Our expedition used the south-west route from Nepal, which passed Namche Bazar which has become a famous centre. The menfolk were seen wearing clothing inherited from many foreign expeditions. It is amazing that one can buy in Namche Bazar almost any kind of mountaineering equipment, including skis used or unused, much cheaper than at the ex-factory price. Once I was short of a sweater, which I suspected was stolen. When I went to buy one at Namche Bazar, I found to my surprise my own sweater at the shop, for which I was forced to pay. After the expedition we brought back the equipment to these stores.

In fact an expedition to a mountain ranging from 20,000 ft. to 22,000 ft. can be completely equipped with mountaineering equipment procured in this village.

We wanted to avoid camping in the village for security and a better view, so we camped on a plateau just above Namche Bazar which was about twenty minutes' walk from the village. From the camp area we had the first glimpse of the white peaks in the distance on the northern horizon. Only the tip of Everest could be seen with its trailing snow plume. Lhotse and Nuptse too were visible. The older members of the expedition pointed out to us the peaks like Thamserku, Tewache and Kwangde, all glistening in the distance. It was difficult to take one's eyes off Everest. Even though only a tip of the mountain was visible, it looked most impressive and inspiring. I spent a lot of time gazing at the majestic peak – the ultimate goal of every mountaineer. My thoughts went back to 1852 when Everest was discovered as the highest mountain in the world. The discovery is attributed to the hard work put in for many years by the Survey of India. Known previously as Peak V it was named in honour of Sir George Everest, who had been the Surveyor General of India. Its Tibetan name is Chomulungma (the Goddess Mother of the Earth). In Nepal Everest is known as 'Sabar Matha.'

It was only in 1893 that the idea of taking an expedition to the Everest was first mooted by General (then Captain) Bruce. It was, however, considered too ambitious and no one paid any attention to it. The British authorities in India were not anxious to persuade Tibet or Nepal to allow mountaineers into that region. In March 1919 a paper was read before the Royal Geographical Society by a young Army Officer, Captain JBL Noel of the Indian Army, in which he described a journey made by him in 1913 to the close vicinity of the Everest. He had managed to penetrate into the Everest region in disguise. He ended his paper saying, 'A fully equipped expedition must explore and map Mount Everest.' The Presidents of the Royal Geographical Society and the Alpine Club supported him strongly. Permission to enter Tibet was granted in 1920 and in the following year an Everest Committee was formed in London to organise an expedition to Mount Everest.

In 1921, the British were the first to send a reconnaissance party to the Everest region from Darjeeling. The pioneers approached the mountain from Sikkim and then through the south of Tibet. They spent three months exploring an unknown part of the world in the area of Rongbuk and the Rongbuk glacier which later provided the north route to the summit of Everest. Rongbuk has an ancient Buddhist monastery which lent support to the expeditions launched from the north side.

In 1922, the British launched the first full-scale expedition and reached a height of 27,300 ft. but suffered the loss of seven porters. In spite of considerable opposition, oxygen was first used in 1922. I am glad that this was so as without the use of oxygen, man may never have been able to reach the summit of Everest. Mallory wrote of climbing Everest: 'The climbers must have above all things, if they are to win through, good fortune, and the greatest good fortune of all for mountaineers, some constant spirit of kindness in Mount Everest itself, the forgetfulness for long enough of its more cruel moods; for we must remember that the highest of mountains is capable of severity, a severity so awful and so fatal that the wiser sort of men do well to think and tremble even on the threshold of their high endeavour.'

The next British attempt on Everest was in 1924 when they reached a height of 28,000 ft. It was in this expedition that George Leigh-Mallory and his companion Andrew Irvine, the youngest man in the expedition, disappeared in the mist when they were just below the summit. They were last seen at about 28,230 ft. on 8th June by Odell who wrote, 'They were going strong for the top.' Today, they probably lie buried somewhere on the shoulder of Everest.

(L to R) June Mulgrew, Sir Edmund Hillary, Bholi and Major Ahluwalia

From 1931 till 1951, the British launched no less than seven expeditions. During the Mount Everest Reconnaissance Expedition of 1951, the first photographs were taken of the footprints of the 'Abominable Snowman' – the legendary Himalayan creature whom Tibetans call the Yeti.

The legend of the Yeti dates back to 1921, when Lt Col Howard-Bury, leader of the first expedition to the Everest, reported that at about 20,000 feet he had found what looked like human footprints in the snow. His porters at once identified them as belonging to the Metohkangmi, which Howard-Bury translated as 'Abominable Snowman.'

The creatures as described to Shipton were half man and half beast, covered with reddish-brown hair but with a hairless face. Some say they live on yaks and men, and that they walk with their toes turned inwards. Others declare that these creatures are the lonely spirits of women who have died in childbirth, or of people who have died a violent death. A man's only hope of escape from them, say the Tibetans, is to run downhill.

In 1952, the Swiss undertook their first major expedition which reached a height of 28,200 ft. This was from the south route where Tenzing climbed with Lambert. The Swiss came back in the autumn of that year and reached a height of 28,300 ft. Then came the first success when the British launched their ninth history-making expedition led by Lord Hunt (then Col John Hunt). This expedition succeeded in achieving its goal and on 29 May 1953, Edmund Hillary and Tenzing stood on the top of the Everest – the first human beings to do so. In 1956, the Swiss put four men on the summit.

It was in 1960 that the first Indian expedition, led by Brigadier Gyan Singh, was organised. Three members of the team, Captain Kumar, Sonam Gyatso and Nawang Gombu reached a point 700 ft. below the summit. The second Indian expedition was led in 1962 by Major John Dias and its summit party reached a height of 28,600 ft. We lost a life in this expedition on the Lhotse face. Then came the first American expedition in 1963 led by Norman G. Dyrenfurth which created mountaineering history by reaching the summit twice from the conventional South Col route and once from the western ridge. The Americans lost a climber, John E. Brietenbach, while climbing the ice-fall during

With Tenzing Norgay

the early stages of the climb. In all they were able to place six members on the summit of Everest. After that came our 1965 expedition.

After setting up camp at Namche Bazar, Cheema, Bogie and I went to the check-post. They were delighted to meet us and offered us *chhang*. Being a check-post, one would have expected some checking there but there was none, at any rate not for us. As we were extremely thirsty, we had a lot of *chhang*. After that we visited a few local houses. One of them was the residence of a very wealthy merchant. It was a double storeyed building, of much the same type which I had previously seen in Sikkim. The ground floor was assigned to livestock which included yaks, sheep and goats. It was dark and dingy and a stranger had to grope his way through it. Experience had taught us that to get to the upper floor of such houses, one should walk straight for about ten yards after entering the ground floor, then turn to the right and go up by a steep wooden ladder. If you are not careful, your head might get hit by loose wooden planks hanging from the ceiling.

The first floor is much brighter than the ground floor. There is an all-purpose big room which has a kitchen at one end and a little room adjoining it at the other, where the valuables, including jewellery, coins and rare stone sculptures are kept. The coins would be stored in an earthen pot and the other valuables hidden in a box somewhere. A long table fixed to a long bench is covered with Tibetan rugs. Any vacant space in the room is filled with heavy brass utensils which to us looked more like antique pieces.

In the houses we visited *chhang* was served by pretty girls who wore garments made of silk and over them brightly-coloured aprons. With *chhang* we were given eats made of yak meat. The yak is a domesticated animal of Sherpa land, extensively used for carrying loads. Yak milk is slightly thicker than buffalo milk and is usually turned into cheese and butter. Its meat is delicious, whether taken in the form of soup, steaks or stew. In a Sherpa's house, something is always being cooked in the kitchen and some smoke may usually be seen floating under the roof as Sherpas do not believe in having a hearth or a chimney.

We found a number of Sherpa women sitting outside their houses weaving carpets. Namche Bazar is famous for its Tibetan carpets and they still use Tibetan wool. Most of us placed orders for small carpets which we collected on our way back.

We left the town for our camp in the evening after having a lot of *chhang*. I am afraid most of us were none the better for it and had some difficulty finding our way back. We met some Japanese who had 'booked' Everest for 1966. Everest has to be booked in advance and a royalty of ₹ 10,000 in Nepalese currency has to be paid to the Nepalese Government. At times the booking is so heavy that the mountain is not available for four to five years. The Japanese had brought three groups of mountaineers from which they would select the final Everest team for their attempt on the summit the following year. As we learnt later, Everest was closed after the Indian expedition of 1965. It was not reopened till 1969.

Next day the march led to the famous monastery at Thyangboche. One could go direct to Thyangboche from Namche Bazar or go via another Sherpa village called Khumzung. The Assistant Sirdar, Phu Dorji, had a house in Khumzung, so some of us took the route through Khumzung. To start with it was a very steep path which gradually became even and passed through pretty meadows and grassy slopes. Flowers grew everywhere and though not yet in full bloom added to the beauty of the meadow. The air was fresh and full of the fragrance of camphor and jasmine. Cheema and I took close-up shots of a number of flowers. We came across a charming Sherpa woman carrying a little baby on her back. I had a glance at her and then looked at Cheema. 'She is beautiful. I suppose you want to photograph her,' said Cheema. She had such a lovely smile. Her jewellery was heavy and she had a prominent headband made of gold. She was clad in a brightly coloured Tibetan dress and wore glass bangles of all colours, indeed, a perfect subject for a photograph. We walked with her for quite a distance, both trying to engage her in conversation in our broken Sherpa language. Every now and then she was amused by our poor diction and giggled. We offered her sweets and some dry fruits which we carried in our pockets. All of us then sat down to rest for a while. Cheema talked to her and playfully pinched the chubby cheeks of the child while I set my Nikon camera. She sat on a raised but fairly flat piece of rock. The sky which was deep blue provided an excellent background. Soon she put the baby in her lap and started feeding him. I took a number of pictures, all in colour. We also took some movie shots of the lovely orchids and other attractive plants. At times we would keep waiting for the honeybees to suck the honey from the flowers, and shoot the entire process.

We finally reached Khumzung just before noon. We visited Phu Dorji's house and met his parents, his wife and his daughter. We also visited the school established through the efforts of Sir Edmund Hillary. The path then gradually became steep passing through

Rongbuk Monastery, North Face

what many a foreigner has compared to the Alpine pastures. Soon we reached the Thyangboche monastery, which stood at a height of 13,000 ft.

Thyangboche has been described as one of the most beautiful spots in the world. Apart from its beauty, it is the site of a famous Buddhist monastery, which is next in importance to the Rongbuk monastery in Tibet. With the destruction of the religious aspects of the Rongbuk monastery by the Chinese, the monastery at Thyangboche has come into greater prominence. Most of the priests at the monastery are refugees from Rongbuk. The Head Lama is an incarnate and is chosen in the same manner as the Dalai Lama.

The monastery attracts tourists from all over the world and every year their number keeps increasing. Thanks to Colonel Roberts who has a tourist agency in Kathmandu, many are able to reach Thyangboche to have a view of the world's highest mountain. Any tourist wanting to visit Thyangboche is flown from Kathmandu to Lukla air strip and the agency makes all the arrangements for his transport, boarding and lodging en route and at Thyangboche.

The monastery rises from a gently sloping landscape which may be compared to the slopes in Gulmarg or Switzerland and makes an excellent site for skiing. All around it are snow-clad mountains. The view of the monastery from the front is magnificent. The Everest massif to the left, with the plume crowning it, offers an impressive sight. On the right of Everest is Lhotse and then the Nuptse wall. Immediately to the right of Thyangboche is the towering Ama Dablam with the deep sky behind it. Ama Dablam looks like a pyramid of hard snow. Earlier a few British boys had tried to attempt this peak and they had applied for permission which was not granted. Yet they attempted to climb the mountain. However, when they were just below the summit, one of the members slipped bringing down the other two. Their bodies were never located. The local belief is that Ama Dablam is the abode of the gods and since the boys did not have the permission of the gods ill luck befell them.

Below Ama Dablam is the Imja Khola valley where birds of beautiful colours and plumage may be seen along with an occasional musk deer. Thyangboche is surrounded by small peaks ranging in height between 17,000 ft. and 19,000 ft. These can be climbed in a day. This makes it an ideal spot for acclimatisation. On the first day here the altitude does tell on you, but soon you get acclimatised and Thyangboche becomes a wonderful place to live in. We occupied the little rest house on one side of the slope in front of the monastery. The Sherpas and the porters spread themselves around in the open space. Cheema, Bogie and I did not sleep inside the hut but preferred to stay outside in a tent. It is more enjoyable and cleaner than the little huts. Behind the rest-house, Thandup, Danu and others set up a kitchen and laid it out very neatly. The only problem they seemed to have was of water which had to be fetched from a nearby fresh water stream. The Sherpas are the happiest people, cheerful and laughing all the time and there is never an end to their drinking of *chhang* and *rakshi*. Bull got busy with his assistant, BP, issuing the colourful personal mountaineering kit to all the Sherpas. Mulki and I issued rations to the kitchen staff and checked the boxes.

The usual practice for an Everest expedition is that the team spends two or three weeks of acclimatisation at Thyangboche. Mohan announced his acclimatisation plan which was somewhat different from others. He divided the members into three small groups. The first two parties after completing the programme at Thyangboche would leave for the proposed base camp and continue the process of acclimatisation by working on the Khumbu ice-fall. The third party would follow. The idea was that the first two parties, on reaching the base camp would immediately start opening the route further as a part of the acclimatisation plan. By the time they were exhausted, the third party would take over. This plan not only worked extremely well but also saved time.

At this altitude man's capacity to perform physical work diminishes. The higher one goes the more severe is the environment. At 19,000 ft. the atmospheric pressure is almost half of what it is at sea level. In this thin and cold air breathing becomes extremely difficult. The lungs are not able to push in the required amount of oxygen for the blood stream, which disturbs the normal body metabolism resulting in loss of appetite, headache, lack of sleep and at times pulmonary oedema which is a serious condition. Acclimatisation is achieved by a gradual and slow process, and responses to it differ from one individual to another. Acclimatisation is best achieved by following the principal of 'go high and sleep low.' Altitude effects soon started taking their toll. Most of us suffered from headaches and breathlessness, which was not very serious.

A very interesting episode comes to mind. An extraordinary Englishman, Captain Maurice Wilson, is known to have reached a height of 24,000 ft. without the aid of oxygen. Howard Marshall in his book, *Men Against Everest*, wrote:

> 'Wilson was a mystic. He had a theory that, if he starved himself for three weeks, he would reach a stage of semi-consciousness in which his mind would establish contact

with his soul, a condition not uncommon among devotees of Yoga. On emerging from this state, he would find himself cleansed of all bodily and spiritual ills, and would then enjoy a great physical and spiritual strength. What is more, it had been revealed to him in a vision that, by climbing Everest, he would attract such publicity that his theory would be accepted by all the world and mankind would be purged of evil.

He knew nothing about climbing; so his first idea was to crash land an aeroplane as high as possible on the mountain, then climb out and complete the rest of the journey on foot. He bought a small aeroplane, learnt to fly, and made off in it for India. At Cairo the authorities intercepted him and turned him back.

But he later managed to get to Darjeeling, and persuaded some Sherpas to smuggle him into Tibet. At Rongbuk monastery he told the abbot that he was a member of the 1933 expedition who had come back to retrieve equipment left on the mountain; and then, taking only a small quantity of rice water for rations, he proceeded up the glacier slopes towards the North Col Early in April, at a point somewhere about Camp Two, he was forced to turn back, exhausted.

For a fortnight he rested. Then, with some Sherpas, he reached Camp Three, where he was delighted to find a dump of food including such luxuries as chocolate, sardines and biscuits, left there by the 1933 expedition. He was quite unable to use the ice-axe he had brought with him, and could make little headway up the slopes to the North Col Day after day he emerged from his tent to attack the bare ice-face, but each time reeled back exhausted.'

On 17 May 1934, Maurice left his porter and started his journey alone. He had with him three ropes, two tins of oranges, a camera, a Union Jack and a tent. He succeeded in climbing the glacier and was caught up below the ice cliff of north Col. He had left instructions with the porters to stay there and wait for him for two weeks and in case he did not return, they could go back. The porters waited for him for four weeks and when there was no sign of Wilson, they came back.

In the following year Eric Shipton, leader of the Everest expedition, when reaching this height found the tent where Wilson lay frozen, dead with exhaustion and cold. His diary showed how he clung to his faith in the divine message which inspired him.

I was in the second party with Gyatso. We spent five days in the region around Thyangboche and climbed as high as 16,000 ft. to 17,000 ft. We climbed a small rocky peak which was in front of the monastery. From the top we had a magnificent view of the Everest massif and distinctly saw its three faces. We looked at Thyangboche which appeared rather small.

In the evening the Head Lama had arranged a Lama dance for us. The costumes were made from very expensive Chinese silk and some of the dresses were seventy to eighty years old or perhaps even older. The clothes, although so old, looked as if they had been made that morning, just for the occasion. The musical instruments were mostly of brass and glittered like gold. With the sounding of the gong, these instruments took over and the dance started. The beat was haunting as the Lamas started enacting the eternal conflict between good and evil. They wore animal masks of the eagle, the tiger, the elephant, and turned with a questing, haunted look towards the cloudy sky. The felt boots of the Lamas tapped rhythmically on the ground.

After the dance was over we dined with His Holiness at the monastery. Thandup, Danu and others went to the monastery rather early to help with the cooking. The dinner started with *chhang*-the best-brewed *chhang* I have ever tasted – and was served with grace and sophistication. We had Chinese food for dinner. There was yak soup, yak fried rice and vegetable noodles.

Acclimatisation at Thyangboche lasted five days and included rock climbing, ice-craft, practice on knots and basic lessons on the use of oxygen. On the morning of 18 March, the first two parties left for the base camp. It was a bright day and the march brought us early into Imja Valley. In the distance stood Ama Dablam soaring into the sky and looking almost inaccessible. We passed through forests enjoying the greenery and the twittering of birds. The pheasants were very beautiful. Some of us even saw *Kasturi* (musk deer) moving about with utmost grace. Shooting is prohibited in this region. After crossing the river we began to ascend a hill which brought us to a village called Pangboche. Pangboche has a *gumpa* (temple) which is supposed to be the oldest in the area. This *gumpa* is famous for its exhibit of the 'Hand and Scalp,' claimed to be of the Yeti or the Abominable Snowman. On payment of a nominal charge, the 'Hand and Scalp' can be seen and photographed. Some time ago they were flown to the USA and to Britain for extensive research. Scientists believe that the hand with its hair may be of an anthropoid and the head that of a human.

Our first halt after Thyangboche was at Pheriche. As we were nearing this place, the weather became bad and remained bad for twenty-four hours. In fact, it started snowing as we were entering the camp at Pheriche. This was the first snowfall we had on this expedition and we enjoyed wandering around in the snow. Pheriche is known as a summer farming area. The fields are well marked by stone walls. It is a wide valley with small streams of crystal clear water which looked almost blue. It has large yak hunts. The villagers move up to Pheriche during summer for ploughing and planting barley and potatoes. In fact, we found quite a few farmers moving in with their yaks. The potatoes of this area are sweet and constitute the inhabitants' main meal. They are boiled, peeled and eaten with a lot of chillies.

Next day we woke up to a bright morning. There was snow all around. The view was breathtaking. There was Ama Dablam, Tewache, Pumori, Everest and Lhotse, all looking magnificent. We leisurely marched over the soft snow which took us to the alp of Lobuje which stands at a height of 16,450 ft. It is perhaps the highest pasture ground in the world. We camped on flat ground close to the rocky ridge. In the afternoon, we went on to the ridge and took some shots of the mountains around and the area ahead of us.

The following day we walked over the soft turf of Lobuje and wondered at the wilderness of the moraine, the hanging glaciers and the icy slopes full of rock and ice and seracs. We then reached Gorak Shep which has a lake more or less like an oasis. We walked over the dry bed of the lake. Yaks are invariably seen grazing here. During the march we came across a big rock on which the name of John E. Brietenbach was engraved. He was with the 1963 American expedition to Everest, the only mountaineer so far to have lost his life in the Khumbu ice-fall.

We marched along on the moraine of a number of glaciers. We then descended into Khumbu glacier at a point where the glacier lies buried under its own moraine and debris. The Khumbu glacier originates in the northern slopes of Lhotse and drains the western side of Everest. After walking over it for a while we entered a small valley which had isolated pinnacles of blue ice rising as high as two to three storeyed buildings. The pinnacles are scattered all around the valley. The Swiss called it the 'Phantom Alley.' It is a beautiful spectacle, almost a wonderland.

As we advanced into the rarefied air and the snow-clad region, I thought of the heat and the dusty tracks we had left behind. The paddy fields and the maize plantations were far below us. So were the rhododendrons, the pine and the fir trees, the green slopes carpeted by mauve primulas. The fragrance of the forest, more vividly of jasmine and camphor, still lingered in the mind along with the twittering of pheasants, cuckoos and *chikoris*. I also thought of the bronze-fronted woodpecker. The rhythmic beat of the dance at Thyangboche still haunted me. Towards late afternoon as we entered the proposed base camp, it started snowing a little. The snowflakes gave a desolate look to the entire region with Pumori,

Phantom Alley on the way to Base Camp (Does not exist anymore)

Nuptse, Changtse and Everest towering against the sky. The feeling of being close to Everest was uppermost in my mind. I thought of the physical difficulties we would soon be confronting.

We reached a fairly level area full of old granite rocks on 22 March. This would be our base camp – height 17,800 ft. above sea level and at the foot of the glacier. Namche Bazar and Thyangboche now lay far below us and in front stood the Khumbu glacier. We were in the moraine island of the glacier. The mighty peaks of Lhotse, Nuptse, Khumbutse, Lingren and Pumori provided a splendid view from the base camp. The summit of Everest could not be seen as it was hidden behind its western shoulder. A huge tricolour, our national flag, was hoisted on a large pole, marking the opening of the camp and the start of our new activities. All the stores were laid out in an orderly fashion. Most of the equipment was unpacked, tents were erected and Sherpas and members got busy in laying out the camp.

On 23 March our day of rest at the base camp, we were still busy establishing the camp. There was hardly any patch of even ground where tents could be pitched. Almost all the tents in the camp were set up on stones. The weather was rough, cold and misty. Gusts of wind did not make our task easy. Despite all this the Sherpas and the members kept working at the base camp. The porters had great difficulty in collecting firewood for the kitchen. Later, in the afternoon, we spent most of the time in our tents. Numerous letters were written to friends and families. Some members wrote as many as twenty letters. The letters are received and sent by runners. We had two mail services a week, that is, letters were received and sent out twice a week. The runner skips swiftly as he does not have much load. A letter from Kathmandu takes about eight to ten days to reach the base camp.

The plans for opening the Khumbu ice-fall were discussed. After all this labour we had a restful night. The wind had died down and there was no snowfall. The next morning was bright and clear. There were no clouds. The first ice-fall party with Sherpa support left to tackle the ice-fall while the other party remained behind to help at the base camp. Thandup, Danu and others built a spacious

Boxes being unloaded at Base Camp

Negotiating Khumbu Ice Fall

kitchen with stone walls and tarpaulin serving for roof. Behind the kitchen there was an ice cave which had an opening at one side. It was a large cave; stalactites of ice from the roof glittered like chandeliers. The roof had a very thick layer of hard, blue ice. Almost the entire supply of fresh water was made by chipping and melting ice from the roof of the cave. In front of the kitchen at some distance the members' tents were spread out, with the medical tent at the centre. Next to the kitchen was Mulki's ration dump from where rations were supplied to the kitchen on a daily basis.

The base camp was the noisiest place I can think of. Day and night avalanches roared down from the mountains nearby. The worst ones used to come down either from the Pumori shoulder or the Lho-La pass. Even when there was no avalanche, the rumbling of rocks or stones was constant. At night moving glaciers seemed to make a lot of noise by their sudden opening and closing.

The work on the ice-fall continued. A group would leave the base camp during the early hours. They would walk up to a place which was at the foot of the ice-fall known as Crampon Point.

Crampon Point is a place at the beginning of Khumbu ice-fall, from where one cannot climb without the help of crampons under one's boots. It was a fairly even area. It also meant an end to the walk on the rocky surface. Beyond it there was ice or a mixture of snow and ice. The party was then divided into 'ropes' – the tying of two or three people to a climbing rope. Beyond this point, the ascent had to be made rope-wise for safety reasons. The ropes would then proceed to open the route beyond the point left over by the previous parties.

The party at the base camp got busy putting the place into shape and rearranging the rations and equipment loads. By now the rest of the party from Thyangboche had also joined us. The activity in the camp increased. The base camp looked like a tiny village in the desolate area and the mess tent soon became a recreation club. Lala opened a library in the medical tent.

As the days went by, I found that the Sherpas were becoming more cheerful and happy. Invariably they were either joking with one another or singing a song. I found some of the Hindi film songs very popular with them. They were very particular about getting the tune of the song right but did not bother much about the words. For them all good Hindi film songs are about love. They know several Nepalese songs and can sing them fairly well. The most popular song was a folk song of the Everest region called 'O Kancha,' which had a pleasing tune and we later used it as a theme song for our film, *Everest.*

Sherpas are a warm hearted, courageous and friendly people. They do not believe in a master-servant or employer-employee relationship. But once a Sherpa gains your confidence he will not hesitate to risk his life for you on desolate slopes or on dangerous climbs. Sherpas believe in dignity of labour and self-respect. They drink a lot and are free from any inhibitions. They have liberal views regarding marriage and sex relationship. They are, however, also very sensitive. I am reminded of an incident at Thyanboche. During our marches Mohan often told me to have biscuits and sweets distributed to Sherpa women and children whom we passed on the way. I discovered after a while that some biscuit packets were missing and asked Danu to account for them. He flew into a rage and promptly went on strike. I tried to explain to him that I was not accusing him of theft but merely asking him to keep an account of the biscuits distributed. But he would not listen, so I took my problem to Gombu, hoping that he would pacify Danu. 'You see,' I explained to Gombu, 'I just want him to account for the biscuits. For example, if he gives you a packet of biscuits, he should tell me about it.' To my horror Gombu misunderstood me and was quite upset. 'If he says I have, he is a liar!' He was so angry that he promptly went away and was about to assault Danu for maligning him. The whole camp exploded into chaos, some of the Sherpas taking Gombu's side and some Danu's, and it took quite some time to restore order. But in a few days Gombu and Danu were once again the best of friends.

We had ample leisure at the base camp. It was utilised in exploring and searching the area which was occupied by the previous expedition. We behaved like a bunch of dedicated rag pickers, picking up anything that was found useful. Once we visited the Swiss camp and found a Swiss cheese tin. We quickly opened it and even tasted the cheese but it had to be thrown away. I am sure even a patriotic Swiss would not have reclaimed it in that putrid state.

There is a belief among the Sherpas that if a village dog happens to run along with an expedition it is a good omen and brings luck to the expedition. A gold coloured mongrel joined us at one of the villages and was well looked after by the members and the kitchen staff. We christened him Tiger. He was a very hardy dog and used to sleep out in the open at the base camp. At times after a fresh snowfall it was difficult to distinguish Tiger from the surroundings except for his eyes which shone like jewels. Tiger used to see each party off at Crampon Point and would be the first to receive the party on its way down.

The route to Everest has three main hurdles. The ice-fall is the first formidable hurdle and the second and almost equally

Sonam Gyatso and Tiger, the lucky mascot of the Expedition

difficult one is the Lhotse face. To overcome these two hurdles, one requires good climbing ability. To open the route either through the ice-fall or the Lhotse face can take anything between ten to twenty days. The last hurdle, which is beyond the Lhotse face, is purely psychological and may be overcome by grit and will power.

The first phase of our climb after the base camp was crossing the ice-fall. Rising 2,200 ft. from the base to the top, it presented one of the most hazardous stretches of the route. During the early days of mountaineering negotiating the ice-fall was considered beyond human skill and endurance. It has the appearance of an area which has been heavily bombed. The British labelled various sections of the ice-fall 'Hellfire Alley,' 'Hillary's Horror' and 'Atom Bomb Area.' Hillary himself called it a 'tottering chaos.' The route through the ice-fall is constantly changing. Large blocks of ice put up a losing fight against gravity until they give in and topple over. Apart from the technicalities of climbing, an acute problem is that of excessive heat on a clear day. At times one had to work on the ice-fall with only a vest on.

In spite of these great obstacles there have been expeditions through the ice-fall in 1952, 1953, 1960, 1962, 1963, 1965 and 1970 and it has taken its toll of human lives. John Brietenbach, a member of the American expedition of 1963, lost his life while bridging a crevasse somewhere in the middle of the ice-fall. His body was buried under tons of ice and could not be recovered at the time, but in 1969 the Japanese expedition discovered a skeleton which was identified as that of the unfortunate American mountaineer. It was buried by some of his old companions on a site close to Thyangboche monastery. The Japanese themselves were singularly unlucky when they lost six Sherpas in one fatal accident on the ice-fall. One of them was Phu Dorji who had earlier accompanied us.

In our own case we were lucky although it took us ten days of hard labour to open the route slowly and cautiously through the ice-fall. By the end of this period much confidence had been gained. The cutting of steps had become easier and the sense of fear had gone. We set up Camp I on top of the ice-fall at a height of 20,000 ft. The following week was spent in ferrying stocks of food and equipment to Camp I. Later a minor readjustment of Camp I was made and it was shifted to a plateau at a height of 20,300 ft. This provided a slightly bigger space to pitch tents and to stock spares and equipment. Camp I, although on a fairly level plateau, was not safe as there was a constant opening and closing of the crevasses underneath. To relate one incident, while some of us were sleeping in the tent, we found to our surprise that the tent was precariously balanced as a big crevasse opened up in the middle of it.

Opening the route to Camp I was beset with other hurdles too. There were several steep, near vertical ice walls ranging from 30 to 120 ft. in height. The bridging of crevasses never seemed to end. The longest bridge erected over a crevasse was 40 ft. with the help of four aluminium ladders. One had to be very cautious both when coming up to Camp I or going down as the route lay through slopes dominated by the towering ice cliffs and unbalanced boulders of ice, often a mixture of both rock and ice. On an average it would take five hours to reach Camp I and about four hours to come to the base camp.

After Camp I was sufficiently stocked, reconnaissance for Camps II and III started. On 3rd April a party of four members and three Sherpas set out from Camp I to open Camp II. The weather was good and the team was able to establish Camp II the same day at a height of 21,300 ft. Camp II was called the advance base camp and was popularly known as ABC. This camp was half way up the Cwm – an archaic Welsh word which means 'valley of silence.' The centre of activity now moved to ABC which was much safer than Camp I. The camping area was fairly wide and could accommodate six to seven tents. It was a good ascent but it hardly involved any technical skill in climbing except for bridging a few crevasses. A wireless link with the base camp was immediately

Camp 1

Advance Base Camp

established with the help of our 'walkie-talkies' which are a great morale booster and a boon for any expedition.

The weather was extremely good and the party moved forward to open Camp III. On 6 April, Camp III was established at a height of 22,300 ft. After opening this camp the party moved down to base camp for rest and recuperation. Further work was undertaken by Gombu's party. After working at great heights for six to ten days, it is absolutely essential to come down to the base camp for rest and recuperation. As one goes higher one's appetite diminishes. At such heights the human body is subject to considerable deterioration and dehydration which affect the body's cells and corpuscles, resulting in loss of strength and weight to the extent of fifteen to twenty pounds.

One of the most boring experiences on any expedition, particularly on Everest, is to kill time as most of it is spent in the sleeping bag. It is particularly so when the activity is around the base camp. The work on the mountain begins at sunrise and must end by noon so that you can be back in camp before the late afternoon when the weather quickly deteriorates. It begins to get cold and you are forced to go into the sleeping bag. On an average I found that twelve to fifteen hours were spent in the sleeping bag; and during bad weather even as long as twenty hours a day. In good weather the base camp was not at all bad. In fact, it was most enjoyable having breakfast and lunch outside in the sun.

Work on opening the route beyond Camp III went on and made good progress. The Sherpas at the base camp made regular ferries everyday, taking the oxygen and other stores across the ice-fall to Camp I and then to the advance base camp. Stores at Camp I were not very safe. When there were no members to look after the camp, a lot of stores were destroyed and eaten away by Goraks – a kind of raven which is slightly better looking than the familiar Indian crow. Goraks would make holes in tins and packets with their strong long beaks, destroying everything that came their way. We had another problem, too. Although Camp III was considered safe, it was very

Everest Massif

Camp below South Col

View of Everest South Face

unpopular with the Sherpas. In 1952, during the Swiss attempt, a Sherpa was killed in this area by an ice avalanche. Ever since then a superstition had developed that the ghost of the watchman wandered around that area. Sherpas, if they could help it, avoided staying overnight at this camp. They complained of being disturbed by a nocturnal visitor – the watchman knocking at their tents. One of our Sherpas, Nawang Tshering, refused in 1960 to stay at Camp

III in spite of very bad weather. Two years later, in 1962, with the second Indian Everest expedition, he was hit by a rolling stone and died in the same area. This only helped to strengthen the superstition and the camp, although well stocked, remained 'haunted.'

Work on the Lhotse face was taken up by Gombu and party. We were well aware of the hazards of this ascent. The Lhotse, rising from 22,300 ft. to 27,800 ft., is the fourth highest peak in the world. The Lhotse face has mostly blue ice (hard ice) which makes it difficult to cut steps into it. It is almost vertical at a number of places and the rope has to be fixed with the help of pitons which are dug into ice like nails. It has a series of small terraces through which the route is made in a zig-zag manner. Much before the top of the Lhotse is reached, at a height of approximately 25,000 ft., you have to traverse some distance to the left. The route then cuts across the yellow band and Geneva Spur. Apart from the other difficulties, the height begins to affect you and the strong winds which blow across the slopes chill you to the marrow.

Under our plan we were allowed the use of oxygen here and the route was opened within four days. We established ourselves at the edge of the slopes. There was not enough space to pitch tents bigger than those accommodating two men. All tents were pitched in a linear formation. We never considered this camp a comfortable place, although later it became important as it marked the stage at which the summit parties would use oxygen. The work in opening the route beyond Camp IV was undertaken by the Gyatso party. This party, again with the help of oxygen, opened the route up to Geneva Spur.

By 13 April, we were all set to move the first ferry consisting of Cheema, myself, and fifteen Sherpas to dump loads at South Col (Camp V). 13 April, according to the Indian calendar, happened to be Baisakhi or New Year's Day, considered very auspicious for all kinds of undertakings.

Our party had moved to this camp on 12 April. We had decided not to use oxygen at this height, at any rate to start with.

Negotiating Lhotse Face

The idea was to check whether living at such a height was possible without the use of gas. To make things more difficult, the weather went bad and it snowed heavily the whole night which we passed in great discomfort. The snowfall was heavy and the roofs of the tents had collapsed over us. Bad weather persisted and the ferry could not reach South Col as planned. We decided to move down although Cheema and a few Sherpas made a vain attempt to advance further. This temporary phase of bad weather continued for a few days when the entire team and the Sherpas gathered at the base camp. As soon as the weather improved, the summit plans were quickly taken in hand again. This would be one of the earliest attempts on Everest.

By 20 April the camp at South Col was well stocked. We were in touch with the Meteorological Department. The weather forecast for the Everest region was broadcast by All India Radio three times a day and proved to be fairly accurate. Based on the forecast, the first summit party left advance base camp on 27 April for Camp IV. The leader had decided to deviate a little from the usual practice of sending a rope of two members to the summit. Instead he decided to send two ropes, each consisting of two members. According to him this would help a lot as the pairs could lead in turns. And in case a member dropped, his companion could join the other rope. This summit party consisted of Gombu, Cheema and both the Sonams. The support party consisted of the leader, Guru, and fourteen selected Sherpas, ten of them earmarked for the final camp. They made rapid progress, reaching South Col on 28 April and were ready to move up the next day. The winds were very strong and maintained their furious pace throughout the night. The summit parties, which were to move up on 29 April could not do so because of this. Another day and night passed at the South Col with the winds still continuing to blow hard. South Col is perhaps the most inhospitable place in the Himalayas– much more desolate than the summit. At the summit one feels a sense of achievement but here there is nothing but depression. All around you is the junk left by other expeditions. But even a junk yard yields valuable booty at times. We collected a wallet belonging to Hari Dang of our 1962 expedition, and a few rolls of 15 mm colour film left or dropped by the American expedition.

A message was sent from South Col to Delhi asking for the latest weather forecast on 'hot link.' The report received within about three hours was not very encouraging and the party decided to move down to base camp. Luck has a devilish way of running out. The prediction of foul weather in All India Radio's special bulletins proved correct. Despite the bad weather, the entire party reached the camp safely but badly beaten by the fury of the winds.

By 1 May the entire expedition gathered at the base camp after lowering the tents at the higher camps. The advance base camp alone was kept open. Danu, assistant cook, and a Sherpa stayed back at the advance base camp. There was a 'walkie-talkie' set kept there which was used three times a day to communicate with the base camp. Further tightening of the tents at the camp was undertaken so that even in bad weather they could hold fast.

The weather forecast from All India Radio was heard thrice a day. The weather continued to be bad at higher altitudes. Since the monsoons were not expected soon, there was plenty of time and it did not worry us much. Life at the base camp was quite busy. Members made igloos in Phantom Alley and explored the areas nearby. At times we trekked to the old camp sites. Although bad weather prevailed at higher altitudes there was bright and warm sun at the base camp. The kitchen staff was generous in giving us rich food and somehow our appetite had also grown. For breakfast we would have parathas, potatoes, eggs, butter, jam and liver. At 11:00 am we would have a coffee break and then there would be lunch consisting of rice, chapatis, vegetables, dal, yak or mutton curry. For afternoon tea we would either have biscuits or pakoras. Dinner was either served in the mess tents or we would have it in the kitchen. Playing cards was becoming a popular pastime. Stakes were rising higher day by day though little cash changed hands. 'Pay when you may' was the rule. Some members would go for long walks. I looked for new sites from where I would make a new composition for my photographs. I remember one day Kumar and I walked for two hours to a place from where only part of the North face was visible. The walk was worthwhile as I was able to get some excellent pictures. With these diversions, time at the base camp passed quickly enough. Parties would go to nearby places to practise rock-climbing and ice craft. In order to keep fit some of us would climb up to the ice-fall and at times would go as far as the advance base camp. We received some visitors at the camp. One of them was Mrs Dayal, wife of the late H. Dayal, once the Indian Ambassador to Nepal, who died in the Everest region during one of his treks. Mrs Dayal had come to perform a religious ceremony for her late husband at several places in the region including one at the base of the ice-fall. Mohan asked Vohra and me to accompany her to the ice-fall. She was a good climber herself, perhaps the first women to have climbed to this height on the ice-fall. After her return from the climb and the ritual, she felt at peace with herself.

Another visit was that of the Japanese expedition to Cho-Oyu. We became quite friendly with the members of the expedition as they marched with us for four or five days. The Japanese attached much importance to this expedition and to another expedition to Lhotse Sar. The aim was to look around the Everest region as they had booked Everest for 1966, and the selection of the final Everest team was to be made from these two expeditions. But as the Nepal Government later banned all foreign expeditions to Nepal, the Japanese had to give up their plans for climbing Everest in 1966.

We also had some rather unexpected visitors from the North. They were Chinese soldiers who moved to the Lho-La pass on the Tibet-Nepal border overlooking our base camp. They created some excitement for us at the base camp. They looked all around giving the impression that they had come to report on our activities. After reconnoitring for a while they went back and were not seen again.

On 14 May, the plume on Everest had vanished, the wind had died down and the weather had improved. It was after twenty-two days of forced rest at base camp that the weather was showing signs of improvement. The weather forecast given by All India Radio was also very encouraging. The time had come for us to move to a higher camp. We were aware of the ban imposed by the Nepal Government on future expeditions to Everest, which meant that this might well be the last chance for us. As no one knew how long the ban would last we had to make the best of the present opportunity. I remembered the motto of our expedition – 'Now or Never.' At this stage, the motto seemed more meaningful than ever.

The summit parties were announced by Mohan. Gombu and Cheema were the first party followed by Gyatso and Wangyal. The third pair would be Vohra and Ang Kami followed by Rawat and Bahuguna, and the last would be BP Singh and myself. It was also decided that the summit pairs would be moved at two day intervals. This would avoid crowding at the last camp. The first summit party would make an attempt on the 20th, the second on the 22nd, the third on the 24th and the fourth on the 26th.

This seemed a very ambitious plan on the basis of our existing stock of oxygen cylinders. I was in the last party, so I sat down to assess the oxygen situation. In all we had 150 oxygen cylinders out of which 44 had already been used in an unsuccessful attempt in April. Six cylinders were kept reserved for medical purposes and only 100 cylinders were left to be used by the summit parties. To make a comparison with the American expedition, it is relevant to note that they had 200 oxygen cylinders and were able to put only six members on top. I wondered how we would be able to support so many with half that stock of oxygen in hand.

On 16 May, the first summit party comprising Cheema and Gombu started their upward journey with their Sherpa support. It was a clear day. The path through the ice-fall had changed, and every now and then they had to strengthen the bridges or at places make a new route. They reached Camp I at noon. After resting for a while, they left for the advance base camp where the stores, equipment and oxygen masks were checked and got ready. On the 17th, the party left for Camp IV. To save oxygen it was decided that the summit parties would start using oxygen only after reaching Camp IV.

Cheema and Gombu reached Camp IV at 4:00 pm. The camp was in a bad shape owing to the foul weather which had prevailed earlier. They re-erected it with the help of Sherpas led by Deputy Sirdar Phu Dorji. The weather was now good and the party left for the South Col on 18 May. Gombu and Cheema were now fitted with oxygen masks consuming oxygen at the rate of two litres per minute. They passed the Lhotse with the help of the fixed rope and reached the Yellow Band. On 19 May, the pair along with Sherpa support, left for the last camp. Cheema in his excitement forgot the juice tin on the stove. They had hardly stepped out of the tent when it exploded and sounded like a gun salute. Nobody was hurt and the party went ahead.

Phu Dorji was entrusted with the task of opening the last camp. The leader had advised him to set up this camp as high as possible. I recall that Phu Dorji became impatient at this repeated advice and said, 'I will have the last camp at the top of Everest. Please stop worrying about it.' Keeping up a fast pace, Phu Dorji and his companions passed both the Indian camp sites of the last camps of 1960 and 1962, and then the American camp site of 1963. Gombu lingered at this camp and spent some moments thinking of his stay there in 1963 when he went to the summit with Jim Whittaker.

The summit party and the Sherpas support led in turns. Early in the afternoon, they reached the hump on the ridge which was at an altitude of approximately 28,000 ft., and decided to pitch the tent on a small area about seventy feet below it. This was then declared the last camp on the route of Everest, the highest ever in the history of the mountain. The area around was levelled and the soft snow was cleared. The oxygen cylinders were neatly stacked outside by the Sherpas. Phu Dorji and the Sherpas, after bidding goodbye to the summit party, left for South Col.

The summit party retired rather early as a hard day was ahead of them. On 20 May at 5:00 am the pair left for the summit. We were all excited and everyone kept a close watch on the progress made by them. Three observation posts were established by us. They were at the base camp, advance base camp and at Camp IV. From these points with the help of binoculars one could follow in that difficult weather the movements of the summit party. One of the posts reported having seen them moving on the ridge close to the summit, having stayed on the summit for thirty minutes and then coming down, reaching the last camp at 12:45 pm.

The news of the expedition's success had been flashed to Delhi without delay. Congratulatory messages soon started pouring in. We got quite a thrill when we heard about Gombu and Cheema's success over All India Radio in the news bulletin of 9:00 pm. It was heart-warming to know that the government and the whole country shared our joy. Meanwhile Sonam's party moved to the last camp under a high wind of 140 kilometres per hour. They were shaken very badly by a blizzard just below the last camp but they continued their ascent. Sonam Gyatso was badly burnt by ultraviolet rays. In spite of the heavy blizzard which threatened to lift them bodily and hurl them below, they continued to struggle along. Unable to communicate with each other due to bad weather, the zig-zag path finally brought them to their destination. The tent had been flung open by the winds and was full of snow. They cleared the snow and prepared to rest. The supporting Sherpas were also hit by the bad weather. It took them hours to search the last camp in an almost exhausted state of health. They had reached their limit of physical stamina when the camp appeared in front of them. The Sherpas too had snow blindness and a minor case of frostbitten fingers. They decided to leave immediately for South Col after bidding farewell to the summit party. To add to this summit pair's troubles, one of the two air mattresses in Camp VI got punctured. Wangyal had a restless night without the air mattress. On 22 May the party left the camp at 6:45 am despite the suffering of the previous day and night. The winds continued to blow strong but they kept going and reached the peak after five hours of a most strenuous climb. Sonam's back injury gave him much trouble but he did not give up. While returning from the summit they had some trouble with their oxygen and with difficulty they reached the last camp at 6:00 pm. They had no alternative but to spend the night at this camp. The following morning they moved to the lower camps.

The third summit party of Vohra and Ang Kami reached the top at 10:45 am on 24 May and returned to the last camp at 4:15 pm. Vohra was able to do cine photography from the top. They too had their share of troubles. On the return journey Vohra's oxygen finished. They spent a very uncomfortable night at the last camp vainly trying to warm their feet. The next day Vohra and Ang Kami came to South Col where they were received by their support party and later moved to the advance base camp.

The fourth summit party according to schedule was to make the summit attempt on the 26th but A.I.R. had warned us of considerable deterioration in the weather. Very strong winds started and the weather was most unfavourable. On the basis of the weather forecasts, 29 May was chosen as D-Day for the fourth party – which was to include me and was to be the last summit group. The oxygen position was not very bright. We were left with some twenty-five bottles, a bare minimum to make an attempt. This factual account of the preparations for the summit and the final assault on Everest is doubtless an inadequate portrayal of the many difficulties, excitements and thrills of the great adventure which I have had the privilege of sharing with my team mates. In the next chapter I have endeavoured to give in greater detail my own unforgettable experience of the last climb to the summit, with its suspense-laden moments, its ordeals and its glory.

Climb to the Summit

The history of man's achievements records numerous instances where success has been snatched away from the jaws of failure. As I look back on the events of the last few days of our ascent to the summit, I cannot help wondering at the miracle which turned an imminent defeat into victory. Was it fate or divine intervention or sheer human persistence which took us to our goal which seemed to elude us?

The morning of 25 May dawned bright but chilly. The cold benumbed our spirits when Dorji, who brought us our morning tea, said, 'Sahib, there has been a big avalanche over Camp III!' Forgetting the tea, Mohan and I rushed outside. What we saw was a frightful sight. The camp, with its colourful tents-luckily unoccupied at the time – had been completely wiped out and nothing was visible except a huge expanse of white. But while there was no loss of life, we had lost something equally precious. The cylinders of life-sustaining oxygen which we had carefully conserved and stored in the camp had now been buried under the avalanche. And with them too, it seemed, were buried the hopes of our summit party reaching the top. The leader had no option but to call off the final assault as without oxygen it was doomed to failure. Could we search for the cylinders, we asked? Such a search seemed both

FACING PAGE: (L-R) Major Ahluwalia and Phu Dorji on the Summit of Everest

pointless and hopeless as whoever heard of bottles being dug out from under a huge mass of snow? But if we were so keen about it, we might as well make the effort, he said. He gave us four Sherpas to assist with the search, and our Nepalese Liaison Officer Rana also accompanied us.

There was no trace whatever of the camp when we reached the site after a two-hour trek – there was no recognizable landmark. It was all white barrenness. The avalanche had poured over our camp in a tide of whiteness. Everything had disappeared under the snow. Only the jet black rocks of the Lhotse face protruded from the thick white blanket. The icy winds of the South Col howled at us without respite and lashed our faces. It was a massive avalanche, and we were lucky that we were not in camp when it struck. Without wasting time, we organised ourselves and started digging in the hope that we might find some oxygen cylinders, if not the rest of the equipment. Doubt and determination kept up a running battle in my weary mind.

So we kept digging but there appeared to be no sign either of the equipment or the oxygen cylinders. It was tough going. Mind and body fought desperately to conquer fatigue and bitter cold, and to win the race against time. Towards late afternoon, after digging for six hours, I was worn out and depressed. I glanced at the Sherpas. They too were downcast. We looked at each other without a word and continued digging. The minutes seemed like years but eventually time – that relentless enemy – entered out calculations. We could not go on like this much longer. And it was at this crucial stage that I happened to glance at the Sherpas once again. They were praying. And at that moment God seemed very near. I too began to pray. 'If not you, Oh God, who will help us?' I began digging again.

Suddenly my axe struck an oxygen cylinder.

My prayer had been answered and the miracle gave me new life. A few more whacks through the thick snow and we soon located another and yet another. What a moment of supreme happiness! We now grinned happily at each other and began to dig feverishly with renewed vigour and hope, and one by one we dug up all the oxygen cylinders buried by the avalanche. Most experts on Everest would say that this was a very rare bit of good luck, but as we believed then, and we believe now, this was a miracle in answer to our prayer which was simple, earnest and full of faith. At that moment, we were at the end of our tether and we literally left it all in God's hands. It was at this stage that I felt a fierce determination flow back into me – nothing could stop us from reaching the summit.

Many famous mountaineers, Shackleton among them, have testified to feeling the presence of a miraculous supreme power when struggling in that inhospitable region of the earth. 'All the time I was climbing alone,' Smythe recalled, 'I had the feeling that there was someone with me. I felt also that were I to slip I should be held up and supported as though I had a companion above me with a rope. When I reached the ledge I felt I ought to eat something in order to keep up my strength. All I had brought with me was a slab of Kendal mint cake. This I took out of my pocket and, carefully dividing it into two halves, turned round with one half in my hand to offer my companion.'

The ordeal of climbing causes strange disturbances in the minds of mountaineers. Smythe recalls another interesting episode. 'I was making my way back towards Camp Six when, chancing to look up, I saw two dark objects floating in the blue sky. In shape they resembled kite balloons, except that one appeared to possess short, squat wings. As they hovered motionless, they seemed to pulsate in and out as though they were breathing. I gazed at them dumbfounded and intensely interested. It seemed to me that my brain was working normally, but to test myself I looked away. The objects did not follow my gaze but were still there when I looked back. So I looked away again, but this time identified by name various details of the landscape by way of a mental test. Yet, when I again looked back, the objects were still visible. A minute or two later, a mist drifted across the north-east shoulder of Everest above which they were poised. As this thickened, the objects gradually disappeared behind it and were lost to sight. A few minutes later the mist blew away. I looked again, expecting to see them, but they had vanished as mysteriously as they had appeared. If it was an optical illusion, it was a very strange one. But it is possible that fatigue magnified out of all proportion something capable of a perfectly ordinary and rational explanation. That is all I can say about the matter and it rests there.'

Back at the camp, Mohan could hardly believe what we told him but the oxygen bottles were, of course, there to convince him that the unbelievable was true. He had been supervising the dismantling of the camp but now quickly changed his plans. 'The summit party will proceed as scheduled,' he said. A fifth member, Phu Dorji, was added to our team, which would now consist of BP, Bogie, Rawat, Dorji and myself.

Phu Dorji, the Deputy Sirdar of the Sherpas, was a slim, genial man who had been of invaluable help to us but was even more superstitious than the rest of his tribe. When the leader decided that in recognition of the Sherpas' good work, one of them should have the opportunity of going to the summit, Dorji was at the base camp. Everyone expected that he would be overjoyed to hear of his selection and of what was after all a unique honour. But strangely enough Dorji was far from elated. He disappeared into a tent and coming out after a few minutes of solitary communion, announced that he would not go with the summit party. Much taken aback and somewhat mystified, everyone at the camp asked him to reconsider his decision. Dorji then repeated his earlier performance: he went into the tent, emerged from it and again said that he was not willing to go. The mystery was cleared a little later when his companions found that inside the tent Dorji had indulged in a quaint little ritual. He had scribbled 'Yes' and 'No' in his own language on either paper or pebble. Each time he drew a lot the answer was 'No', so he concluded that the gods did not favour his going. Eventually I suppose the prospect of joining the select band of Everest conquerors proved too alluring even for

Dorji's superstitious nature and, while still troubled by doubts, he was persuaded to go with us. He made up for his earlier vacillation by double marching and joining us with his party at South Col.

We had left the advance base camp on the morning of 26 May. The sky was cloudless and the weather seemed to hold no threat. Bidding me goodbye, Danu, the chief cook at the camp, said, 'God will look after you. I shall await your return here.' He gave each of us a hug and chanted some Buddhist prayers. It was a touching gesture and we began the climb. But before long misfortune dogged our steps. BP and I were sharing a rope, Rawat and Bogie the other, followed by twelve Sherpas. We had ascended about a third of the Lhotse face and gone past the site of the avalanche which we had dug the day before, when BP complained of a pain in the chest. We halted for a while and gave him some hot coffee but it did not help. We did not want to leave him behind but he felt quite uneasy and insisted that we proceed without him. 'You must go on,' he said. Somewhat perplexed and while still pondering what to do, we fortunately encountered at this point Vohra and party who were returning after their summit climb and a night's rest at Camp IV. He was worn out but greeted me warmly. 'The climb upwards from South Col is a simple affair,' he said. This was cheering news and revived my flagging spirits.

When we reached Camp IV at a height of 25,000 ft., it was still sunny and warm. After a dinner of fried rice and yak meat we crawled into our sleeping bags. We had to use oxygen from here onwards and set the flow for the night at half a litre per minute. I remember I could not sleep because of the thought that should I happen to turn on my side, the entire tent would roll down the Lhotse face. There was hardly any place for the tents to be pitched. The four tents which constituted this camp were all placed in a single-line formation. My tent which was supposed to be a two-man tent, could hardly be pitched. Almost half of it was hanging without any support underneath, and I had to be very careful. While I had a little nap, I soon discovered that due to a slight snowfall, the whole roof had come down on my face. I tried to lift the roof but found it extremely hard. I shouted for help but nobody could hear me because of the high winds which kept lashing at the tent. I nearly froze inside. I was literally pulled out of the tent next morning.

It was bitterly cold. Setting the oxygen flow at a litre per minute, we started at 10:15 am. It was a steady climb to the South Col which we reached in the early afternoon. As a preliminary to our camping here for the night, we looked round the camp sites of previous expeditions to see if we could retrieve anything of value. The sites used by the Swiss, the British and the Americans were all easily recognisable. Someone has called South Col 'the highest rubbish heap in the world.' This description was borne out by the many discarded items of stores we found at the site. On the way up we had come across an especially useful find – a full oxygen bottle left at Geneva Spur by the American expedition.

Phu Dorji and his party caught up with us soon. In spite of his protracted and arduous march, he was in excellent spirits. We re-checked our stock of oxygen and were not worried by the fact that if we did reach the summit we would not have any left for the trip down. After a delicious meal of hot tomato soup, chicken and fried rice, we were buoyant and looked forward to the last camp. Although outside the winds were raging and threatening to blow up the tents like so many balloons, we were snug in our sleeping bags.

We woke up to find that all was well and, after consuming mugs of hot tea, were ready to move up by 7:30 am. The winds continued to be high. As we moved along the ridge – Phu Dorji, myself, Rawat, Bogie and the seven Sherpas, in that marching order – Makalu was on one side and the distant slopes of Tibet, wreathed in clouds, on the other. The oxygen was set at two litres per minute. We moved to the couloir, cutting steps into the ice and making slow progress. Then we moved on to the rocks.

Remnants of old expeditions lay scattered along this route. At 9:15 am we passed by the camp site of the 1962 Indian expedition and half an hour later the American camp at 27,450 ft. We collected extra tent pegs at the Indian site and two bottles of oxygen – both at full pressure – from the American camp. There were also piles of foodstuffs. I cut out strips of material from the colourful tents to keep as souvenirs. It was 11:30 am when we reached our camp site, 27,930 ft. high, just below Razor's Edge – so called because it is a very sharp edge extending for about 500 yards and walking over it is extremely difficult and dangerous. At this point the Sherpas bade us goodbye and left. There were now just the four of us – four men to pit their strength and stamina against the world's highest and most formidable peak.

We had levelled the site to make room for two tents. The speed of the wind had shot up to about 100 kilometres per hour and we pitched the tents close to each other. Phu Dorji and I were in one and Bogie and Rawat in the other. At this height, with its low humidity and low air pressure, plenty of fluids was the recommendation, and Phu Dorji was only too happy to follow it. He kept hopping around serving fruit juices, tea or coffee, and we must have amply made up for the cupful of water per hour which one is supposed to consume at this altitude. Rawat came into our tent to enquire if we had any oil and spices as he wanted to fry some chicken. We had none and he had to be content by steam-heating it over melted ice. Earlier, taking advantage of the bright afternoon, I had gone out to take some movie shots. I fixed the camera on top of my ice axe which I had dug into the hard ice. It was freezing cold and my hands were shaky. But the panorama of the mountains around me as they stood majestically against the sky was too glorious to be missed. I photographed those which were within reach of the camera – Makalu, Lhotse, the South Summit and Ama Dablam. The others I could only reach with my longing, wistful eyes.

When I returned exhausted but happy to the tent Phu Dorji had the evening meal ready. The steam-heated chicken was not easy to munch. In the cold our jaws worked slowly and I took an hour to bite into a few pieces. Changing into a new pair of socks and stockings, I crept into my sleeping bag for the night. The weather forecast over the wireless had not been too reassuring. It indicated that the weather might deteriorate by the next afternoon. We, therefore, planned to start early and return, if possible, before it took a turn for the worse. I took with me into the sleeping bag my reindeer boots, boot covers, the movie camera and the turret lens, so that they could all be kept warm for use in the morning. Together with the oxygen apparatus, they made rather troublesome bed companions.

Although there was just space for one tent, since our summit party constituted two ropes, we had to make space for another tent. Here again, like at Camp IV, our tent could not fully rest on the ground. We tried to anchor it as best as we could but it kept lifting up from one side with the force of the wind. While my sleep was disturbed to some extent, Phu Dorji kept snoring. To him the lifting of the tent from one end probably felt like a rocking bed which he seemed to enjoy.

The wind kept lashing at the tent and my slumber was fitful. I woke up first at 9:00 pm and finally at 3:00 am when I decided that I had enough sleep. Phu Dorji, fully dressed and accoutred, was sound asleep and still snoring, and it took me almost half an hour to wake him up. But once on his legs he was his usual energetic self. Surprisingly, in spite of my disturbed sleep, I too felt quite refreshed. I had a peep outside the tent to reconnoitre my surroundings. The sky was azure and cloudless, and the sun, yet hidden from my view, was beginning to tinge the mountain peaks with a golden hue. I brought out the camera and took some shots. Rawat and Bogie too were awake. Returning to the tents, we all had some hot coffee, checked our equipment, and by 5:00 am were ready for the final ascent.

But an unexpected hitch occurred. Just before starting I heard a hissing sound and found that the regulator of my gas cylinder was leaking and the pressure in the bottle had come down considerably. This might have proved a catastrophe as two of my other regulators had already let me down. Fortunately Bogie had a spare one and came to my rescue. It was 5:30 am when we began the ascent on

Razor's Edge. Phu Dorji and I led, with Rawat and Bogie following a few minutes later.

The wind was blowing at tremendous speed and there was not much foothold on Razor's Edge. Lashed and buffeted by the wind, I found it difficult to keep my balance. We dug our ice axes in and tightened the ropes but the winds were merciless and kept lashing us while the cold penetrated to the very marrow of our bones. The going became tough and there were moments when I felt like giving up the struggle. The main ridge had now ended but our path was hardly less hazardous. As we took a turn to the right, we were faced on the left with an unbroken wall of slate rocks. Pressed against the loose, black slates, we clung to whatever handhold or foothold we could manage as we moved across like tiny flies against all that immensity. Below us was a straight fall of some 10,000 ft. into Tibet.

The nightmare of the black rocks finally ended and we entered the area of Yellow Band where the going was comparatively easier. But now another problem cropped up. I discovered that my oxygen pipe connected to the bladder of the oxygen bottle was leaking. One of the spikes of my crampon had evidently punctured it. Binding it with a handkerchief did no good. Then my mind, working rapidly, found a solution. We tore a piece of adhesive tape off one of our film cartons and glued it over the puncture. The escape was effectively blocked. From then on I was careful to keep track of the long pipe so that it would not trail under the spiky crampons again.

Greatly relieved, we would now have continued the ascent but Phu Dorji spotted a lone figure which was trudging towards us up the rocky part of the path we had left behind. I thought of the Abominable Snowman but Dorji was more realistic. When the figure came nearer we discovered it was Rawat. Waving and panting, he reached us where we sat under the base of the South Summit after repairing the leaking pipe. What had happened to him is best stated in Rawat's own words. Below is an extract from his diary.

'Ahlu and Phu Dorji had left. We followed them ten minutes later. I was leading. Bogie was abject, however, finding the climb very difficult and was taking each step after considerable delay. We had hardly gone fifty or sixty feet from the camp when Bogie sat down and after awhile said he said he could not proceed any further. He had developed a rash the previous night and kept scratching his body the whole night. He felt weak and exhausted and had to make a lot of effort to take even a few steps. He decided to unrope and asked me to go ahead and join the first rope.

I repeatedly asked myself whether it was wise on my part to continue alone and to leave Bogie all by himself. A quick decision had to be taken. Bogie's condition did not appear very serious and he could wait for us at the last camp. I was prepared to take the risk of a lonely climb. I reasoned that if I experienced any difficulty, I could always come back to the last camp. After a few minutes' deliberation I decided to go on. With a heavy heart I released Bogie from the rope and bade him goodbye.

The wind was blowing at sixty to seventy kilometres an hour. Being alone I was concentrating hard on the climb and took each step carefully on the sharp ice ridge. In my heart were feelings both of urgency and fear. Would I get to Ahlu and Phu Dorji or not, was the vital question. I knew that one slip or one small mistake could plunge me to my death on either side of the ridge. There was nothing to break my fall for a mile or more. Mustering all my courage, I inched my way up. Strong gusts of wind almost swept me off my feet and it became increasingly difficult to maintain my balance. It was almost impossible to stand up straight on the Razor's Edge.

Finally my progress was at a standstill. I then decided to walk on all fours with my thick eiderdown gloves on my hands to prevent frost-bite. This certainly saved me from the strong winds but the going was not easier. The balance of the oxygen bottles was disturbed and as they dangled down like pendulums they hurt my back and shoulders. Notwithstanding the discomfort I kept up the struggle. I had hardly gained a height of about a hundred and fifty feet from the last camp. It was nearly 6:00 am and there was a mild sun which had little effect on the bone-chilling morning cold, made worse by sharp winds.

At this point I descended about ten feet from the Nepalese side to a small flat area. Resting for a while, I took out the walkie-talkie set and tried to contact the lower camps but without success. Since there was not much point in carrying that dead weight to the summit, I dug some ice and left the walkie-talkie set there. I tied the oxygen bottle with a rope and secured them firmly to the rucksack. Then I resumed my march.

I could see Ahlu and Phu Dorji going slowly along the right side of the black rock. The Razor's Edge ended and I reached the base of the black rock region. I walked across a small area where the rock and snow met. The rock consisted of loose, small slates and upset my balance. Slowly I continued between rock and snow, taking to rock when necessary and kicking the edge of the snow when there was no proper foothold in the rock. Often I had to cut the ice with my axe before I could find a place to hook my fingers. When I had gone about half a furlong on the rock I had trouble with my oxygen supply I was breathless and did not know what to do. I kept shaking my head and waving my hands to attract Ahlu and Phu Dorji's attention but it did not help. Again, I started ascending the black rocks. There were now enough hand-and-footholds and I did not have much trouble finding my way up. After progressing about a furlong I came to the yellow rocks which I traversed a hundred yards or so. I had now been

> struggling all alone for almost an hour and a half. And then I joined Ahlu and Phu Dorji waiting for me at the base of the South Summit. I could hardly believe my eyes.'

Rawat having joined us, we took him as the middle man on our rope and moved on. The rope was meant for two and it was against accepted theory to use it for three.

The winds shrieked and flayed us mercilessly. We dug our ice axes in and kept cutting steps but the higher we went the fiercer the wind blew. A raging thirst tormented me but my rope mates had their heads well down and were marching doggedly. I could not suggest a halt. With my companions I kept plodding on mechanically while an inner voice urged, 'You can't quit, you must keep going, you must succeed!'

Slowly and cautiously we negotiated the big boulders of the South Summit. We did not go over the top but took a traverse to the left about seventy feet below till we came across a narrow gulley in the snow which we named India's Den. This gulley is on the main traverse from the South Col to Hillary's Chimney. We were quite relieved to see it as this was the only place sheltered from the high winds and had a small spot where we three could stand and sip some fruit juice. Beyond this point we wanted to be as light as possible. We left the fruit juice tin here and also the oxygen bottle which we would use for our return journey from India's Den to the last camp. We set out again at 9:00 am, with one bottle each of oxygen left to take us to our destination and bring us back to this point. We regulated the flow at two litres a minute.

The foremost thoughts now in my mind was whether we would be able to climb Hillary's Chimney and come back to this place safely after achieving our goal, or would it prove an insurmountable obstacle and rob us of success when it seemed within our grasp. Descending vertically for about thirty-five feet we came to some rocks and a narrow path that led us to the Chimney – an almost vertical obstacle between rock and snow cornice, which I had

Negotiating the Final Ridge

dreaded ever since I was selected for the expedition. Phu Dorji, who was ahead, tried climbing it but kept slipping. He would cut a step with the ice axe and gingerly place his foot on it but would slip all the same. His abortive attempts disheartened me but at last I saw him swing the ice-axe into the wall on the top and it held there with the blade driven in fully. Helped thus, he slowly crossed the Chimney. He asked Rawat to come up another way, from the rock side. Rawat too slipped and had to be pushed while I, who followed them, had literally to be pulled up.

In fact, negotiating the Chimney proved to be a most hazardous affair. Since I was at the rear of the rope and quite far away from Phu Dorji when he made his final attempt, I could not see the exact holds which he took. Rawat, not being able to push forward from the same place, had moved slowly to the left over a big boulder and thus ascended the top of the Chimney. I being in the corner could hardly see him moving up but tried to follow him. Not realising that I had gone too far left, when I stepped over the big boulder, it started rocking. I knew that with a little more pressure on it, the boulder would fall down along with me and I might possibly also bring down the other two climbers, in which case nobody would be able to stop us during a fall of 8,000 ft. I must have wasted at least fifteen minutes or more trying to push myself forward. From that point I could not see either Phu Dorji or Rawat nor attract their attention by shouting. I could only signal to them by pulling the rope twice which meant that I was in trouble and that they should anchor themselves and make preparations to pull me up. While tugging at the rope I nearly hit my back, with the oxygen cylinder, on a rock. If this had happened, the oxygen would have leaked out and I would have been left stranded.

We now found ourselves perched on an ice platform. From here the slope slackened gradually and there was rock to the left and snow to the right. We followed the path between the two. The climbing was not steep now. There were only humps of rock or snow and often a mixture of both. Breathing, which had never been easy, became even more difficult. We would take a deep breath but it would shorten into a hiccup and we gasped for breath. Would the ascent never end? Each step now was a totally exhausting effort. Time and again I wondered if our quest was worth this terrible ordeal. But each time mind overruled matter and I found myself taking yet another step, cutting the ice if need be or merely climbing into steps already made by my rope partners.

The humps undulated endlessly. Sometimes there would be only rock, sometimes a snowy rock or a shoulder of snow. I kept asking myself how much longer and how much farther. Maybe it was far off; maybe we would have to turn back without reaching it. On every climb one is assailed by these doubts, and there comes a time the mind and body dwell on the sheer bliss of going downhill again. I was in

Major Ahluwalia on the Summit

such a state. Yet, another part in me urged me to go on. It couldn't be more than a few feet now – perhaps fifty or even less. But the slope led on and on. Heavens, was there no end? And then, suddenly, there was an end – no more little humps, only a white little dome curving slightly above us. Incredible! It was the summit of Everest.

Yes, we were there. Linking arms, we climbed the last few feet together. The tricolour planted by our first summit party was flying, tattered but jaunty. There were other flags too and some souvenirs and offerings left by the summit parties which had come before us.

From this point, there was a sheer drop and I looked into space. It was freezing, may be 30 degrees below zero, but suddenly the wind dropped, and I remembered thinking: this is a special gift from the Goddess Mother of the Earth. We took a long, wheeling look from the highest point in the world. There were Makalu and Lhotse, Nuptse, and Kanchenjunga looming on the horizon, and many other peaks, all far below us – in a maze of rock and snow-fluted ice-falls plunging into glaciers and glaciers thrusting into valleys. We gazed north towards the Tibetan plateau, and south towards the plains of India. The roof of the Thyangboche monastery glistened in the distance, an up-turned mirror, floating as it were on the opal mists of morning. The view was unforgettable. Off all

View of the Summit with Harish Rawat

the emotions which surged through me as I stood on the summit looking over miles of the panorama below us, the dominant one I think was humility. The physical in me seemed to say, 'Thank God, it's all over.' I thought of all the Everesters who had gone before and those who would follow us. The British, the Swiss, the Americans, and my own countrymen. I thought of the few who had tried and triumphed, and the many who had tried and failed.

I knelt down to bury a photograph of Guru Nanak and a rosary that my mother had given me. Phu Dorji buried a silver locket containing a photograph of the Dalai Lama. Rawat burnt a little incense and left an idol of the goddess Durga. And then I thought I would make a personal offering too. I removed my wrist watch and strapped it to the post of the flag planted by the American Everest Expedition in 1963.

We took some photographs, anxious to film as much as possible of this vastness and grandeur. The film finished faster than I had imagined and coming down about six feet from the summit, I removed my 'down' gloves and tried to load a new film into the camera. But the film would not go in; it would crack as I wound it. The movie camera unfortunately had already let us down. My hands were cold in the silk gloves but after a few abortive attempts I thought of a plan which worked. I let about a third of the film roll over the spool and then closed the camera and tightened it. When I now wound the film it did not crack.

Back at the summit Phu Dorji – bless his soul – had a cup of hot coffee for us. He alone had offered to carry the flask of coffee we needed so badly. My heart went out to this simple, selfless companion of ours.

We had already spent half an hour on the summit and the oxygen in the cylinders was running out. It was time to move and take leave of the Goddess Mother of the Earth. She had been a grand mountain in the distance, and she was a beautiful mountain now that she had lifted her veil and shown us her resplendent face.

View from the summit of Mt. Everest

As we began our descent, I thought what a coincidence it was for us to have chosen 29 May for our last climb. That was the date on which Hillary and Tenzing had stepped on to the summit – the first time ever – twelve years ago to the day. We descended the summit ridge slowly and came down to Hillary's chimney. Then came the thirty-feet ascent. We changed the oxygen flow to three litres, and later adjusted it to two litres a minute as we traversed the South Summit. Reaching India's Den, we changed our bottles for those we had left here on the way up. The pressure in my bottle had been reduced to forty pounds and this might have given me trouble later on, but we were on our way down and that was a comforting thought. We had left the summit at about 10:30 am, and it was now 1:15 pm. We were negotiating the grey limestones, the crampons digging into the loose rock of the Yellow Band. Lhotse looked black against the deep blue sky while on the left Makalu was white with snow. Makalu would be a good mountain to climb, I thought, but the thought was tinged with sadness. Was it because I had already done the 'ultimate' in mountaineering and hereafter there would be nothing higher to climb and all roads would lead down?

Phu Dorji had found an oxygen cylinder with some oxygen in it. This came in handy as I was running out of oxygen. It had been a hard day's work and I was getting slower and panting for breath. I changed the cylinder. The wind had risen from a hum to a moan and then to a roar. Around Razor's Edge my oxygen ran out again. I began to pant convulsively. Snow coated my goggles. My legs would not move and they were lifeless.

I would take a step and feel as if I had run a mile. We descended very slowly, stopping to fight for breath. The wind raged over the ridge from the gulfs of vast space on either side. Hands and feet went numb. It was a terrible and at times frightening experience. The effort was agonising as I began to gasp – I thought my lungs would burst. I crawled over Razor's Edge, in the teeth of this fiendish gale, sometimes collapsing on my belly.

Phu Dorji was in the same plight and could not help me. But we spotted the tents of our last camp; they were no more than a hundred yards away. We thought we might attract Bogie's attention if we shouted 'Bogie, oxygen! Bogie, oxygen!' But our cries went unheeded as Bogie had already left for the lower camps. As Phu Dorji and I lurched and floundered down the long slopes, Rawat kept supporting us. At each step we had to take a long deep breath. Phu Dorji took the lead and with much difficulty I made it to the last camp. I can never forget how my companions helped me in those crucial moments. Companionship and friendship are vital factors on a mountain. You can never forget a man who has shared a rope with you.

It was 3:30 pm when we reached the summit camp. Bogie had left two oxygen cylinders outside the tent. This was indeed remarkably unselfish on his part; he sacrificed his share of the precious oxygen for us. Rawat helped us open the oxygen bottles, and Phu Dorji and I tried to regain strength by using oxygen at four litres a minute. Phu Dorji warmed up some fruit juice which we sipped slowly and felt much better.

As the weather was bad and we were short of oxygen we decided not to stay any longer at this last camp but move on to South Col. When abandoning the last camp, it is customary to leave there a full complement of store. When we left there was enough food for four people for three days, sleeping bags and air mattresses.

At about 5:00 pm when we were about to start for the main east ridge, my oxygen regulator again started making a hissing sound, which meant that oxygen was leaking. I tried to hasten the descent so that I could make do with whatever gas was left in the cylinder. Within fifteen minutes, however, the cylinder was empty and had to be discarded. From then on, although it was a gentle descent, my pace was so reduced that I felt I would never reach the plateau of ice. It was nearing sunset and from a distance we could see the plateau diffused with the rays of the evening sun, making the snow crystals and ice glisten in the crimson light.

Col Cheema, Sonam Gyatso, Bala, Cdr Kohli, Col N Kumar, Major Ahluwalia and Ang Kami erupted into Bhangra when all members and sherpas reached safely at Base Camp.

This was one of those moments when my energy was at its lowest ebb. I had lost all strength and my legs almost failed to move. I tried to move them forward but my steps were falling all over the place. Phu Dorji and Rawat, who were holding my arms, also felt tired and exhausted. At one place all three of us fell on our feet like pieces of log and did not have the strength to get up. The wind was rising and it was becoming dark. We thought of making a manhole in the ice and staying there for the night. With the high winds our feet and hands had become absolutely numb. There was no oxygen to breathe. All our attempts to get up proved futile. I remember Rawat saying, 'One, two, three, up!' He tried to shout but we could hardly hear him. His repeated shouts brought no response from us. I could not even look at my watch but it must have been about 6.30 pm. We had been walking for almost twelve or thirteen hours with hardly any rest except for thirty minutes on the summit during which we had half a cup of coffee and some fruit juice. We had no water at all and now there was no oxygen. We did not know what to do. Sitting down, I tried to dig for an ice cave. I tried to hit the ice with the pick but the blow was nothing more than a scratch. There was no energy left and we were on the verge of a total collapse.

Just then we saw Sherpa Pema Sunder approaching with a torch in his hand. He rushed towards us and refreshed us with hot juice which gave us a new lease of life. With great difficulty we then got up and made our way to the South Col camp. We reached South Col at 7:30 pm, weary almost beyond endurance, and none of us had the energy left to contact the base camp on the wireless and pass on the 'O.K.' report. Pema Sunder had warmed some fruit juice which we thoroughly enjoyed and there were plenty of juices to drink. By 8:00 pm we were ready to sleep in our comfortable tent but the complete lack of oxygen was a serious handicap and badly affected me.

It was about then that I started getting hallucinations. I imagined that Rawat was trying to close the door flaps of the tent to choke me to death. (Rawat had not moved so much as an inch.) Furious with him, I tore open the door flaps and wanted to tear the walls of the tent too. Then I staggered out collecting whatever discarded oxygen bottles I could find. I did not bother to see if they were full or empty or had just a little oxygen left in them. Like a maniac I continued to collect these bottles till midnight, making a heap of them, and then sat on my bed the remaining part of the night striking a Buddha pose. When Pema Sunder brought a hot mug of tea in the morning, I looked sick and weak. He was amazed to see the mound of oxygen bottles at the entrance of the tent. Rawat told me later how rude I had been to him that night and how I accused him of hiding his pen-torch which all the while I had been using when screwing and unscrewing the regulators of the oxygen bottles.

We left South Col for the advance camp at 7:30 am. On the way, at the Yellow Band, we were greeted by a party of Sherpas who were going to the South Col to close the camp and collect essential items. At 9:45 am we reached Camp IV where we had a breakfast of apple juice, coffee and dry fruits before starting our descent to the advance base camp. About a hundred yards below Camp III, which we had reached around 1:30 pm, I came to a sudden halt at the sight of huge footprints in the soft snow. The Sherpa babbled nervously that the Yeti must be around and that a curse would befall him if he ever gazed at those footsteps. Was there really a chance of my coming across the fabulous Snowman? For fifteen suspenseful minutes I waited with my camera just in case the creature should turn up. It proved a futile wait and I had to be content with a close-up of the footprints. As I was operating the camera something hit me on the back and I was toppled off balance. The thought flashed through my mind that the Yeti had got there after all, and at a most inopportune moment. But when I eventually collected my wits and looked around I saw that what had hit me was a mass of hardened snow. Embedded on its outer edge were some pebbles and as it bounced in a zig-zag fashion down the hill slope, the pebbles left prints on the soft snow which closely resembled the footprints of a huge animal. An anti-climax, but my experience might make a useful addition to the numerous tales about the Yeti.

It was 3:30 pm as we neared the advance base camp. Danu and his kitchen staff came forward to meet us. Danu insisted on carrying my rucksack to the camp. 'Phu Dorji and Rawat have already reached the camp and are resting,' he said. Arriving at the camp, we were greeted warmly by Mohan and Lala. They removed my crampons and reindeer boots. The mess tent looked luxurious. Mohan offered me some brandy. I looked at Lala, who promptly said, 'Oh, this won't harm you, Ahlu.'

I woke up refreshed the next morning. The camp was closing down and leaving it after breakfast we reached the base camp in the afternoon. A warm reception awaited us here. It was now 1 June and time for us to bid farewell to Everest. The members of the expedition were out in the early sun gazing at Everest, Lhotse, Nuptse and the other peaks. The gigantic mountains, everlasting and unpredictable, lay far behind us, but for Everest we had a special feeling of closeness as it had become an intimate part of our daily lives for some time. We were now leaving the Goddess Mother of the Earth in her snowy vastness, thankful that she bestowed her favours on us and helped us achieve our objective. We thought of the many mountaineers who had attempted to reach the summit but had to return disappointed. We gloried in our success but it was a sobering thought that we would perhaps never come to Everest again. As we left without loads of food, equipment and medicines, we had a last look at the mountain which was shrouded in mist and clouds.

We were much lighter now and needed only 200 porters to carry the load back. A bulk of the load was equipment and food for the return journey. Everyone was in a happy mood and there was singing all the way. Thandup and others were active again. Thandup had risen from the honorary rank of 'Brigadier' to 'Major General.' While our task was more arduous we not only looked for good food but also in larger quantities.

We passed through the Phantom Alley. It was already midsummer and most of the glaciers had melted into small rivulets. They offered a good subject for my cine camera. With every step that we took we were getting farther away from Everest. The ascent of Everest was an event of yesterday but with the lapse of time it would become more and more remote and then what would remain? Would my memories eventually fade away? All these thoughts led me to the obvious questions: Why do people climb mountains? And why did I climb Everest? It is not easy to answer this question. For me the mountains are nature at its best and their beauty and majesty pose a constant challenge. Many of us believe that they are a means of communion with God or the creator.

But why Everest? Because it is the mightiest. It takes the last ounce of energy – a brutal struggle with rock and ice which once taken up cannot be given up even when one's life itself is at stake. With the peak climbed, there is the joy and the sense of achievement, exultation, triumph and of a battle won, a feeling of happiness and victory very difficult to describe. Whenever I have glimpsed a peak in the distance, like Everest seen for the first time, I got transported to another world and experienced a change within myself which can only be called mystical. The peak draws me to its beauty, aloofness, might, ruggedness and solitude, and offers a challenge which is irresistible. There is a sense of connection with some power beyond you. This curious sense of nearness to the sublime or the infinite is what sustained us in our final physical effort to climb Everest. It fostered courage and confidence amidst the snows and winds of that cold, unfriendly and ruthless altitude. Our bodies became mere vehicles of this new determination imbued with a new will to reach new heights.

With these thoughts in my mind, we passed through Gorak Shep. Its lovely meadows with the soft, young grass looked exquisite, a priceless carpet of beauty. We passed by two big rocks on one of which was engraved the name of our late ambassador, Harishwar Dayal and on the other of John Brietenbach. These were monuments to their everlasting memory. Then we came to the Lobuje and its grassy slopes. Covering a three-day march in one day, we soon reached Thyangboche monastery. Cheema, who was with me, carried the stand of the cine camera while I carried the camera. We made every effort to photograph this area in detail. We even set the lens on a flower and waited for a bee to come, and then photographed it.

Thyangboche was in full bloom with different types of rhododendrons. Nature had put on its best garb here to welcome us. There was the incarnate Lama and other Lamas who greeted us at the huge welcome arch at the entrance of the monastery. We stayed at the same place in the huts where we had lodged before. While we had achieved a great deal, nothing had changed here. The same quiet Thyangboche, with the occasional whirling sound of the prayer wheels and the calm, peaceful Lamas. Their prayers continued uninterrupted and so did the routine of their lives. The Lamas were not in the least affected by the rumbling of ice blocks and avalanches or the thundering noises of the ice-falls. The evening was marked with the usual festive activities. The local drink, *chhang*, was available in abundance.

During the day messages of congratulations from all over the world kept pouring in. I received telegrams from my friends and relatives. In the evening, the President of the Indian Mountaineering Foundation, S. Khera, arrived and with him was a press party. They flew in from Kathmandu to Lukla just below Namche Bazar. We were overwhelmed by this gesture of welcome. Khera greeted each one of us with great warmth. In the evening he presented medals to those Sherpas who had reached either the last camp or the South Col. This was a memorable occasion for all of us.

We left Thyangboche on the 6th. I had woken up quite early in the morning and kept gazing at Everest which now lay far behind us. Before moving down, I had a last look at the summit. As I looked, the plume on its cap vanished into the sky. We then passed through Namche Bazar and Khumjung – the home of many a famous Sherpa. There were receptions everywhere and in all the houses we visited we were served *chhang*. In fact, drinking began immediately after breakfast and would continue till late in the evening. The news of our success had already reached all the villages and it would have been wrong not to accept such spontaneous hospitality. Whenever we halted, there was plenty to eat and much to drink. After having stayed so long in an area where the snow never melted, it was a delight and a treat to be on green grass again. We were now following a slightly different route from the one we took on our way up. We were now going to Kathmandu instead of Jaynagar. On the morning of 9 June while we were crossing the woods we saw a plane flying high above us towards Everest. We later learnt that it was Sarin in an Indian Air Force plane, going to pay his homage to Everest and to take aerial photographs of the massif.

On 19 June we finally reached Banepa where many friends were awaiting our arrival. Among them were a number of relatives of the members of the team and many people from the Diplomatic Corps in Kathmandu. It was here that I first met Duff and his family. He and his wife and two daughters. Joanna and Fuzz, had come to greet us. We were then driven in a procession to Kathmandu. Here again there was a round of receptions and parties. At one party we had the honour of meeting His Majesty the late King of Nepal.

At another party given by M. Ramunny, Chief of the Indian Aid Mission in Nepal, the national honours of Padma Bhushan and Padma Shri awarded to us by the President were announced. This was the first time that such awards had been given other than on Republic Day. We greatly appreciated the honour. After three days in Kathmandu we left for Delhi.

In the capital large crowds had gathered to receive us. There were several Ministers, our friends and relatives and a huge press party. In the absence of the Prime Minister, on tour abroad, the acting Prime Minister had come to greet us. There was also YB Chavan, the then Defence Minister, Sarin and other members of the IMF. Many of my relatives including my mother, father, brother and sisters had come to meet me. We were received like national heroes. Our stay in Delhi was marked by many receptions, public and private. We were greatly touched by the warmth of the welcome accorded to us everywhere.

Later, the team was split up and the members sent to various states in response to their invitations. Kumar, Cheema and I went

Prime Minister Gulzari Lal Nanda, accompanied by Defence Minister YB Chavan and other Ministers, and several thousand enthusiasts headed the historic reception at the tarmac of the Palam airport.

Members of the successful Everest expedition

to Punjab. In Patiala we stayed as personal guests of the Maharaja of Patiala for two days. I was then living in Amritsar and the biggest reception in Punjab was given to us in that city. Huge welcome arches had been erected on the entire route through which we passed and it reminded me of the welcome accorded to foreign Heads of State visiting India. I was also included in a party which went to Mumbai and Pune, and later in another party which went to Darjeeling. A number of other visits were proposed but since I had to be back on duty at the High Altitude Warfare School, I cancelled my visits and left for Kashmir.

It was August when I reached the summer camp of our school in Sonamarg. Colonel Chadha sent me to Gulmarg for a week's rest and recuperation. It was nice and pleasant there. I made friends with some people staying in Gulmarg. There was Madam Schlumberger who was staying in a nearby hotel. I met Prem Nath, an Indian film actor, who loved the mountains. He is known to get away from the hustle and bustle of Mumbai every now and then for trekking in the mountains. I had quite an interesting time with him. The lovely holiday came to an early end as war broke out with Pakistan. I had to put away my mountaineering kit and get back into uniform. The sten gun replaced the ice-axe and the hand grenade the piton.

It was an unexpected war for us. It began with infiltrators coming into our part of Kashmir from the Pakistan Occupied-area of Kashmir. They entered our territory at different places, crossing the high passes in large groups. From the documents captured from a couple of infiltrators, their orders were to assemble either in Srinagar or in Gulmarg. They were told that by the time they reached these two places, the Pakistan army would be in effective control of the areas. To fight a regular war is quite different from fighting infiltrators. They would be dressed up like ordinary local inhabitants and often it was difficult to distinguish between friend and foe. Most of the infiltrators enlisted the help of the Bakarwals – a tribe like the gypsies who camp in summer heights with their herds of goats, horses and donkeys and in winter move down to lower altitudes. The infiltrators somehow managed to coerce this tribe into forming part of their caravan and crossed over. It became extremely dangerous to move out as they could be anywhere. All the areas around Gulmarg were by now infested with them. While we were busy clearing the infested areas, counter measures were taken by our Army to halt the offensive launched by the Pakistan Army. A new tactic used by the Pakistan Army was to give artillery cover fire to the moving infiltrators. Our task became even more difficult as we had to take care of both the advancing Army and the infiltrators, a kind of fifth column who were already inside. At this time we had only our small detachment at Gulmarg. The summer camp at Sonamarg was now deployed in tactical formation and the main assignment given to us was to clear various pockets of infiltrators whose aim was to disturb our convoys going from Srinagar to Leh and Ladakh. They attacked these convoys a number of times.

Reception at Golden Temple with Col N Kumar

One evening we got information that a small patrol party of infiltrators was likely to enter the main Gulmarg valley. So far we had successfully foiled all their attempts to enter the valley. This beautiful holiday resort now turned into a battle area and one could not come out unsecured for fear of being attacked by the infiltrators. My assignment was to prevent the patrol from advancing. I took some jawans with me to the area where the infiltrators were expected to cross. I reached there well before dusk and positioned my jawans in tactical formation around a culvert. Not being able to identify the enemy and not knowing from which direction he would come was a prospect I did not very much like. There was no one in the area. One could hear shots being fired in the distance. The booming of the artillery guns or at times raids by the aircraft gave one an eerie feeling. The jawans with me were Gorkhas and Rajputs and I had full confidence in them. There was also my batman Sher Singh. It was pitch dark. We kept awake the whole night.

At about 4:00 am we heard the sound of some movement among the trees and bushes nearby. As luck would have it, one of my boys who was nearest to their approach opened fire in fear or excitement without being ordered to do so and the fire was returned by the infiltrators. We kept firing and then suddenly there was no response. The firing stopped. We waited. By now there was some light and we could make out the things around us, while we were still hidden behind the little culvert. We then searched the entire area. Except for a few discarded items, there was no trace of anybody. We returned to our post.

Back in Gulmarg, there was a message for me to join the others at the summer camp as activities in Sonamarg were on the increase. In Sonamarg I found that the camp had shifted to a nearby place with barracks. From here we took part in a number of operations. In one of the operations which was personally conducted by the Commandant, Colonel Chadha, on one of the high grounds overlooking the Srinagar-Leh highway, he was shot by an infiltrator and died on the spot. The atmosphere in the camp became gloomy after this tragic incident. At the same time our anger against the infiltrators grew. On the regular war front the Pakistanis could not gain much. But the fighting continued.

One of our convoys of about two hundred vehicles which was taking supplies to Leh got trapped in an ambush. This convoy had been ambushed very close to our area of operation. We were already in touch with the convoy as it was our duty to give them cover. The moment we reached the spot we could only see a few vehicles of the convoy in front and the tail was not visible. The firing had continued. We had a small mortar detachment. Major Vasudev who was in charge of the entire operation ordered fire. After half-an-hour's battle we overpowered the infiltrators and their guns were silenced. Very few could escape. They were all tall and well-built and hailed from the North West Frontier. They wore shirts and *shalwars*. Of those on the run, we took six or seven into custody.

Our convoy, besides arms stores, was also being used by a company of Gorkhas who were being shifted to a new position. When the convoy was ambushed, the entire Gorkha company took cover on the side of the hill and opened fire on the infiltrators. Supplemented by Major Vasudev's mortar fire, the situation was controlled quite fast. Among the captured was one officer from the regular Pakistani Army – a fair and handsome looking person from the North West Frontier. It was from him we learnt that their information was that the convoy was carrying rations and had very few troops to escort it. They got a shock when this company of Gorkhas got down and started firing. The two front vehicles had been completely riddled with bullets. Looking at the infiltrators and the set-up employed by the Pakistanis in this particular ambush, we made out that there were people both from the regular and the para-forces but each operation was commanded by a regular officer of the Pakistani Army. From the captive officer we also gathered that they had plans that night to blow up the iron bridge next to our location. I was quite surprised at the officer's lack of tactical knowledge as he had laid the ambush at a very inappropriate place. Also the infiltrators were together in a bunch, which accounted for nearly twenty-four to thirty being killed. They had no place for retreat. They had not thought of any place to which they could escape should the ambush fail. When Major Vasudev started firing from the mortars they began running in all directions and were easily picked up by small arms fire.

It was almost evening when we returned to our base. Negotiations had been going on to stop the war and again an unexpected cease-fire was declared on 23 September. Fighting in the border areas where the regular armies were engaged in a battle came to a stop but the activities of the infiltrators still continued. So did our operations in tracking them down.

It was the last day of September. There were some officers with me and we were coming back from a nearby forest after clearing it of infiltrators. Just as I was entering my base area, I heard a bullet shot from very close quarters. I fell down and lost consciousness. When my memory returned, it was fitful and for many days I had only the haziest notion of what had happened to me.

Doctors and Quacks

I am now back to the point in time from where I began my story. My progress in the Delhi hospital was slow and tortuous. I found summer in the Indian capital particularly tiring. It was now the end of June and the hottest part of the year. Because of the heat it had become impossible for me to sit in the veranda during the day as I used to do earlier. However, early in the morning at about 6:30 am I would ask the orderlies to help me on the veranda and I sat there watching the birds and the flowers and reading the morning papers. By about 10:30 am I would be back in my room. It became very hot and uncomfortable outside. It was difficult to sit in the veranda in the evenings, so till next morning I would be locked up within the four walls of the room. I found this tedious and boring. Luckily, I received several visitors in the evening besides my own relations. My mother would sit with me till half past ten in the evening and would be the first to reach the hospital at eight in the morning. I got fed up with hospital food and the unchanging routine. My mother then started bringing me morning tea in a thermos flask, and lunch was sent to me later from home.

About this time there was some talk that I should go personally to receive the Arjuna Award from the President. My relations

FACING PAGE: An Open Air 'ICU' in a bazaar at Kashgar, Central Asia

and friends thought the little outing and the ceremony might do me some good. The other award of Padma Shri which had been given by the President in April had been received in person by all members of the expedition except me. General Joseph, who had already given me a clearance, insisted that I must go and collect the award. But I was reluctant to go and thought it would be awkward to be wheeled about in the President's presence. There was hardly a week left for the ceremony. I wanted to think on my own about it but each one of my visitors who knew about the award insisted that I should go. The award ceremony was to be held in Rashtrapati Bhavan on the afternoon of 8 July. Sarin had come to visit me that morning and doubtless the main object of his visit was to persuade me to receive the award in person. The hospital had arranged for me to be taken to Rashtrapati Bhavan in an ambulance. My mother also accompanied me. It was terrible being driven in an ambulance in the blazing summer afternoon. I sipped water every now and then. A sister and a member of the nursing staff looked after me. I was helped on to the wheelchair when we arrived in Rashtrapati Bhavan. When I sat on it, in that heat I could not keep my head straight. In spite of my sipping water frequently I felt that great fires were consuming me, and I wished somebody would press ice against my body which seemed to be literally aflame.

Somi, my brother, quickly wheeled me inside through the long corridors of the President's house and then, using the lift, I was taken to the main hall. Most of the members of the expedition were already there and so were Sarin and other members of the Mountaineering Foundation. They all greeted me. I felt terribly shy and nervous. Blood rushed to my face and I felt as if I belonged to a different world. I almost regretted having come there. A place had been earmarked for my wheelchair. Somi put me there and one by one all the members of the expedition and other friends who had gathered there to witness the ceremony came up to me to say hello. Some of them said I was looking much better, while there were others who had not visited me in the hospital and from the expression on their faces they seemed to think that I was in a hopeless condition.

Before the main ceremony there was a short rehearsal. The Arjuna award is given for excellence in sports. Hardly seven or eight persons get this award in any year. The number this year was the maximum because of the successful expedition team. One feature we all greatly appreciated was that the award was to the whole team and not to individual members. I knew that this was Sarin's idea.

Soon the ceremony began. Everyone got up when the President, then Dr S. Radhakrishnan, arrived. He stood at the dais with his smartly turned out ADCs on either side. I was the only one who remained seated. We were called one by one to receive the award. My turn came. I was shy as ever and every little drop of blood in my body seemed to rush to my face. Amidst the applause I was wheeled up to the President. The President brushed aside all protocol. He stepped down the red carpeted pedestal of State, gripped my hands, handed over the scroll to me and patted me on the back. I was overwhelmed by this gesture. The ceremony was short and brief. In his address the President made special mention of me, which was very encouraging and raised my spirits. After the ceremony and the departure of the President, the entire press, the camera men and television technicians who had gathered there, all came up to me.

Back in the hospital, I nearly fainted as it had been a tiring afternoon for me. My face had become hot and flushed. I thought the exertion had been too much for me and I should not have gone. It was after the ceremony that Sarin told me for the first time that he had discussions with General Joseph who was of the opinion that I should be sent for rehabilitation to Stoke Mandeville Hospital in the UK. Sarin said he was already considering this suggestion and ways of implementing it.

It was now autumn and I again began to sit out in the veranda. My room in the officers' ward had a small lawn in front where I could spend most of my time reading. I started reading all kinds of magazines and innumerable books given to me by my friends. The hospital authorities decided that since I had spent over a year in this hospital, I should be moved to the Naval Hospital in Mumbai which had slightly better amenities for rehabilitation. I welcomed the change and agreed to go to Mumbai.

I reached Mumbai on 7 January by a military plane and the journey was not too uncomfortable. All through the flight, lying on a stretcher, myriad thoughts passed through my mind. I had taken off from Palam in Delhi. The last time I was here was when I had returned from Everest with the Indian team. A rousing reception had then been given to us. There were crowds of people at the aerodrome, a huge platform carrying reporters and press photographers, smiling faces, clicking cameras. A military band resplendent in its uniform was only too happy to be doing its chore. We were the heroes then. I thought the band seemed proud playing its vigorous tunes as the bandmaster's stick flashed up and down, the drum resounded and the bagpipes kept up their incessant cheer. I remembered how when I came down from the plane, my brother lifted me up in his arms in sheer exuberance. There were many friends and relatives, all jostling with one another in the crowd. It was quite a moment in my life. My mother and father were overjoyed. Nobody could have imagined what was going to happen to me.

My mood of reminiscence did not last long. I had now to face the reality of the grim present and uncertain future. I wondered if Mumbai would do me any good. The doctors had said that it was the best Naval Hospital in the country. But, I thought gloomily, they had also said that I would have to be in bed, a confined patient. That was one possibility I dreaded. I could never believe that I would be so completely helpless – that throughout my life I would have to stay bed-ridden. I did not know how it would be like at Mumbai, but was sure I would miss Delhi and my relatives and friends there. In fact, for the last few days I had not felt very bright. And now that I was on the plane, getting closer to

Mumbai each moment, my morale was low and frankly I was quite miserable. My mind had begun wandering again. This had become quite a habit now. It was in flights of fancy that I sought refuge at such times. I would stay lost, thinking of treks I had done while at school, mountains I had climbed, or photographs I took while in the hills – a woman smoking a bamboo pipe, children on ponies, or infants in cradles or tied to their mother's back, looking out as if from a pouch.

I had still not lost faith in myself and God and tried to keep as strong as I could mentally. My aunt had exhorted me to have abiding faith in God's grace. I felt good when I remembered that. I knew God would look after me. I was certain I would get better. As to when that would be, I did not know, but I was sure that the time would come.

The plane touched down at Santa Cruz. We reached Mumbai well after lunch time. As it was hot, I asked the nursing orderly to remove the blankets. A few people in naval uniforms entered the plane. They were the nursing staff from the hospital. They carried me to an ambulance car and set out for the hospital.

I remembered the drive through the main streets. I had been to Mumbai before. Santa Cruz, Bandra, Dadar, with their restaurants flitted past us as we sped on our way. And then Peddar Road, Marine Drive and the Taj. The last time I had come here was just after our return from Everest in July. The All India Wool Federation had arranged a reception for us. We had stayed at the Taj where my room overlooked the sea. My companions and I had received a lot of attention. It was different now, speeding past the Taj on to the Colaba streets and then into the quieter area of many trees and a shaded road leading to the hospital. The journey was rough. I was relieved when the ambulance car stopped. We had reached the reception counter. Papers were handed in. We moved on to the officers' ward, and the ambulance stopped in the arcade. The nursing attendants got down to carry me in. In the veranda, there was much rushing about of people in white uniforms. The hospital looked neat. The officer-in-charge received me with the Sister. The nursing attendants showed me the room. It was large and spacious. They set me on the bed at last and they opened the windows. There was the sea again and the rushing waves, and the ships anchored and the lighthouse just in front. It was good to have a view of the sea again. There would be plenty to do now, I thought. I would watch the ships come and go, and there would be boats and there would always be the waves rushing to the shore.

All the nursing staff, I found, were happy workers and those that stayed long enough soon became good company. I passed my days in the hospital in reasonable comfort. The only drawback was that in the beginning I could not cure myself of homesickness. I missed my mother most of all. Curiously, I lost my appetite and much of the food would be left uneaten in the tray. I wanted to be left alone. I had many friends in Mumbai, but somehow I felt embarrassed meeting old friends and tried to avoid them. I was also not sure whether they would like to have any association with me. I hoped that in time they would perhaps learn about me and would come to see me. I tried to reason with myself why I felt this way. The only answer that occurred to me was that some people who met me earlier had made me feel embarrassed and uncomfortable and perhaps unwanted. I had been in hospital now for more than a year and a half, and lying in bed, seeing old friends fade away one by one, had made me wary. I often thought of a person whom I called 'Uncle' and of the time when he had hailed me as a hero, hugged me and proudly exclaimed to the company, 'My nephew, you know.' But when I was sick and disabled, he passed me by as if I were a stranger and did not recognise me. There was a lot that I learnt about human behaviour and human nature during those days of prolonged illness. Of course there was also a lot of good that happened to me. I came to know love and compassion better. There were many who had rallied by my side – old friends, new companions. Colonel Gurdev and his wife visited me regularly and their lively conversation and generous ways (they always brought with them some delicacies) brightened my life considerably.

The hospital had started training me for my rehabilitation. I would be taken to the Physiotherapy Department and a young Parsi lady, Miss Vania, who was in charge of the department, set for me a very ambitious programme. First, there would be a course of heat treatment under lamps and other electrical machines. Then there would be the physical exercise. These would be given to me by the dedicated attendants, and although it was rough going I thought it would do me good, so I did my utmost to co-operate. Miss Vania and I kept up this serious effort till the end of my stay and she was most helpful and encouraging. I shall always remember their ceaseless care. An Occupational Therapy Department was part of the Physiotherapy Department and here they had a set of simpler exercises for my limbs. First, they took charge of my hands. There was an apparatus to activate them. It was painful to keep my hands in its grip and though I could take it off whenever the pain became acute, it continued to be a dread for me – its iron hooks holding my fingers and a band stretching back the palm from the wrist. But it did help a little and soon I got used to it, as one does to all such contraptions.

There were some other patients with me undergoing similar rigours, and one of them was Major Verma who was in a similar condition. We would often set out together for the departments and there between exercises or treatment, while waiting, we would talk and exchange notes. Later, back in the ward, we would often have our lunch together. Mrs Verma, who with the children had shifted to Mumbai, would have some choice dishes ready and while the two kids, a boy and a girl, played outside chasing cats in the hospital, we would be attended upon by the lady and would be eating and talking of our activities in the hospital.

Before long I was visited by members of some Mumbai climbing societies or there would be some other enthusiastic climbers planning an expedition to the Himalayas. Although I was miles away from the mountains and realised that my own climbing days were over, anything to do with mountaineering fascinated me.

It was March now and about three months had passed since I left Delhi. On 25 March I got a message from Delhi to the effect that Sarin was coming to Mumbai and would visit me the following day. Apart from the important work that he does for the Government of India, Sarin is always able to find time for furthering mountaineering interests in the country. I eagerly looked forward to meeting him. He has an infectious enthusiasm that always makes my spirits soar. His robust optimism makes light of difficulties and he has the knack of solving the most formidable problems. I wondered what he would have to tell me when he came.

The next evening Sarin walked into my room, a smile on his face as usual. He said there were plans to send me to the UK for treatment at Stoke Mandeville Hospital in Aylesbury. I was delighted to hear this as I had heard of this hospital and was quite aware of its high reputation. I was also aware of its long waiting list of applicants and I knew that if ever I had a chance of getting treated there it would only be through Sarin's efforts. This was, therefore, great news for me. He said that the papers had already been dispatched and that they waited only for confirmation from Stoke Mandeville. I could well imagine the efforts which he must have exerted in getting clearance from the Army medical authorities for this treatment abroad and for carrying out other relevant formalities. Sarin, who had another important engagement, left soon after giving me the news.

It was friends and incidents like these which nourished my flickering faith. I could then think only of the good things that had happened to me. I did not pass on the news about my likely departure to the UK to anyone but I was undoubtedly glad and excited. If I could ever hope to divest myself of dependence on others, I knew Stoke Mandeville might show me the way. For a time things went on as before in Mumbai. I was waiting for the final news. The daily trip to the Physiotherapy Department and to the Occupational Therapy Department were an essential part of my routine.

Back in my room, people started coming to see me, and along with them came numerous suggestions about what treatment would help me the most. Someone suggested a Chinese recipe treatment, with pins and needles. Other well-wishers recommended that I try other systems of medicine. 'Why not try the homeopathic system?' A visitor would ask. Another would enumerate the merits of the Ayurvedic system. But both flesh and spirit were too weak for new medical experiments, and while politely listening to them I could hardly accept any of this well-meant advice. I would wait till their inspiration ran out and they got on to other dispiriting subjects such as rising prices. But the most good natured were the hardest to be put out. Their hope was profound and their eloquence ceaseless. However much I would wait, they carried on their argument.

I noticed that my friends Colonel Gurdev and his wife were not as cheerful as before. I found the daily quota of gossip diminishing. Their conversation and their jokes were now few and far between. It seemed they were keen that I should try one of the treatments suggested to me. 'There is a *hakim*, Hari,' Gurdev said one day, 'and he is very good too.' And Mrs Gurdev, happy that the subject had been broached, started expounding the merits of the Unani system of medicine and the achievements of this particular *hakim* – the patients cured by him, the desperate cases who made good and the miraculous results he had obtained with his treatment. They knew I had little faith in *hakims* and their methods, and I knew they did not expect me to take them seriously. I had a call from my mother from Delhi. She said, 'Hari, what's wrong? Why don't you try *hakimji*?' And she closed the argument by remarking, 'If it wouldn't do you any good, it wouldn't do you any harm either.'

And so the *hakimji* was announced one evening. Gurdev ushered him into the room. An admirer of *hakimji* – a burly Sikh – parted the curtains to make way for him. The admirers were not let down. First, the *hakimji* revealed to me the various diseases for which he had a cure. Then followed a list of the patients cured. A long narrative it was. As for the diagnosis and the treatment of my malady, he opined that it would hardly take any time. The medicine would be pounded out of *motis* (pearls) and *kasturi* (a substance with a persistent odour, obtained from a gland of the male musk deer situated in its rectal area extensively used as a perfume fixative, incense material and medicine, since ancient times.) He added in the same breath that these ingredients would of course be somewhat expensive but the expected result merited the expense.

The treatment would cost between two or three hundred rupees a day. Apart from the medicines, I would need daily a quarter pound of ghee and half a pound of milk to be mixed together for breakfast and a dozen pigeons for soup measuring about four glasses. (This, I was told, would have to be taken twice a day with the medicines.)

I was absolutely bewildered. I wondered if *hakimji* was prescribing a diet for a wrestler. His Sikh admirer, intervening, said, 'Sir, for this diet I shall be happy to provide the milk and the ghee for you.'

'Yes, that would be no problem. Sardar sahib will look after that,' said Gurdev. Sardar sahib gave us a very satisfied look. As for the pigeons, Gurdev said he would be glad to arrange for them. The arrangement was finalised and I was to be ready for treatment the next day when *hakimji* would confirm the diagnosis and the remedy. The charges? I was told a charge would be made only if the treatment helped. So all was ready. Sardarji was obviously pleased and *salaam*ed us as he left. He owned a dairy, Gurdev told me later, and I thought how well his buffaloes must look if he was equally generous in treating them to rich fodder.

The next morning *hakimji* came to diagnose my case further and recommend the treatment for my cure. Mrs Bali, a charming young lady from Delhi who had come to look me up also happened to be in the room. All the time *hakimji* was trying to diagnose my trouble he kept looking at this young lady and was probably admiring her good looks. Breaking the silence I said, 'So, *hakimji*, let us start the treatment – I am ready.' At the end of the session, I wasn't too sure if I was the subject for diagnosis or my fair visitor – she got more of *hakimji*'s attention and I got very little. I said to myself, the treatment has started after all and it will continue till, perhaps, like one of the twelve pigeons, I would take to wings and fly into unknown valleys.

The treatment started on a Monday. Gurdev came early in the morning with ghee and milk, and the pills that *hakimji* had made. I took breakfast. It was tough but I wasn't sick yet. Then the soup came. Gurdev brought it in two thermos flasks. I took that too but this time there was trouble. I was sick. I would have thrown up my hands, but it occurred to me why not take the other pill which *hakimji* had said would help to digest the food. So I swallowed that pill too although I was sure the *hakimji* was a hoax. In spite of my misgivings and discomfort I persisted with the treatment but could stand the ordeal no longer than a week. I thanked *hakimji* and Sardarji and I asked *hakimji* to name his fee. Sardarji proudly declined to accept any payment for milk and ghee and said he would pay *hakimji* too. I was firmly asked not to insist on payment and cause him embarrassment. This touched me deeply and I thanked them both. The Unani experiment was over and I returned to my normal diet.

Some changes for the better now came about in my routine. The difficult times in Mumbai, I thought, were over. A friend had loaned his typewriter to me and I had begun learning how to use the machine. My fingers were weak. I could not hold a pen yet, and my letters had to be written by others. It was this that gave me the idea of acquiring a typewriter and doing my private and personal writing unaided. I could use the keyboard but could not hold a pen, and so on a wheelchair, the typewriter in my lap, I would sit for long, learning how to use the keys. In a few days I found words beginning to form on the page and though I could barely manage to type out a page or two it was enough encouragement for me. Soon I plunged headlong into typing and cleared the backlog of pending replies, thus bringing some order into my disorderly life. It was a great step forward for me. The fact that I could communicate unaided with people dear to me was a great consolation. I began to make extensive use of my newly acquired facility, sitting in the veranda, slowly locating the keys and forming the words letter by letter. The words would get strung into a line and lines would grow into pages.

Another change that came about in my routine now was that I was able to leave the hospital in a car once or twice a week to go to the Films Division on Peddar Road. The movie shots that the Everest team had taken while on the mountain were being edited there and since I was in Mumbai I could go now and then to the Films Division and see how the work was progressing. Thapa from the Films Division was in-charge of the project there. He was a great friend of mine since we had climbed Frey Peak together in 1961. That was another reason why I found myself frequenting the office of the Films Division.

He brought back some lovely pictures from Frey Peak. While he was engaged in this assignment, he taught me how to take movie shots. In fact, he taught me a lot about cine photography and what I learnt from him proved very useful. Photography had been my hobby. It blended with mountaineering very naturally. To me climbing a mountain had always been like loving it and when later I started to take photographs of the climb too it was as if I had touched new heights. Photography gave a new dimension to climbing and the two interests complemented each other.

All my Everest team mates were amateur photographers. The team had been selected purely on mountaineering ability and we took no professional photographer with us. None of us had much experience, especially with cine photography, but since some of us had made 8 mm movies, we were, to all intents and purposes, the official cinematographers for the team.

With our meagre experience in this line, we kept our aims simple. Our budget for the expedition was limited because of import restrictions and we had by compulsion to adopt a humble attitude to film-making. We carried four movie cameras. I used a Swiss camera, Paillard Bolex. It was winterised I was told, and could be used right up to the summit. It worked well till our last camp, above South Col, but fifty feet below the summit it froze. This was a disappointment to me, particularly as the camera had functioned so satisfactorily up to that point. I wanted to roll it down the slope into Tibet but Phu Dorji was there to stop me from doing this. And now that I talk of my cinematographic adventures, I must give credit to Phu Dorji for the assistance he gave me at those heights. I took some still shots at the summit with a Nikon camera. I was also able to get about forty movie shots from the summit. Later I felt that my anxiety over the Paillard Bolex was more a case of nerves than a result of any sensible assessment of the situation.

The film unit of the team did quite well. From the base camp up to the lower half of the Khumbu ice-fall, the whole area was scanned. Some good shots were taken of the varied natural phenomena at those heights. There were the ice caves and pinnacles, avalanches and crevasses and some glacial mills in the shots. There was enough material to make a full-length feature film, so the Films Division were given this job, and they in turn selected Thapa to be in charge of the project. A short film, *Challenge of Everest*, had already been made by him and it had been released. Now Thapa was working on a full-length film and when I appeared on the scene, the sequences were being combined and a rough-cut was being made. I could help him only in recognising the shots and then setting them in their correct sequence. As we sat in his studios for this task day by day, I would relive my experience on the mountains. It was a very good change for me and I always looked forward to my visits to Peddar Road.

Making an 8 mm movie is one thing; making a full length film is quite another. But as we laboured, we realised that making a full-length feature film that would compete in the commercial market was a highly specialised job. We decided to invite some important movie-makers to see our work and suggest improvements, keeping in mind the commercial feasibility of the whole project. Thapa and I promptly sent out invitations to some of our friends in the film industry. They were good enough to come over and we showed them the shorter film. It was a good thing we did so because the suggestions that they gave proved extremely useful.

An important suggestion made at this meeting was about the background music. The orchestration should be strong we were told, and if we could get the services of one of the popular music directors from the film world it would not only improve the music but would also enhance its market value. A few names were suggested and Shanker-Jaikishan, a popular duo, were recommended as most competent if we could obtain their services.

All this was good but we had some problems to solve. Ten to twenty times more money would be required. The Films Division's allotment of funds for music would take us nowhere we found. I contacted them and with the help of a friend in the films, soon got in touch with Shanker. He came over to the hospital to see me, which, for a busy man, was a very kind gesture. He immediately set out to understand our requirements. I had with me the photographs of the climb and I took very little time, not more than ten minutes, to outline to him the story of the expedition. The rough cut of the film apparently met his expectations, as after seeing it he was keen to get on with the project.

The problem now was that of costs. 'Our budget …' We apologetically set out to explain. 'That shouldn't be your worry,' he said. To cut the story short, he said they would not charge anything for their services. He remained true to his word. Not only that, Shanker used a 75 to 100-piece orchestra at his own cost.

For the rest of my stay at Mumbai, work on the making of the film combined with my routine at the hospital. To get Thapa and Shanker together was not easy. Both were busy men and Shanker was a much sought-after man in the film world. Locating him was difficult and even when he was located he was often not able to spare any time. I would go to his Mahalaxmi Studios where he had his music room on the third floor. He always came down to meet me no matter how busy he was and however great the rush of people around him – such was his humility despite his high reputation and great talent. In the car, the matter would be talked about and arrangements made. In fact now that I look back, I find that much of the planning for the film was done either over the telephone or in the car. Photography was one of my interests but music was a new line for me. However, as we worked together I found myself eager to know more about Indian music with its rich tradition and became especially interested in Indian folk songs.

The film progressed steadily and as it emerged in its final shape, we were gratified that our labours had borne fruit.

I had now been in Mumbai for six months. It was the beginning of July and the monsoons had broken. Across my windows I would see clouds over the sea and when it rained a light breeze would start blowing. The ships would come and go in the rain and the boats on the sea nearby would set out in rows with the boatmen singing. But I knew that soon I would be leaving all this behind, as I would be going to the UK.

The expected message from Stoke Mandeville Hospital, Aylesbury, arrived. A room was available for me and I had to leave in four days. Although I had anticipated the message, now that the flight to England was imminent, the many problems relating to the journey appeared formidable and even insoluble. First, there was the clearance by the medical authorities of the Army. The doctors in Bombay thought it unlikely that they would approve of the trip. Then there was the problem of an attendant during the flight. There were other difficulties too arising from my peculiar condition. I began to doubt if I would be able to leave on 6 July as planned. But I was lucky. Sarin, accompanied by some senior Army and Navy officials, visited me on the afternoon of 2 July when some papers were signed and the formalities completed within a few minutes. After this I was no longer apprehensive about commencing my journey according to schedule, although some other misgivings remained.

Before my departure I was anxious to find out what progress had been made with the Everest film, and called at the Films Division. The film had yet to take shape and as for the music, Shanker explained that his envolvement would begin only after the rough cut was ready. I gathered that it would take him two to three months to compose the tune, then write out the notations and have the music recorded. But he had the project well in hand and I didn't have to worry, he told me. Somewhat reassured, I turned now to personal affairs.

My mother came from Delhi to help me with the last-minute preparations. I was told that I need not worry about an attendant during the journey as Air India had kindly undertaken to look after me. Sarin had also telephoned the Indian embassies in Moscow and London and there would be people to help me at both the airports. Suddenly the confusion of the preceding days had resolved itself and all was clear like the morning of 6 July which dawned bright and clear after a night's rain.

Gill, a close friend was with me and my relatives as we made our way to Santa Cruz airport. In another fortnight Gill himself would be able to look me up as he had been awarded a scholarship for advanced studies in the United Kingdom. His arrival there would also solve one little problem about which my mother had been worried – who would tie my turban at Stoke Mandeville Hospital? Indeed she had given much thought to finding an answer to this seemingly trivial, but for a Sikh very important question. One day she had come beaming into my room in Mumbai and said, 'Hari, I am told that there is another Gill family at Aylesbury. They will be a great help to you. I have written to them.' But a few days later she seemed perturbed again. She had found out that the Aylesbury Gills had given up wearing turbans long ago and would not know how to tie one. After an anguished parting with loved ones, Somi, my brother, and Gill helped me get into the plane – a Boeing named 'The Lhotse.'

Soon we were airborne and I had a last look through my window at the vanishing airport and city. I began ruminating on the name of the aeroplane, Lhotse. Was it a mere coincidence or was there some hidden significance in a mountaineer like me travelling by a plane named after a Himalayan peak?

It was a lovely morning and the flight was smooth and comfortable. I asked for tea and had hardly finished my cup when Delhi was announced. The plane landed and taxied to the main building of Palam airport, Delhi. Looking through the window I saw a crowd milling around a newly married and heavily garlanded couple. I wondered if the newlyweds were emigrating in search of new pastures.

Suddenly I spotted Sarin. There were my other friends and relatives too, who I recognised one by one. Their presence was a pleasant surprise. Situ Mullick was there with his team of reporters and photographers – his 'boys,' as he called them. And there was 'Burra Sahib' (Commander Mohan Kohli), and Bull (Col Kumar). It was a happy reunion amidst the clicking of cameras and the popping of flash bulbs. Sarin told me that the Indian High Commission in London had been informed of my visit and their representative would be at the airport to receive me. Brigadier Hari Singh, Military Attache in Moscow, had also been contacted. Perhaps the best part of what he had to convey to me came at the end when he handed a cheque to me with the words, 'This will take care of your pocket money in England.'

After a brief stopover, the plane left the Indian landscape now changing into an unfamiliar vista of arid hills with patches of greenery. The mountains kept getting bigger and bigger. We were over Afghanistan. Kabul and Kandahar – those ancient cities with many historic and romantic associations – nestled in these hills. As a child I had often wondered what they would be like. I recalled reading about the siege of Kandahar and the famous Khyber Pass. How many armies in quest of plunder and territory it had dislodged on to the rich, fertile plains of India. I visualised the

Mughal invasion – hordes of riders, uttering war cries, their swords flashing and trundling along some cannons too. From the medley of thoughts an English name arose, that of Godwin Austen, and the mountain named after him K-2, which must be here somewhere towards the east. 'Captain Austen,' I asked in thought, 'what made you, a young British officer, come all the way here in the nineteenth century, to a land so far removed from your own country?' But even as I posed the question, I knew the answer. In the words of a famous mountaineer: 'You climb the hills because they are there.' Not far off was another well-known summit – Nanga Parbat. I thought of Herman Buhl and how he had conquered a great mountain alone. Many a glorious battle may be fought without swords – or bombs – I mused. As we passed by the scenes of those heroes' exploits, I felt like a pilgrim and saluted them.

With Thapa, Sunil Dutt and Nargis

'Major Ahluwalia?' A tall, handsome man whispered close to my ears. 'Can I sit down here, please?' he said, 'I am Sunil Dutt.' I was having my coffee. The face was familiar but I could not recollect immediately where I had seen him. But when he sat down and started talking to me I realised that he was one of India's leading film stars. A very pleasing person, he talked about how he had followed our Everest expedition and how fascinating he had found it. I talked to him of the film, Everest, that was in the making and he gave me a few ideas about titling and mixing. He spoke to me about the film that he had recently made and which had won an international award. What interested me most about it was that it was enacted in one room like a one-act play and was shot in a single sequence. He was now on his way with his wife to attend a film festival, first in Moscow and then in London. I remember the absorbing interest that I found in my conversation with Sunil Dutt. He talked of numerous other ideas that he had in mind for some future films. After a while his charming wife, a great film star in her own right, also joined us. Time passed very quickly.

We were flying at a height of about 30,000 ft. Below, the desert was giving place to forests with an occasional clearing and a solitary hut. I could soon spot some fields and little, round-shaped houses too. The rustling of the air-hostesses' silk saris reminded me that it was lunch time. I asked for an Indian lunch as there was no knowing when I would have one again. The rice pulao and vegetable curries were delicious.

A few minutes later we landed at Moscow. After a brief stopover, the scene changed once more and there was nothing below except a vast expanse of deep blue sea. I began to think of England which we would reach soon, of the English kings and queens about whom I had read in school and college, and of how the English countryside would look at this time of the year. Before my mind's eye were the English moors, the daffodils and lilacs.

My Days at Stoke Mandeville

It was evening in London when we landed at Heathrow airport. An officer from the Indian high Commission came and introduced himself. Arrangements had been made to drive me up to Aylesbury; a black car was parked near the gangway. Thanks to the assistance of a lady Customs Officer, the Customs formalities took only a few minutes and we were on our way to Aylesbury within a quarter hour of our arrival.

The countryside was all I could wish it to be. There were grassy slopes and in the falling light I could still see the meadows full of flowers. Were they daffodils? I could hardly bring myself to ask the driver. Instead I talked to him about the car and our smooth drive. When I said, 'It's a beautiful car,' he turned to me in surprise, 'Why, Sir, I wouldn't pay thirty quid for it.' I was amazed. It was a Hillman and seemed to have been very well kept. The Indian Major who was accompanying me explained that second-hand cars did not fetch much in England. As we passed by a garage, he pointed out the prices it advertised, these ranged between fifteen and twenty pounds. I thought of the low depreciation allowed on automobiles in India and how even old cars were almost as expensive as new ones. Our driver was an Indian who had settled in England and had lived there with his mother for fifteen years. He had a lot of

FACING PAGE: Escorted by Nurse Grace and Physiotherapist Robbie, at a reception in London, 1967

petty grievances to air and did not seem much interested in his motherland. When I asked him if he would like to return to India, his response was unenthusiastic.

On our way we passed a number of pubs – those unmistakable landmarks of the English countryside. They brought back to me memories of our beer drinking bouts at Gulmarg in Kashmir. We were now in the vicinity of Aylesbury which seemed a bigger place than I had been led to expect. Noticing the signboard of the Royal Buckinghamshire Hospital, I recalled that Lala Talang worked there. We stopped for a while at this hospital which had a beautiful lawn where roses and dahlias were in bloom. But we were told that Lala was not in. He and his wife Sulu had gone for a week's holiday to Scotland. I left a message for him and we drove on to Stoke Mandeville.

A hospital is usually conceived of as a somewhat forbidding place where doctors and nurses go about their task mechanically and even ruthlessly. But my first impression of Stoke Mandeville Hospital was that of orderliness, friendliness and beauty. It was a big hospital with neat rows of hutment-type wards and flower-studded lawns. Small groups of patients and their relations sitting in the open made a friendly sight. As I was escorted through the corridors to my ward, I came across more patients and some doctors and nurses who smiled as I went past them. The nurses in their white or blue uniforms looked very smart, cheerful and beautiful.

At my ward – with the mysterious number 5X-1 I was greeted by a gentleman named Norman. My room was spacious, with a large bed on one side and a dresser on the other. There was a cupboard and a chest of drawers with a telephone on top of it. Also some freshly cut flowers in a vase.

Norman gave me a big smile and set about organising things. He was middle – aged with grey hair, silvery at the temples. He told me in detail of the treatment planned for me and of the various arrangements already made. He seemed quite knowledgeable and I wondered if he was a doctor on the hospital's staff. Later I learnt that he was a male nurse assigned to the ward. Although Norman briefed me very adequately, he regretted that he would not be able to look after me as he was shortly going on a long holiday to North Wales. He now brought me a cup of tea, toast, butter and eggs. After the light meal I lay in bed trying to get some sleep.

From Mumbai to Aylesbury – what a leap in distance and environment! When I woke up in the morning, it was clear and bright. I had slept and felt refreshed. The hospital had already stirred to life and there was brisk activity all around me. The Ward Sister came into my room. She was very tall and wore a blue dress. Some staff nurses accompanied her. I raised myself to greet her but she was talking to the nurses. 'He is an Arab!' She exclaimed. 'I thought I was getting an Indian patient.' A nurse said, 'Oh, the language problem again.'

I thought it best to keep mum. The Arabs, of course, wore turbans too and many of them grew beards, so I might well look like one. Meanwhile the inspection of my room was going on. The Sister opened my box and examined the cupboard. She then asked one of the nurses to bring my breakfast. When I said, 'Thank you, Sister,' I caused a minor sensation. The proceedings halted abruptly. 'Oh, he speaks English,' someone remarked. They were evidently all relieved and pleased. The Sister came up to me and I introduced myself. 'I am the Ward Sister. My name is Sister Grace,' she said.

After this somewhat dramatic breaking of the ice, business proceeded smoothly and apace. Sister Grace gave some rapid instructions and then turned to me. 'TV set is out for repairs but I will lend you a wireless set,' she said. Within a few minutes she returned with a radio. The set was small and old, with only a single knob. I thought it looked like a museum piece. Sister placed it on the side board and turned on the switch. It soon got warmed up and a tremendous noise ensued. She banged the top and the noise ceased. Pop music was emanating from the set now. 'How do you change the station?' I asked. 'Simple!' she said and slapped it on the side. There was another station on the channel now. It gave me a great thrill to learn that we had caught a pirate station. It was after all a good if somewhat unorthodox set and I looked forward to many hours of enjoyment with it.

Mary, a helper to Sister Grace, helped me eat my breakfast and insisted that I should leave nothing on the tray. 'Everything English is really good and you must eat it,' she said. As I came to know Mary during the weeks which followed, I was much impressed with her professional ability and obvious sincerity. She was middle-aged, religious-minded and thoroughly English. She ran a little poultry farm not far from the hospital and would come each morning from the farmhouse where she lived. I formed in my mind a delightful picture of Mary in her yellow dress as she walked to the hospital through the green, dew-laden fields. I marvelled how she braved the morning cold when she crossed the fields. Were there cicadas in the fields which entertained her with their thrill music and did she talk to them?

Mary told me of the many patients from abroad who came to the hospital and how they were treated. Patients in the private wards had to pay about fifty to sixty pounds a week. Fourteen beds were reserved for such patients from overseas. Obviously they were very rich and she thought I was rich too.

During breakfast Sister Grace informed me, 'The Therapy Departments have sent in your programme. Tomorrow and the day after – Saturday and Sunday – are holidays, but from Monday onwards you will go for your therapy exercises.' The exercises would begin at 7:30 am and continue till 5:00 pm with an hour's break for lunch from twelve to one. Dinner would be at 6:00 pm. It seemed an exacting routine, but all I said was, 'Yes, Sister.' Soon I had other visitors from the hospital and from London and also a number of telephone calls. A small news item had appeared in the press about my arrival in Aylesbury for treatment and this may have aroused some curiosity. Some of the telephone calls were from people whom I had met in India long ago and I was surprised that there were so many of them in England. When they asked if they could come over to see me, I was naturally pleased and looked forward to their visits. Some of them came the following Sunday and we talked of old times and old happenings. Sometimes the incidents they recalled were a little hazy in my memory but little details helped to reconstruct them. As a mountaineer, I thought of my visitors as companions with whom I had travelled some distance on life's journey in the years past. And as I lay on my bed alone in the evening after they had left, I was happy that Sunday had turned out to be such a wonderful day.

My physiotherapy routine began at 7:30 am on Monday. I was first taken to the swimming classes. The swimming pool was

Therapist fixing the callipers at Stoke Mandeville Hospital

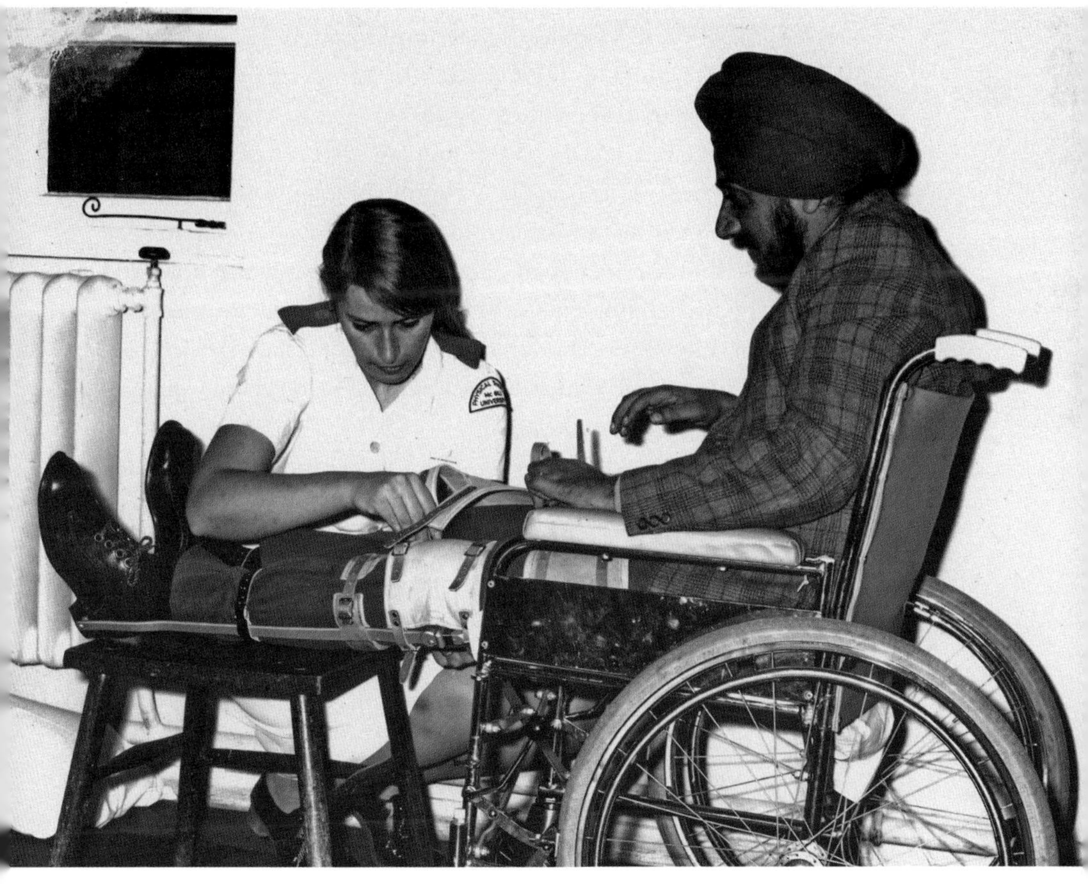

indoors and was centrally heated. The physio girls took charge of me. I wondered how I would fare as I had never swum before. But it was not difficult. We didn't have to swim all the time. There were numerous exercises to be performed in the water and most of them were easy and interesting. After an hour or so when I was tired, I was taken to the other end of the hospital for a course of occupational therapy. This includes, among other things, training in handicrafts with the object of combining exercises with some kind of creative activity. I decided to make a table lamp. Other patients were making flower vases, leather bags and lamp shades. There was a carpentry shop, too, where one could make various articles ranging from salad bowls to centre tables. There was also a machine shop where a variety of machine parts could be turned out. A typing section was also part of the Occupational Therapy Department.

After lunch came the physiotherapy. The first period was allotted to archery. This too, like swimming, was new to me, but it was interesting and when I was told that archery strengthened the arm, I practised it assiduously. The archery session was followed by parallel bar exercises. Here the instructor showed you the right posture for movement, and plastic moulds in the parallel bars helped you to move forwards or backwards. Finally, there would be sports – ping-pong or volleyball.

This was somewhat tiring but an interesting and essential routine. In the course of the day I would meet a number of people and exchange experiences and pleasantries with them. When I returned to my room in the evening it would be supper time and I would sleep early unless I spent some time chatting with other patients in the main ward after supper. I would wake up refreshed in the morning and a new day would begin, filled with the same exciting, ceaseless activity.

In my handicapped condition tying my turban was a problem. But it was solved for me one evening. Chris, a young patient in the hospital, had spoken of an Indian doctor who came to meet me. Bajaj, or Baj as he was popularly known, introduced himself. The young man had established a reputation as a surgeon. He was wearing a white gown and a blue turban. Chris had remarked jocularly, 'We call him the doctor with the lid on.' While his turban may have been a source of amusement to Chris and the other girls, I was much relieved to see it. I knew that my immediate problem had been solved.

Mary thought of India as a world entirely different and remote, and the Himalayas as the abode of God. She was surprised to see in my room articles which I told her were made in India, for she thought we still imported all consumer goods. When I showed her some Indian linen, she said it was of better quality than that made in the United Kingdom. Seeing me take some Indian biscuits, she could hardly believe that India could make such good biscuits. And her doubts seemed to be confirmed when she saw the brand name 'Britannia' on the tin. I am not sure if my explanation that the brand had no relevance to the country of manufacture entirely convinced her.

As already remarked, some of the hospital staff had mistaken me for an Arab. This led to a rumour that I had four wives and numerous children. They were a little confused about my age but they knew that Arabs married quite young. But how on earth one could afford four wives, they wondered. This fantastic rumour was finally set at rest when one of the physio girls mentioned it to me and I told her that I was an Indian and not yet married.

I had begun to settle down in my new surroundings. I took more notice of my environment in the hospital and became acquainted with more people. At the swimming pool one day a member of the nursing staff remarked how happy he was to meet someone from India. And he went on to ask, 'Where is it, this little country of yours? Is it somewhere in Africa?' Such questions might sound incredible but this was by no means the only instance I came across of complete ignorance about India. On another occasion an enthusiastic philatelist commented, 'How nice it would be if India issued its own stamps!' It seemed that he had been collecting stamps for about eight years but had none from India in his collection. When later I gave him some Indian stamps, removed from the envelopes containing my home mail, he was both surprised and delighted. It also surprised me when one of the patients asked me how we lived as according to him India was nothing but an expanse of jungles infested with snakes, lions and elephants. To convince him I had to give him long explanations and to show him some photographs of Indian cities. I had a photograph of our house in Dehradun. When he saw it, he exclaimed, 'Why, this is much like a house you would find in England!'

When on a Thursday morning I received an unexpected call from Dr Walsh, who was Director of the hospital, to meet him in his office, I was somewhat puzzled. He told me that an X-ray examination had revealed some stones in my bladder, and he said it would be necessary to operate on me the following day.

Next morning I was operated upon and the stones removed. Showing the stones to me, he remarked, 'Look at the debris you collected from the top of Everest!'

The guests who visited me seemed to have told Mary about my climb to Mount Everest. 'Why Hari, you never mentioned it to me!' She complained. And then followed a volley of questions. 'How did it feel to be on the top of the world?' 'How did the stars look?' 'Wasn't that your moment of greatest triumph? You sure were very near to God!' Her eagerness was only momentarily suppressed when Sister walked in with a cup of hot milk for me. 'Sister, do you know that Hari has been on top of the Everest?' She exclaimed. But Sister had more immediate things to attend to. She checked me and told me that the operation had been quite successful but I must remain in bed for four days. I felt relieved as I had been told that I might have to remain immobile for a much longer period.

Monday began as a dull day with a slight drizzle in the morning but later the weather improved and it was bright and sunny. After the usual morning routine I asked the Sister to lay some coffee for the visitors I expected. The room had been tidied up and Mary had brought some fresh flowers. Colonel Sinha, and old friend posted in the High Commission, telephoned from London to say that Sarin would be visiting me around ten o'clock that morning. Sarin arrived accompanied by Admiral Samson and Colonel Sinha. Lala, who was working in the Royal Bucks, also arrived. There was much shaking of hands followed by solicitous enquiries about my progress, and for the three of us it was a happy reunion. Sarin said that if Dr Walsh felt my stay at the hospital should be extended he would get this sanctioned by the Government of India. He had asked Dr Walsh to keep him posted about my progress. This was indeed very reassuring, although of course, I was not aware at the time how Dr Walsh rated the possibilities on my rehabilitation. It was only later – in fact sometime in 1969 – that Sarin told me what had transpired that day during his visit to Stoke Mandeville.

As he came in, he did not go to the receptionist but asked a patient – a girl in a wheelchair – if she could direct him to Dr Walsh and Major Ahluwalia. Wheeling away briskly, the girl soon came back to say that Dr Walsh was busy but if they would follow her she would take them to Major Ahluwalia. It was she who guided them to my room. My visitors were much impressed with this active and warm response from a handicapped patient; it was a testimony to the effectiveness of the hospital's treatment. About my own case, I learnt that Dr Walsh accosted Sarin with these words, 'First of all please tell me if you will give a suitable job to Ahluwalia when he returns to India. If you confirm this I shall be with you for as long as you like and answer any questions you may have.' Sarin had replied, 'Yes, Ahluwalia will be given a job when he returns.' When my visitors left, I felt lonely and depressed.

At the time preparations were in full swing at the hospital for the forthcoming Stoke Mandeville games. Temporary structures were being built round the lawns at the back of the hospital to accommodate the international teams which would participate in the games. Teams were expected from the USA, Japan, Czechoslovakia

Sir Ludwig Guttmann, founder of Stoke Mandeville Hospital, UK

and several other countries. I was told that the games, which had developed into an international competition for the paralysed, were a big draw. They had originated in 1948 when Dr Guttmann, the first Director of the hospital, arranged a contest between some English paraplegic units which had grown after the Second World War. Not many people thought at the time that the project would be a success and fewer still could have visualised that within a short span of twelve years these games would acquire almost as much importance as the Olympic Games.

It was in 1952 that Dr Guttmann first invited a foreign team from Holland. Since then this competition for paraplegics has drawn entrants from many parts of the world. In 1960 the games were held along with the Olympics in Rome, and in 1964 with the Olympics in Tokyo. These games were, of course, adapted to the peculiar needs of the paralysed. As early as 1944 Dr Guttmann and his remedial gymnast Quarter Master Hill had thought of and tried out wheelchair polo. This game was, however, considered rather rough and was replaced later by basket-ball. (But isn't basket-ball equally rough, I wonder.) Archery followed and in course of time the tournament comprised ten different events. In the Sixteenth International Games for the Paralysed, for which preparations were then afoot, twenty-three countries were expected to take part. Although the normal routine of the hospital continued uninterrupted, everyone talked about the games. Mary was agog with interest and often brought news of the building activity going on around us.

Thanks to good friends like Duff, former British High Commissioner in Nepal, and his delightful family, I was able to do quite a bit of sightseeing of the surrounding countryside and London. It was Sunday morning when Duff drove me to his house Frith-Haye in Berkhamsted, a lovely bungalow in the countryside. I was meeting the Duffs after two years. There was Mrs Duff, a charming lady who prepared an Indian lunch for me. I also met the other family members. Fuzz, their little daughter, had grown taller. Joanna, their elder daughter, looked as charming as she did before. After lunch, Duff drove me to London. At London I saw the famous Hyde Park, Kensington; and Buckingham Palace with its guards in their resplendent uniforms. As we were driving along the Thames, Duff showed me Cleopatra's Needle erected on the riverside and told me how it had been ferried across in specially made boats all the way from Egypt. We halted in front of an old ship which was moored on the quay. This was the famous ship Discovery in which Scott voyaged for his explorations of the South Pole. It was now set up as a museum piece. Duff said that his maternal grandfather, as a young naval officer, had taken part in an expedition to the Arctic and travelled in an earlier Discovery. As a memento of that voyage, the Duffs had in their home the ship's bell with the date 1875 engraved on it. I was shown this bell when we returned to Frith-Haye in the evening and could well appreciate their pride in the exploits. It had been a memorable day and I felt greatly indebted to my friend and his wife for having made it so enjoyable for me.

My hospital routine was resumed the next morning. Robbie, the physiotherapist assigned to me, was the Deputy in the Physiotherapist Department. She was a hard taskmaster and under her vigilant eye my exercises became more rigorous, any casual movements being immediately checked. 'Physiotherapy has to be taken the hard way,' she told me. I was tired when I returned to my room after exercises. But in time I got used to them and felt both energetic and enthusiastic.

Robbie was Welsh and very proud of her nationality. Her father was an ex-Army officer and had served in India during the days of the British Raj. She was a keen climber and had been able to climb Snowdon in the worst possible weather. Talking about mountaineering one day I asked her if the Welsh term 'Cwm,' which means 'the valley of silence,' had any special significance. Did it not connote the national characteristic of the Welsh who had a reputation for silence and softness of speech? 'But perhaps you are an exceptional character,' I said, looking at Robbie with a straight face. She guessed my meaning and laughed as she went out of the room.

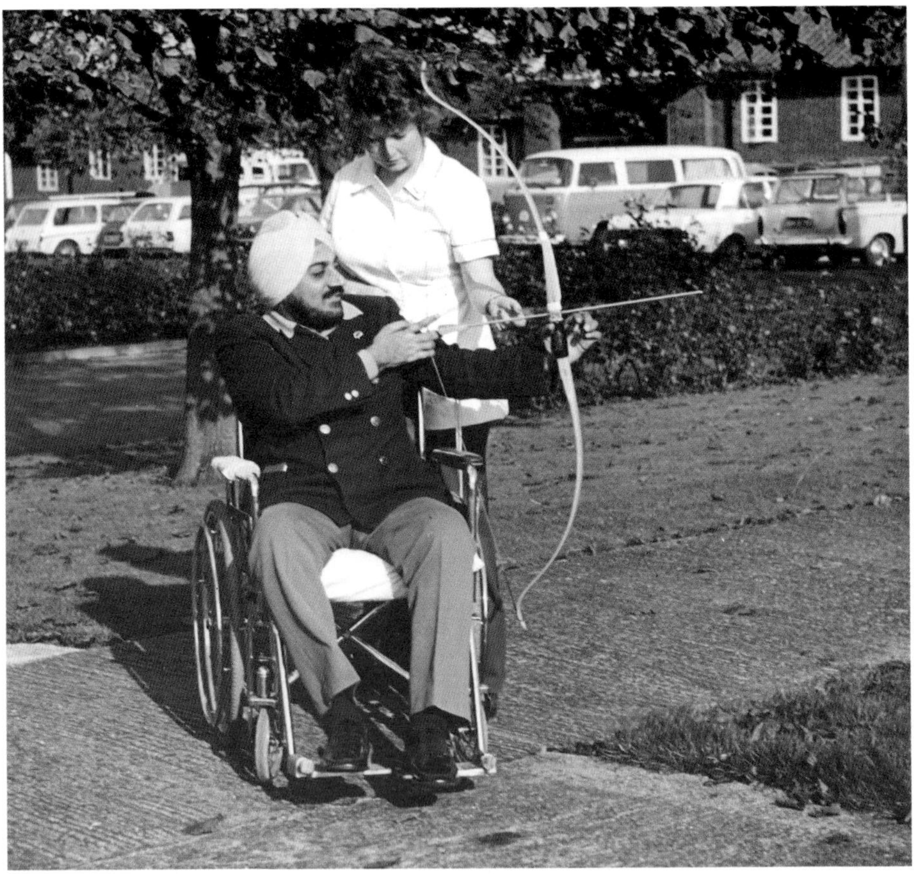

Archery practice at Stoke Mandeville Hospital

One evening Robbie took me to her house for supper. She had also invited a number of physiotherapist colleagues and some nurses, most of whom I knew. After supper I was asked to show the guests my Everest colour slides. Robbie also had some slides of the places she visited during her recent holiday in North Wales, particularly her climb on Mount Snowdon. By inviting me to this party at her home Robbie unwittingly paved the way for a number of similar meetings at which I was asked to show my slides and talk about my mountaineering experiences and the Indian Everest expedition. I was invited to many homes including some in London, and sometimes I returned to the hospital quite late in the evening.

The 1967 Paraplegic Games began in Stoke Mandeville Hospital on 25 July. Among the participants were people belonging to almost every nationality. It was a great occasion and a unique gathering. Much hard work and pioneering effort had gone into it, notably by Sir Ludwig Guttmann and Dr Walsh. A spirit of camaraderie and friendship pervaded the camps. Even the participants who had been disabled in war bore no grudge to the nationals of their erstwhile enemy countries. They all mingled with one another as friends. They enjoyed the opportunity to live, play and eat together. These games are a great morale booster for the individual participants and help to promote goodwill and international understanding. I was sorry that India had not entered a team for the tournament. No selfish reason prompted this sentiment. I was nowhere near fit to participate in any of the events.

The games were to be held on the fields at the rear of the hospital. They were to be inaugurated by Princess Marina, Duchess of Kent. That morning the large crowd of players and spectators was eagerly awaiting her arrival. Sir Ludwig Guttmann and Dr Walsh were busy giving last minute instructions to their assistants and the umpire. Suddenly from behind the tall trees the Queen's Air Force helicopter with the Princess on board was sighted and it landed on the helipad specially constructed for it. Sir Ludwig and Dr Walsh hurried to receive the royal visitor and escorted her to the dais. In his introductory speech Sir Ludwig Guttmann briefly traced the beginnings of the games and announced plans for the construction of a covered stadium in Stoke Mandeville Hospital where future games would be held. I came to know later that Sir Ludwig Guttmann personally raised a very large sum of money – over a quarter of a million pounds – to build the new stadium.

The Princess's speech was short and precise. She was as graceful and dignified as I had imagined. But she left soon after watching the opening events. The games continued according to schedule for several hours. I also left early as I was expecting some Punjabi visitors from London. In attendance at the inaugural ceremony and throughout the games was the military band of No. 1 School of Technical Training, RAF, Halton. Some of the tunes played by it reminded me of similar music played by our own military bands.

My visitors at the hospital that day were Mr and Mrs Gill, two other Sikh gentlemen from London, Kohli who was a resident of Aylesbury, the editor of a local Punjabi newspaper, and a press photographer. One of my visitors had brought a large bouquet of flowers for me and the others brought garlands. As they greeted and garlanded me, the camera kept clicking and there was a good deal of flashlight photography. I found all this somewhat embarrassing but Mary was quite fascinated by it. My friends spent about an hour and a half and left.

The results of the games were announced shortly before the closing ceremony. The Americans had done well but the performance of the Israeli team was superb and they won several gold medals. The trophies were given away by Walter Winter Bottom OBE, Director of the Sports Council of Great Britain. And thus ended the Sixteenth International Stoke Mandeville Games aimed, in the words of the organisers, 'to unite paralysed men and women from all parts of the world in an international sports movement … and promote understanding amongst nations.' The participants dispersed, not without a feeling of sadness at parting from many new friends they had made at this unique meet.

The first Sikh family to meet me in UK, The Gills

I was told by Gill that elaborate plans had been made for my reception at Shepherd's Bush and Southall Gurdwaras. Gill also talked about a projected reception at Gaylords, an Indian restaurant. Gill came to England in 1951 after the sudden death of his father-in-law who had emigrated from India about fifteen years earlier. He started his career as a factory worker on a wage of seven pounds per week but before long became a partner in a wholesale textiles trading concern. Later he bought his partner's share and set up his own firm in the name of Gill & Company. Soon he had built up a yearly turnover in textiles of about half-a-million pounds. In 1960 he entered the property business and bought three hotels and some apartment houses.

Meanwhile my physiotherapy exercises were continuing. I was already in plaster which is preliminary to the use of callipers which help one to stand erect in parallel bars. Robbie would make me stand and go up and down the parallel bars a number of times, often without letting me rest in between. After one of these exercises she said, 'Hari, if you continue like this I'll soon be recommending you for measurement for callipers. It would be marvellous if I could train you for short callipers.'

As the days rolled by, I visited many places and met many people. By now I had a number of friends both in Aylesbury and in London and at times my engagements overlapped. To avoid this I planned my programme so that people could visit me in the hospital on Monday, Tuesday and Wednesday. On Thursday and Friday I would go out either in Aylesbury or to places nearby, while the weekends were kept for engagements in London. I found that this arrangement worked very well. I was frequently invited to meetings of local climbing clubs. I enjoyed giving them a short talk illustrated by Everest slides. This seemed to fascinate my audience for most of whom the Himalayas and Everest belonged to another world. I estimated that on an average eight out of ten persons who listened to me were keenly interested in climbing.

Unfortunately, the increasing number of engagements sometimes resulted in my not being able to return to the hospital on time. The hospital rules laid down that on working days one could leave only after 6:30 pm and one had to be back by 10:30 pm. When this came to the notice of Sister Grace she was annoyed.

One morning she came to my room and said, 'Hari, you were late again last night. I understand you came in at 11:50.'

I replied, 'Sister, it is difficult to come back from a talk and dinner party in London by 10:30. You know how embarrassing it is to leave when a party is in full swing.' But the explanation did not satisfy her.

'I don't agree, Hari,' she said. 'You will have to adhere to the hospital timings, otherwise I shall perforce have to report it to Dr Walsh.'

A somewhat serious situation thus developed and I did not know how to cope with it. Some of the Sisters on night duty were quite lenient and did not report my late arrival but others were strict and I had to be careful to return to the hospital on time when they were on duty. One evening when a friendly Sister from Wales was expected to be in attendance, I accepted an invitation to a party. The inevitable discussion on mountaineering and exhibition of slides terminated quite late and I reached the hospital about midnight. I was not worried, however, as I was confident that the friendly Sister would overlook the lapse. But to my surprise on entering the ward I found a nurse with a forbidding exterior on duty at the door. She said, 'You are late!' and I vainly sought for an excuse. I wondered what had happened to the Sister from Wales. The next morning Sister Grace came to me and I guessed from the way she banged the door open that she was angry. She said, 'Hari, enough is enough. I cannot tolerate your late arrival at night any more. It is bad for the discipline of the hospital. I shall have to report it to Dr Walsh.' She continued lecturing me for about ten minutes. I did not know where to look or what to say. After some hesitation, I said, 'Sister, I solemnly promise that I shall never go out again. I shall leave this place only when I am ready to return to India.' Her anger had not entirely subsided when she left me.

The entire ward came to know of this little episode. While clearing the room, Mary said, 'Sister Grace is very angry with you, Hari. Why can't you cut your parties short? I suppose your slides of Everest keep everyone absorbed. I would like to see them too.' For a few days after this incident I did not leave my room except to attend my classes in the hospital. Sister Grace peeped into the room whenever she passed that way and she always found me in. After a week or so she came in and said, 'Hari, you don't seem to go out at all these days.' I merely smiled and she smiled back at me. Then she said, 'You may go out by all means but please, Hari, try to return as soon as possible. If you are late, it is bad for the discipline of the hospital.' A little later she came back with some bottles of stout which she placed on the table. She then started banging the ancient radio, and I knew we were friends again.

On the last Sunday in August I attended the reception at Southall Gurdwara which the Sikh community had arranged for me. This Gurdwara was built in 1966 on a site previously occupied by a factory owned by United Dairies.

The locality is inhabited mostly by Punjabis and I saw a number of Sikhs on the streets. One of them, quite well-dressed, was pulling a handcart laden with crates. It was drizzling when we arrived at the Gurdwara. Several people stood on either side of the road. In the absence of Gill, who was away on a visit to India, I was received by the Vice president and Gill's eldest son Jagmail, a smart and energetic looking man.

At one end of the hall, *Granth Sahib*, the Holy Book of the Sikhs, was placed on a dais and priests were singing *Shabads* (hymns). After the *kirtan* was over, the Secretary got up and made a rather long speech. While I was grateful for the compliments he paid me, I was embarrassed by his frequent eulogistic references to me and I thought he exaggerated my achievements both as a mountaineer and as a soldier. After the ceremony was over we all shared the community lunch.

The Shepherd's Bush Gurdwara, where I had another reception that evening was built in 1913 by the Maharaja of Patiala. It was known as Bhupindra Dharamsala, and provided temporary hostel accommodation for Sikh students arriving in the United Kingdom. In fact it looked like a palace, with the Maharaja's pictures adorning the walls. The temple of the Gurdwara was on the first floor. At the time of my visit negotiations were going on for further additions to this property by purchasing a nearby Salvation Army church. I came to know later that a fortnight after this purchase had been made, the building was destroyed in a fire. This might have entailed a loss of £20,000 to the Gurdwara but luckily the transaction had been financed by a bank which had insured the property. Subsequently the place was rebuilt at a cost of about £57,000 and is now a spacious structure. It has a large hall for meetings, a dining room, a kitchen and other amenities.

After the reception in the Gurdwara Jagmail took me to his house, introduced me to all his family members and finally drove me back in his Rolls Royce to the hospital.

With the family of Narinder Sawhney at a function held in honour of the author at Shephered Bush Gurudwara, UK

Time passed quickly. The hospital routine continued, with the swimming classes in the morning as usual. I had gained confidence and could now swim without the help of the physiotherapist and at times I could do three to four lengths continuously even doing backstroke. Although the swimming pool was covered it had a large glass panel in front and immediately after a swim it was soothing to sit and enjoy the warmth of the sun. Back from the swimming pool to my room, I would change and be just in time for the other physiotherapy classes which were more or less in the form of games. From eleven to twelve I worked in the Occupational Therapy Department. I had already made a table lamp including a shade and now I switched over to the carpentry shop. There I started making a salad bowl in two kinds of wood, rose and teak. The lady in charge of Occupational Therapy was extremely kind and took a lot of pains teaching me typing. I was soon able to type my letters although I did it very slowly. She allowed me to come to the department in my spare time to complete my letters. All my home mail and local letters were typed by me in the Occupational Therapy Department. This I found was very helpful. I also began to use the electric typewriter which was very easy to operate. Since I could operate a typewriter efficiently and it was not always easy to spare time to go to the Occupational Therapy Department, I requested Col Sinha to have a typewriter purchased for me. On his request, a representative of Remington called on me one evening with three different models of portable typewriters, of which I chose one. I could now type letters in my own room and the typing was a useful step forward in my recovery.

In the afternoon the classes would begin with physiotherapy by Robbie. By now I had started walking on callipers in parallel bars. Robbie had planned to let me walk on the floor with the help of crutches. The callipers were short and were easy to put on. Dr Walsh and Sir Ludwig Guttmann used to visit the Physiotherapy Department once a week. It was during one of their visits that Robbie insisted that instead of walking with parallel bars I should walk on the floor with crutches. Since Robbie was to hold me from the back at my waist I was not at all nervous. This was the first time that I used crutches. I would swing from left to right while Robbie would try to keep me steady. I could hear Robbie saying, 'Steady up, don't hold your breath.' I tried to move forward but found it extremely difficult. 'Your steps are rather long!' shouted Robbie from the back. I would try again and take shorter steps. 'They are still very long,' said Robbie, helping me from the back. 'Let the steps be very, very short. This will give you better control,' said Dr Walsh who was on a round of inspection, and then proceeded to the next patient. 'In future, Hari, you will come a little early, stand with parallel bars for some time and then I will make you walk.' The exercise continued from day to day and I walked on the floor, each time trying to increase the distance with Robbie's help. Although walking on crutches was tiring, it was a wonderful feeling to stand upright once again.

During my stay in Stoke Mandeville I met several keen mountaineers. Mountaineers, I have always felt, are a close-knit band of people. They may hail from different parts of the world but whenever they meet there is the mutual feeling of familiarity and closeness. There are no formalities and, of course, there is a lot in common to talk about.

One of my visits to Frith-Haye, the home of the Duffs, was on Bank Holiday weekend in September when a country fair was being held in the vicinity. We stopped for a few minutes on a hill overlooking the town of Hemel Hempstead and the site of the fair. Thousands of people in bright summer clothes had gathered there and all kinds of stalls were doing a roaring business. They sold sweets, ice-cream, balloons and souvenirs. There were also roundabouts, swings, electric cars – in fact all the 'fun of the fair.' Music from the loudspeakers mingled with the shouts of children and their parents. To add to the confusion – or so it seemed from our vantage point – suddenly a parachute display began and daring sky divers began to drop into a small field just on the edge of the crowd.

After having lunch with the Duffs we moved on to a different but equally friendly meeting in a field where dozens of old, obsolete, steam-rollers and steam traction engines had been gathered. For their proud owners, who had spent months rubbing and polishing and getting their unwieldy machines into tip-top shape, this was the big moment of the year. Not only did they parade their gleaming monsters before their friends and discuss with one another the technical details of the engines and equipment designed half a century ago, they actually raced them against each other. In one race the object was to see how slowly the vehicle would go without actually stopping, the winner being the last to cross the finishing line. I was fascinated by this show as we never witness such an event in India.

During the afternoon of 29 September I had a pleasant surprise when Lord Hunt visited me. He came into my room in the ward holding a small basket containing fruit. Although this was the first time I met him, his face was so familiar from the photographs I had seen that I felt I had known him for years. With his grey hair, he looked very distinguished and dignified. He said, 'I have just returned from my trip abroad, and in India I came to know about you. Lady Hunt has sent some fruit for you,' he added. I was very happy to meet him. He placed the fruit basket on the dressing table. Lord Hunt also presented me a book titled *Alpe Neige Roc*. Although the book was in French, it contained lovely photographs. Perhaps he knew about my interest in photography. I opened the book and found this inscription by Lord Hunt on the fly leaf:

> For Hari, fellow Everester and member of the
> *growing* family of those who were 'there'
> from
> An old stager in admiration and friendship.

I was touched by this kind gesture. We started talking about Everest and some of the Sherpas whom he knew. We got so engrossed in recounting our experiences that I even forgot to offer him a cup of tea till Sister dropped in. 'Meet my friend Lord Hunt,' I said, and then asked her if she could arrange for some tea for him. 'I am sorry, Hari,' she said, 'the staff are off at the moment and I am busy with patients in the ward. I am sure your friend can make some tea. I will show him the kitchen.' I felt quite embarrassed but Lord Hunt promptly got up, went into the kitchen and in a few minutes I saw him returning with two glasses of tea made in typical Indian style. He had served in a Gorkha Regiment in India where it is very common to have tea in tumblers. This incident provided another example of the complete informality among mountaineers. The hour Lord Hunt spent with me passed very fast and he left with the promise that he would meet me again.

Besides Baj there were other doctors on the staff who became friendly with me, particularly Robin and John Cage. I had a number of parties and outings with them.

An enjoyable occasion was my visit to the Bucks Country Fair which was held in Aylesbury on a weekend in the compound of the Finishing School. As there was a big rush at the fair, the traffic police were rather strict. All the cars had to be parked away from the entrance to the fair. 'It will be convenient to drop you near the gate,' said Robin, 'but I am afraid we will have to drive away quickly otherwise the police will catch us. They are very strict around here.' The moment Robin slowed down the car, Val, a physio from the hospital, alighted from one side but as she did so, a policeman came up to Robin and asked for his license. Robin was trying somewhat ineffectively to explain why he had driven up to that point and kept saying, 'Yes, officer!' When the policeman, after taking Robin's name and other particulars, spelled out his offence, he came over to me and to my surprise, put his hand on my shoulder, and said, 'Hari, how are you?' I looked at him, a little bewildered.

He smiled and said, 'I enjoyed your slides at the pub the other day.' It then occurred to me that he must be one of the members of the club I had recently visited. He then went up to Robin and said, 'It's all right. You can park your car here, and hurry up as the fair has already started.' Robin felt relieved and Val remarked, 'So, you have friends among policemen too. I never knew that.'

The fair was spread over a vast area. There were agricultural stalls where agricultural implements were neatly displayed. Good breeds of cattle were on display, also horses and carts. We visited almost all the stalls. After a while, people crowded at a place where the display was to start. It began with various horse shows and equestrian feats. The riders were as skilled as the horses and jumped with ease over the obstacles kept in the field. This was of course not new to me. I had seen such performances at many horse shows in India. Then came a march past of cattle which was followed by various types of buggies ranging from a one-horse trap to buggies driven by eight horses. The most interesting item I thought was the 'hunter's call'.' A horseman would blow a bugle and hunting dogs would begin following him. There was a prize distribution before the close of the fair. While the prizes were being distributed, we moved away as it would be easier to cross the ground before the crowd started rushing out. This was an interesting fair and different from the others that I had seen. It made me realise that even an industrially developed country such as the United Kingdom could not afford to neglect agriculture. I was told that the fair was held once a year, generally towards the end of summer. I could see from the large crowd how interested people were in such fairs.

It was now October and I knew that I would be leaving England towards the end of the month. It had become quite cold by now and central heating in the hospital had already started. It was cosy everywhere as the veranda, the wards, the Physiotherapy Department, the swimming pool, and the laboratory were all centrally heated. Outside there was always a breeze, even though there might be bright sunlight, and most times a cold breeze blew. My physiotherapy lessons went on extremely well. In Occupational Therapy I had finished making a handbag and a shade for my table lamp and in the carpentry shop a salad bowl. I was now learning engraving on brass plates. This process needed quite a bit of practice but was more enjoyable. Apart from engraving brass plates I had also begun to engrave on plastic transparent plates. I made some name plates by engraving on plastic transparent sheets.

I saw that every patient in the carpentry shop devoted more time to it than I could and made bigger things. I could only spend an hour on Occupational Therapy and found this was not sufficient. There was so much to learn and to do in this department. There was a drawing section where I would have liked to spend some time but could not manage it. It was a drawing-cum-designing section. Here were special tables along with various attachments to facilitate easy handling of various drawing instrument. Since drawing was one of the subjects I studied for my engineering degree, I could have availed myself

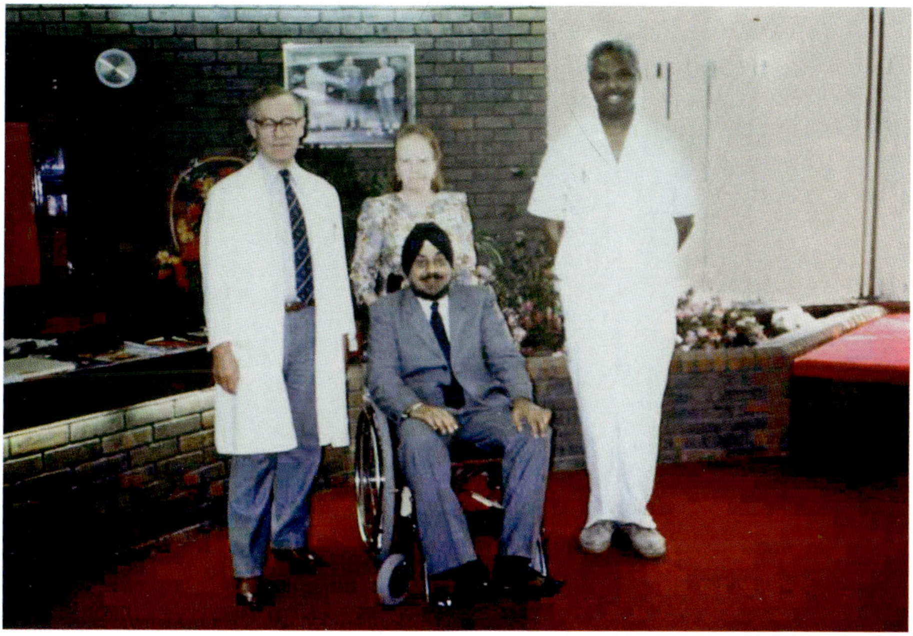

Dr Frankle and Anglieo Hospital Staff of Stoke Mandeville with author before departure to India

of these facilities with advantage. I saw some patients draw a complete design of a house by themselves.

An event I recall with pleasure was the dinner the Youngmen's Sikh Association had arranged for me at Gaylord Restaurant, Mortimer Street. Lord Hunt had been invited as the chief guest. The association had also extended invitations to about fifty British friends of mine, many from the hospital.

Lord Hunt spoke in chaste Hindi and was applauded by all the people gathered there for whom it was a pleasant surprise to hear him address them in Hindi.

Duff, in a brief speech, made a pertinent point. He said, 'When you pour beer into a mug the froth which floats at the top does not mix with the beer down below. So you blow it off. But if you wait a little the froth settles and becomes part of the beer.' He wanted our people to merge themselves with the British and live like them and not be separated as froth is from beer. This speech left a deep impression on the Indian audience.

Stoke Mandeville Hospital staff. (L to R) Dr Warner, Dr Frankle, Frankie and Normen, (Sitting) Anglieo, author and Nurse Grace

Another important function was organised by our High Commission in London. This was a preview of the film *Everest.* It was a shorter, twenty-five-minute version of the original film. I again invited a number of friends from the hospital. The entire arrangement was supervised by film officers of the High Commission. The show was also covered by press reporters. The same evening the BBC televised some extracts from the film. Although everyone liked the film, somehow I was not very impressed as I thought it needed a lot of improvement. The film had been made by the Films Division, Bombay, and specially flown to London for screening.

My friends and engagements had kept me so busy that I did not realise that I had already spent five months in England. It was time to leave. The day I left, the entire hospital staff who had worked for me and had looked after me extremely well were all there to see me off. Parting is always sad. Although I was looking forward to meeting my people and my friends in India, I felt sad at leaving behind the friends I had made in England. I might never meet them again but I will always remember their friendship. Whether it was Mary or Sister or Dr Walsh or my other friends, one thing was common to all of them and that was the sincerity with which they treated me, it was a very important factor in my mental rehabilitation.

While a handicapped person has to be rehabilitated physically by means of exercises, his mental rehabilitation is even more important. Just after the accident and before coming to England, I had become afraid of people and places. I had become extremely shy and had started getting an inferiority complex. It was here in Britain that this barrier was broken and I had once again started meeting people, going to parties and giving talks on mountaineering which I would never have done otherwise. This restoration of self-confidence was the most important factor in my rehabilitation through the methods adopted at the hospital.

A New Life in India

I was back in the Naval Hospital in the same room overlooking the sea. The sea was as calm as it was when I had left. It was the month of November now and quite pleasant. The breeze from the sea was soft and refreshing. I felt active and energetic. After doing my exercises in the physiotherapy ward, I invariably went out. The work on the film was almost coming to an end. Thapa had by now joined the rough-cuts in the proper sequence, making them into a film with a running time of ninety minutes. During the first week I was busy with Thapa, going to the Films Division almost every day to check the sequences and making minor alterations. I also got in touch with Shanker, who had composed the various tunes for the film with the background of folk songs from the hills. Only one major hurdle remained – coordination of the music with the film strip. It was tough work, involving a large, 80-piece orchestra which had some Indian and some western instruments. It took ten hours of work to coordinate the music for half of the film. The film was entitled Everest.

My work for the film now came to an end and I turned my attention to more vital matters concerning my future. Sarin had informed me during his last visit that a suitable job was being found for me. Although I was not unduly worried, I was naturally

FACING PAGE: With Bholi at the Pangong Lake, Ladakh

concerned about my future and was keen that I should get a job in Delhi.

I left the hospital shortly and it was nice to be back in Delhi with my parents. I was grateful for the comforts of home and enjoyed the food cooked by my mother. As Somi, my brother, was engaged there was a new member in our family. His fiancée, Dolly, was an attractive and intelligent girl and was great help to me with my correspondence, as she had done a secretarial course.

About this time DP and Guddi came on a holiday to Delhi. Their little daughter, Ishu, was now nine months old and a beautiful baby. I somehow got very much attached to the child. When I was not doing anything, it was fun to watch her play on the bed, rolling all over the place or throwing up her hands and feet. Wherever we went for an outing, we took her along with us and she seemed to enjoy the drives in the car. One day while I was sitting all alone at home, Guddi came to me and said, 'If you like, I can leave the child with you. With Biji around, I know she will be very safe and moreover I keep coming to Delhi, so it would be all right.' I was quite overwhelmed by this gesture on her part. I decided to keep Ishu with me, as a child is always fine company I thought.

Finally, on 17 April I got a job in the Ministry of Defence. I reported to the office of the Director General, Ordnance Factories. The Head Office of the Director General is in Calcutta, and in Delhi is an executive office consisting of six officers and a staff of about forty people. It was an important office of the organisation. The officer in charge, R. Srinivasan, greeted me. He explained to me the type of work expected of me. 'At this stage, I cannot be more specific but gradually we will see,' he said.

From the little chat that he had with me I could gather that he was genuinely interested in rehabilitating me in the particular job assigned to me. I was quite decided that in case I was not capable of some kind of output or unable to work and felt the strain, I would candidly admit this to Srinivasan. In fact all along it had been my principle not to either overestimate or underestimate

With Mrs Indira Gandhi at the opening ceremony of the Asian Games in New Delhi.

my capacity. But in most cases I always subjected myself to a trial before coming to any conclusion and I would never take anyone's word or belief about my ability to handle any particular job unless I tried it myself. I was not sure what exactly he meant but I gathered that no concession would be given to me and he meant business.

Later, during one of his visits to Delhi, I met RM Muzumdar, Director General of Ordnance Factories, and I was completely charmed by the kindness and understanding he had for me and for my problems. For an officer enjoying one of the highest positions in the country, Muzumdar's disarming nature and his highly dignified informality was a novel experience for me especially in the context of my own army background.

There were other officers but the two I got close to were Chidambaram and PN Jha, son of the former Lt Governor of Delhi. Initially it was hard to work with the civilian staff. In the Army we were used to giving orders to the staff and getting the

Launching of the book *Faces of Everest* in Kathmandu (L to R) My youngest brother, Kuljit, Bholi, sister-in-law Minni, Rekha Poorie and Aroon Poorie

work done, but I found that this business of ordering people about did not work here. I had to adapt my Army ideas to the different environment of the office. I began picking up slowly, and, of course, Chidambaram and Jha were of great help. The more I came into contact with Srinivasan the more I found him a thorough gentleman. A soft-spoken person, he gave me the impression of being a good Commanding Officer.

Jha, who was popularly known as Papu, would invariably spend most of his time with me in my room. He kept himself fairly busy. If it was not files, he would be speculating on the prices of shares. Papu, apart from being an excellent mechanical engineer, was extremely good at designing houses. After having known him for a while I had an opportunity of meeting his father and other family members and thus I became one of their family friends.

I was also lucky to have as my Personal Assistant Harbans Lal Tandon who did not take much time to adjust himself to my requirements. He was almost as dedicated as a Gorkha soldier to his battalion. He was indeed of great help in keeping my correspondence intact and up to date.

After I had moved from Mumbai to Delhi, many friends and neighbours often came and called on me. In particular there were two girls from the neighbourhood, Bholi and Daljit, both university students, who often came to see me. For me at that time when I had just moved to Delhi and was feeling unsettled it was indeed pleasant meeting these girls who were both good company and had many stories to tell about their college and companions. With their delicate features, they looked charming. Bholi had a soft musical voice which enthralled me.

I had still not started going out to restaurants but on Bholi's birthday she invited me to lunch in a restaurant with her other friends. Although I was hesitant about such visits in the beginning, I soon got over my shyness and attribute this mainly to the encouragement I received from these two girls and the way they looked after me. Within a few months, Daljit married and has since settled with her

Father showering blessings after the marriage

husband Harjit in America. I hear from them occasionally. Bholi continued to meet me, and she is a delightful companion indeed. Naturally, we got married.

About this time I met Melville de Mellow who made a fine radio feature entitled 'Concept of Courage' based on my life. Melville de Mellow's radio features have always won great acclaim. The preliminary work on this feature had already begun and when the script was ready, he called me over to his office for the final recording. I thoroughly enjoyed working with him.

A major factor in my rehabilitation was my white Viva Vauxhall with hand controls. It took me just two days to get used to the car. It was fun driving my own automobile. It added to my self-confidence and feeling of independence as I could drive unaided everywhere in the city and without any difficulty. By now I was well settled in Delhi. Although I was known to a number of people, I kept my circle of friends rather small. One of them was Jagmohan who was looking after a hotel which belonged to his father. I was introduced to him by Papu. Jagmohan was proud of his culinary skill and used to say, 'I can cook any dish, Indian, Chinese or continental.' I avoided heavily spiced dishes but whenever I was looking for an evening's entertainment, I dropped in at his hotel.

In May 1968 the Indian Mountaineering Foundation had planned to celebrate its tenth anniversary. The Foundation was formed in 1958 when it launched its first major expedition to Cho-Oyu. The 1968 celebration coincided with the third anniversary of our ascent to Everest. The hall was packed. There were diplomats from almost every country, Ministers, Members of Parliament and a large gathering of other distinguished invitees. Prime Minister Indira Gandhi honoured us by presiding over the function. After Sarin's inaugural address we were awarded the Everest silver medals by the Prime Minister. Some of us were also given the Indian Mountaineering Foundation's gold medals. The most interesting part of the programme was the film, *Everest.*

I was quite surprised to see the Prime Minister sitting through the entire film show as we were told that she would leave for another engagement soon after the show began. She kept greeting people in the hall after the film was over. After seeing Mrs Gandhi off, Sarin came over and said, 'Congratulations! The Prime Minister is very pleased. She wants to take a print with her on her tour of Australia and New Zealand.' This function provided an opportunity for reunion for all of us. I felt elated and very much a part of the Everest team.

I had made a number of friends in Delhi and social engagements kept me busy. My neighbours, Joy and her husband Major Michael, were keenly interested in drama. In fact the 'Yatrik' group of amateur actors is their creation. During the season, they would put up some fine play which I attended. I felt involved in the organisation of Yatrik to some extent. I was soon enrolled as a member of the Yatrik Committee which would decide the policy of the organisation and its working. With all these activities and my office work, I found myself quite busy.

Standing on Parallel Bars with father Sarjit Singh, mother Harbans Kaur, nephew Sonu and niece Ishika.

I often visited Frank Moraes and Marilyn Silverstone, and about this time his son Dom Moraes came over to Delhi. Although I had read a number of Dom's poems and books, this was the first time I met him. From our very first meeting we became good friends and often met each other. Later Leela Naidu, the well-known film actress, married Dom. She looks much more charming in real life than she does in films. Both Dom and Leela became very close friends of my family and whenever they were in Delhi they would visit us and spend some time with us. I found Dom's company very enjoyable.

Among my friends were several mountaineers. With mountaineering activity increasing in Delhi, a few other leading mountaineers and I met and decided to form an association which we called the Delhi Mountaineering Association. Kohli became its first President.

Somi got a son who was named Sonu. Sonu, like Ishu, began living with me. Both were extremely fond of each other. Since Ishu was going to Mrs De Mellow's Nursery School, Sonu also joined this school. I was quite pleased with these two children and also with the two sons of my eldest sister, Bunty and Polly, who had grown into healthy, cheerful lads. Being far away in Kolkata, Bunty and Polly would only spend their summer vacations with me.

Thus the last few years have rolled by without many excitements except the usual minor ones in everyone's life. At times I have found my new routine somewhat boring and on such occasions I have longed for a change. I took a trip to Dehradun and Mussoorie with Sarin and his wife and their son Tunny. With me were my mother, Dolly, Sonu and Ishu. It was lovely driving my car first to Dehradun and then to the hill station of Mussoorie. This reminded me of my good old days at school and college. I met a number of old friends, and had occasion to address my old school in Dehradun. Mussoorie was fascinating. I was delighted to meet my old friend Ruskin Bond. I could not, however, go to St. George's College as it was closed for vacations.

In 1972 I was elected President of the Delhi Mountaineering Association. More responsibility now fell on me. I tried to change the entire structure of the Association. With the passing away of Lt Governor Dr AN Jha who was the Patron-in-Chief of the Association, a great vacuum was created. The new Governor, Baleshwar Prasad, took over and I found him equally interested in the activities of the Delhi Mountaineering Association. With his help, the activities of the Association were revived and at his suggestion, we requested Dr GS Dhillon, Speaker of the Lok Sabha, to become our Patron-in-Chief. I called on the Hon'ble Speaker. I had met him earlier when we returned from Everest, and after many years I now met him again. I found him extremely interested in our activities.

Even though I had several friends in India I often thought of the friends I had left behind in England. Fortunately, I soon got an opportunity to meet them again. Five years after my return from England, it was suggested that it would be desirable for me to go to Stoke Mandeville again for a check-up. In fact a similar suggestion had also been made to Sarin by Dr Walsh, who continued to be in charge of Stoke Mandeville. Our medical advisor Gen. AK Barat who had taken over from Gen. PT Joseph and Lt Col Rautry also agreed to the proposal

This time my mother accompanied me. The first glimpse of England, as we drove from the airport, fascinated my mother. We stayed in a hotel in Wendover close to Stoke Mandeville. Wendover is a delightful small town lying at the foot of the Chilterns on the Icknield way in North Buckinghamshire. It is ideally situated, as it is in the heart of the countryside and is yet within only an hour's train journey from London. Its busy high street spans many centuries of trading and on it is located the Red Lion Hotel where I stayed. The hotel dates back to the 17th century and its register records such famous names as Oliver Cromwell, Robert Louis Stevenson and Rupert Brooke.

Another link with the town's past is the attractive Cold harbour cottages which were given by Henry VIII to Anne Boleyn as part

With Mother and Chris Briggs at his Hotel Pen-Y-Gwayed, North Wales

of her dowry. It is interesting to note that for more than 700 years Christian worship has regularly taken place in the Parish Church of Wendover, and on record is a continuous list of vicars from the year 1221. Although little remains of the original church building, the peace and serenity of its setting have remained unchanged with the passage of time.

A large RAF station at Halton, less than two miles from the centre of Wendover, provides a very positive link with the present as does the close proximity of Chequers – the official country residence of the Prime Minister of Great Britain and Northern Ireland.

Back at the hospital meeting old friends and acquaintances was a pleasant and exciting experience. I was greatly touched by the warmth of their greeting. Sister Grace (now Ms Pouyoucas) was now in charge of Ward 4 where I often met her and had tea or coffee with her. My mother was present at some of these meetings and, in spite of her limited knowledge of English, managed to communicate with our English friends.

I had taken with me a 16 mm print of our film, *Everest*, and this was shown to a select gathering in the hospital auditorium. News of the show soon travelled round the area and I was invited by various schools and other institutions in Aylesbury and Wendover to show them the film and talk to them. The Aylesbury Climbing Club also got in touch with me and I attended one of their meetings which are usually held on Tuesdays at a pub.

At about this time, Air India had hosted a formal lunch in Café Royal for the leading mountaineers of the country. Cdr Kohli and his wife Pushpa especially flew from India to London for the occasion. I was delighted to meet at the lunch Lord Hunt and other British mountaineers. The guests included my mother and many officers of Air India and tourist agencies in London. While in England I was keen on visiting the National Mountaineering Centre in North Wales. I wanted to stay at Pen-Y-Gwayd Hotel. The proprietor, Chris Briggs, was a mountaineer himself and Lord Hunt had sent him a note about my visit. Jenny Walker of Aylesbury Climbing Club made all the arrangements.

Driving through Wales was like driving into a hill station in India. It had snowed a little and I felt excited as I was seeing snow for the first time after climbing Everest. We reached the hotel in the evening. Chris Briggs, who had been away on a holiday in Cyprus, had just returned to receive me. On entering the famous Pen-Y-Gwayd Hotel I saw a large slate (incidentally the area is famous for its slate quarries and exports slate to many countries), with the following inscription:

'This plaque commemorates HARSH BAHUGUNA, Major in the Indian Army, who died in Everest, on 18th April 1971, during the International Himalayan Expedition.'

I was touched by this memorial. Harsh Bahuguna was one of my companions in the last camp on the Everest climb.

(L to R) Bholi, Mrs Briggs and her daughter, Jane with author in North Wales, UK

The hotel, decorated in the Welsh farmhouse style, is more or less a mountaineering centre. It has mountaineering records dating as far back as 1837 and articles of historical interest such as rocks from the top of Everest and mountaineering equipment used by the early explorers. An Everest autograph book contains the autographs of noted mountaineers including Eric Shipton, Tillman, and coming to later times, Lord Hunt. In the bar there is a row of silver beer mugs autographed by prominent mountaineers. Whenever they visit the hotel they drink from their own mugs. The successful British expedition of 1953 stayed here and has a reunion every year in the hotel.

Chris had invited all his friends to see *Everest* and a show was arranged on the first day of our visit. The next day he accompanied me to the mountaineering centre, an institution run more or less on the lines of the Himalayan Mountaineering Institute but with more varied training courses including skiing on artificial ski slopes and canoeing.

My trip to Wales had been very enjoyable and I was indeed grateful to Gundula a German friend for driving us all the way to Wales and to Chris for looking after us so well. I began visiting the hospital again and expressed to Dr Walsh my desire to return home as soon as possible. I had planned to spend only four weeks in England but almost ten weeks had passed. My mother too was keen on a speedy return. Dr Walsh agreed to my discharge, and to expedite our bookings for the journey I called on the Air India people in London. Raj Vaid of Air India had made an appointment for me with his Regional Director, Manek Dalal. Dalal was extremely helpful and got everything sorted out. I was free to move the next day. Immediately after leaving the Air India office I had lunch with Jagmail at Gaylord. Jalota of the High Commission was of great help to me throughout my stay in England and tackled many minor problems for me. The manager of Gaylord greeted me and recalled the party which the Sikh community had given me during my last visit in 1967. The restaurant was warm and cosy and I enjoyed the Indian food, which I had missed for several weeks.

In the evening, Sister Grace invited us to dinner at her home, and a number of common friends were there. My mother cooked an Indian meal for the party. This was a good opportunity for me to bid goodbye to all my friends who had been so kind to me and whose friendship I would always cherish.

Later I visited Stoke Mandeville a number of times with my wife Bholi and invariably met our friends, Chris and Jo in North Wales. Chris and Jo became very close to us and we met almost every year; either they would come to India or we would visit them in the UK.

The Silk Route Expedition

Every journey, even before it physically commences, is first completed in the mind. The Central Asia Cultural Expedition which reached Delhi on the 20th July after travelling across 12,000 kms of the Silk Route in five Indian made vehicles started many years earlier. It was eight years earlier that the seed of an idea was placed in my mind: let us rediscover for India's youth the spirit of adventure and thirst for knowledge that has driven civilisations to seek to expand the frontiers of excellence. An eight year journey through books and manuscripts researching the Silk Route; talking to officials; seeking links in China and finally a visit to Beijing in September-October 1993 to sign the historic Agreement about cooperation on the expedition.

Now when I sit back in the recess of my garden and contemplate this experience, I wonder what was it that originally propelled me to stalk the path of merchant adventurers like Marco Polo and countless others from the annals of history who have now been forgotten. Why did I want to trek along the pilgrims' path – the road which Padmasambhava took to spread the light of Buddhism; and the road along which Fa-Hien and Huien-Tsang travelled barefoot in search of sublime truth.

FACING PAGE: The ruins of a madrasa in Bukhara

ABOVE: Author, Sudesh Kumar and Liang Limin, Director of the Chinese Academy of Sciences, signing the agreement on cooperation for the expedition

BELOW: Elders in the holy city of Bukhara

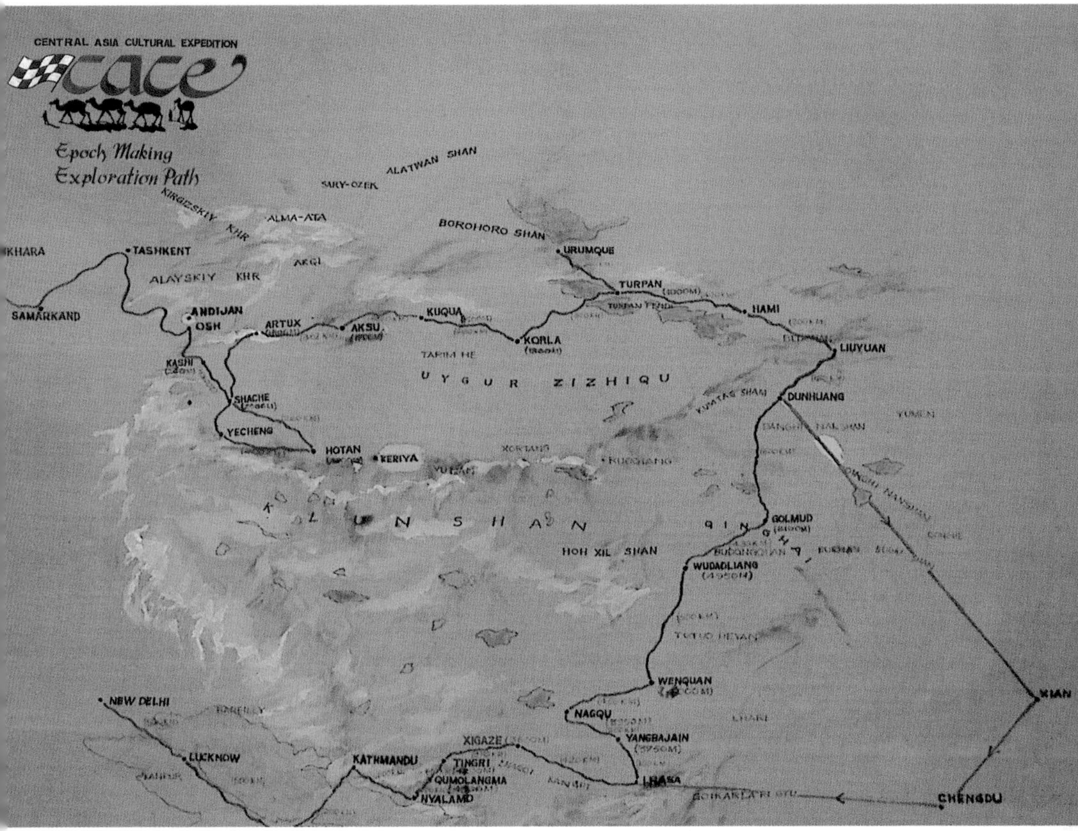

An artist's rendition of the route taken by the members of the Central Asia Cultural Expedition. Map not to scale. (pg208) *Pics from the book Tracing Marco Polo's Journey

To seek my answer I had to only raise my gaze and look at the massive walls of the Old Fort which is just opposite my house. It was manifest in the blue tile decoration on the traditional Rajput Chattries adorning the massive gate. Suddenly, the oasis of Samarkand and Bukhara, which we had just left behind were hauled from the recesses of memory and planted on the Indian soil.

The Silk Route is much more than a jagged line drawn across the Asian heartland running from Constantinople at one end to Xian at the other. The road has been the connecting cord of civilisations. The recorded history of Silk Route dates back to approximately 138 BC when General Chang of the Chinese Army set out on a horse buying mission for the Imperial Court. He went to Fergana

Bholi and Nawaz Bhathena in the local traditional dresses of Samarkand

valley which was famous for its heavenly horses believed to be the fastest in the world. Legend had it that whichever army possessed these horses was sure to win the battle. Later this route attracted the attention of the traders whose merchandise consisted of silk, spices, gold and other precious stones.

The great East-West trade route and vehicle for cross-cultural exchange was named in the middle of the 19th century by the German Scholar, Baron Ferdinand von Rechthofen as 'die Siedeustrasse' – 'the Silk Route.'

Adventurers, conquerors, traders, philosophers, academicians and poets have journeyed across desolate and inhospitable terrain to Central Asia over the centuries – Alexander the Great, Marco Polo, the Kushanas, the Mongols, Chinese scholars like Fa-hein, Huien-Tsang and a host of others, all of whom travelled on foot to India to collect and study the original Buddhist scriptures. These men undertook spiritual journeys of enormous hardship. They showed courage, determination, stamina and vision. They knew what their goal was or they would never have survived. They were heroes of mythological stature who were responsible for taking Buddhism – the jewel of Indian culture – to China.

Central Asia Cultural Expedition set out on the 17th May 1994 from New Delhi with twenty members. The mission was one of peace, friendship and brotherhood and to have a 'people to people contact.' This was the first expedition of its kind to have been given permission to journey through Central Asia. The first leg of our journey was to Tashkent by air. We flew over some of the most majestic mountain ranges of the world. It was an exciting air journey of two and half hours.

It was my good fortune that my twelve-year old daughter Sugandh studying in Modern School had vacations at that time. So she and Bholi, my wife, were able to become expeditioners in their own right. Bholi had started photography as a hobby and her abilities to take candid shots had blossomed with quality to match any professional's skills. She had done the photography for all my earlier travel books on the Himalayas including Ladakh.

In front of the Qin Terracotta Army Museum with Bholi

My daughter Sugandh with a local girl in Bukhara

Bholi thus took this opportunity of arming herself with new equipment, both for still and video shooting. The manner in which she has captured the spirit of Central Asia is what makes her pictures so very special.

Sugandh was growing up in a mountaineer's home and I was really waiting for an opportunity to introduce her to the challenges of understanding nature, a region and its people. She made the most of her chance and was with the expedition in the erstwhile USSR sections of Uzbekistan, Kazakhstan and Turkistan. She flew back to India from Alma-ata along with Ruhi and Matilal just before we entered China.

Her return to India gave both the expeditioners and me some breathing space. With all the impishness of her youth she would give me a report at the end of the day about who was drinking what, smoking how much and saying what about whom, to whom. At the same time, she would conveniently overhear my unguarded comments to Bholi and then with the delight of a little pest, set up one against the other. This good natured mischief kept us all on our toes. Sugu had made a powerful triangle with Ruhi, who is a film maker trained at the prestigious Jamia Media Centre in New Delhi and Nawaz Bhathena twice winner in the lady's division in the Himalayan Car Rally and now an advertisement executive after an MBA from England.

These three musketeers travelled in the same jeep with Hormazd Sorabjee, a professional photographer and son of the noted jurist Soli Sorabjee. Hormazd is a lovable fellow, but it seemed to me that the constant company of three young ladies, always giggling, continually up to mischief and dazzlingly attractive made him miss his wife far too much. So while others spent their money in making purchases, Hormazd spent the last dollar in speaking long distance to his wife, Naheed in Bombay.

We had come to a city where time had stopped. The city of Tashkent was destroyed in an earthquake which struck in 1966. The entire Soviet Union had participated in reconstruction of the city, a task which was completed in a surprisingly short span of just four years. Tashkent is indeed a beautiful city with planned boulevards and well laid out rose gardens. A lovely canal criss-crosses the city. After enjoying the most gracious hospitality of the Minister for culture

Drinking Holy Water from the Well of Hodja Uban

Mr Naim Gaibov and our Ambassador Mr Dalip Mehta and his charming wife, Nandini, we took off for the hoary town of Bukhara.

Dalip is surely one of the best Ambassadors of Indian culture. The manner in which the local people have started appreciating Indian things is a direct consequence of his efforts. He made wonderful and detailed arrangements for our expedition in Uzbekistan. The starting few days of an expedition are always the toughest since we tend to remember the comforts left behind at home. While Nandini, Dalip and their team at the Embassy made us feel at home. BK Singh, a young Foreign Service officer must be singled out for our compliments.

En route to Bukhara is the significant city of Samarkand. The one thing that struck us about both Samarkand and Bukhara was the sense of déjà vu as if we had been here before, as if nothing is unfamiliar. People could have been talking in strange tongues but we had little problem in comprehending them. Many buildings in

In the Taklamakan Desert with the double-humped camel-which was once the only means of travelling across this region

Samarkand, which was once the capital of the world conqueror Timur Lane were inspired by what he had seen in Delhi. A large contingent of masons and crafts persons were part of the booty that he carried with him from Delhi to Samarkand. Alexander the Great in 329 BC described Samarkand as: 'Everything I have heard about the beauty of Samarkand is true except that it is even more beautiful than I could have imagined!' Expeditioners Babar Hameed and Ruhi Tabbassum, with interest in architecture and design, were able to draw many parallels between the buildings, jewellery and costumes of these areas and India.

Samarkand is Uzbekistan's second largest city, with a population of 6,00,000. Its most important monument is Registan, which compares well with the Taj Mahal for its monumental beauty because of its most spectacular architectural work. Today Timur Lane lies buried here in the imposing mausoleum under a slab of green jade, the largest in the world.

From Samarkand, a drive of eight hours brought us to Bukhara, the holiest city in Central Asia. It has 360 mosques and 80 Madrasas. It has a population of 2,50,000 people. The city is 2,000 years old, some even say 3,000. The name Bukhara, dates back to 1st century AD. There is a lot to see here, like the Ulaq Bek Madrasa, Kalyan Mosque, Iyabl-Khauz and Chor Minar, the blue domed minaret which is a crude miniature form of the Char Minar in Hyderabad. We were in Bukhara during the Eid-ul-zoha festivities, 'We are now brothers for life,' we were told everywhere. It is considered extremely auspicious to visit during this period.

Bukhara still reverberates with the legendary stories of Timur Lane, his uncle Changiz Khan and Alexander the Great. It is said that Timur Lane carried back craftspeople and masons from Delhi after his conquest so that they could reproduce in Bukhara the beauties and splendour of India's capital.

We were given a very warm and traditional send off by the local administration, the people and the school children of Bukhara. There were clergymen from eight different mosques who read out prayers and blessed us before we moved to Tashkent. Our lady expeditioners Bholi, Nawaz, Sugandh and Ruhi joined the local girls in a send-off which had a lot of dancing.

From Tashkent, the team was divided into two groups. The main caravan led by Akhil Bakshi crossed over to Kazakhstan as the Government there was very keen to have them. The second group along with Nita, Goutam Ghose and his crew flew with me and Bholi to Andhijan. Andhijan has had historic ties with India, Babar being the main link.

Akhil has an outstanding academic record with an MBA from USA. This he combines with a love for the outdoors. Even as a student in USA he dreamed about Central Asia and of travelling across it. Most of all though, he has an ice cool temperament and never gets flustered even in difficult situations. Seeing these qualities in him, I felt he would be ideally suited to be the leader of the expedition that included academicians, scholars and adventures; not to speak of the international members and the Chinese.

I think Akhil beat the Chinese at the game of keeping a poker face. His leadership abilities blossomed fully and he played a significant part in keeping all the members as a cohesive unit, very often under conditions of great stress. I am sure all these factors contribute to his success in his job as Officer on Special Duty to the Prime Minister of India.

His wife Sharmila, an elegant and gracious lady met the team at Kathmandu. Sharmila is tall with sparkling black eyes and long, beautiful hair to emphasise the fact that she is a Bengali. Sharmila means 'Shy' and her shyness truly adds to her grace.

Goutam Ghose, the celebrated film maker was invited to join the expedition and to lead the film team. The logistics were frightening: shooting in the desert and in the mountains; at temperatures varying between sub-zero at night and 45^{0}C during the day. We were keen to share the beauties of Central Asia with the world by making a film on it. I realised that the budget I had been working with would prove wholly inadequate to the needs of making a world class product. With Goutam in the team, I had no hesitation in meeting the challenge of the now doubled film budget and then to raise the additional funds. I am sure that Goutam's ability to capture the mood and essence of a region and its people and recreate it on the screen will mean a film that the world will be inspired by.

A painting of Babar in a museum in Andhijan

Andhijan is a city that breathes Babar. They have Babar Foundation and Babar Square. They are very proud of the fact that Babar established the Mughal Empire in Hindustan. They regard him as a great poet, a kind and perfect father and son.

The Babar Foundation is doing intensive research on the life of Babar. Its premises lie at the very place where Babar was born and care has been taken to have its buildings in the same old style. It is a round single storeyed building, with a grand entrance and a beautiful courtyard full of flowers and the central fountain in the shape of a samovar. A statue of Babar in a sitting posture overlooks the area. The building houses a museum where beautiful paintings of Babar, his family as well as other prominent personalities of his time are displayed.

The Babar Foundation made us an honorary member and we were received in the home of Zokirjon Mashrabov as a relative of high standing: We found Zokirjon and his family full of love and affection. Zokirjon narrated very interesting incidents of how they dismantled Lenin's statue and erected Babar's at the centre square of the city at the time of the Independence. I promised Zokirjon that I will be present for the marriage of his granddaughters.

Andhijan is situated in the lap of the Fergana Valley, the home of the legendary Heavenly Horses. It was believed that whoever rode these horses to battle would be invincible.

It is said that Babar always pined for his beloved Fergana Valley, fed with a natural spring with the most lush green areas and mouth-watering fruits – cherries, apricots, raspberries and strawberries.

Andhijan is a very well laid out and well maintained city. The roads are sprayed with water twice a day to make them clean. The centre partings on the roads as well as the sidewalks have fruit trees. Every house has its own little orchard and the people feel happy to offer their fruits to guests. Even the Airport has its own vineyard.

After spending three days in Andhijan, we took a flight to Bishkek, the Kirghiz capital, from Osh. The city of Osh is 40 kms from Andhijan. This was another place for which Babar had a great nostalgia during his lifetime. Before we left Osh, we were served breakfast in a beautiful garden overlooking the whole valley – the very place where Babar rested for three days on his way to India and named it Khwajabad after his teacher whom he loved very much. We felt we were on the same trail as some of the great adventurers of times gone by.

FACING PAGE ABOVE: Arrow straight roads cut through Xinjiang's bleak expanse. The road network and traffic has increased following the discovery of large deposits of crude oil in this area

FACING PAGE BELOW: Cars of the expedition departing from Issiykkul Lake for Naryn

The second group, the main caravan under Akhil, entered Kazakhstan on 25 May and passed through some of its most important cities such as Chimikent, Djambul and Talas famous for its epic hero, Manas and Chengiz. According to Akhil, the genuine warmth and love showered in abundant measure on the Indian expedition by the Kazakh people came straight from the heart. The traditional welcome with bread and salt at the Uzbekistan border; the sumptuous lunch served with fermented mares' milk on a grassy meadow.

The expedition then drove for almost eight days through Kirghizstan, picturesque country famous for its Tian Shan

mountain, known as the Heavenly mountains and Issyk-Kul Lake, beautiful streams and meadows rich in flora and fauna.

It was a feast for the eyes and more so for the scholarly vision of Dr Vikram Thakur, the Geologist on our team. He would examine rocks with the intensity of viewing a work of art in a museum. 'To me these rocks are like a museum, since they reveal the past,' he said. Thakur collected four suitcases full of rock samples which he carried back for detailed scientific analysis at the Wadia Institute of Himalayan Geology at Dehradun, of which he is the Director.

From Issyk-Kul we drove to Naryn, a border town adjoining Xinjiang. On the 3rd of June we crossed over to China at Torugart pass where we were met by a team from the Chinese Academy of Sciences.

Here I was able to re-establish my ties with Liang Limin, Director in the Chinese Academy of Sciences who was leading the Chinese team. We had exchanged dozens of letters and fax messages in preparing for this historic expedition. Limin and I had become close friends through our frequent communications. I had not yet spoken to him on telephone as he knew no English; and I no Chinese. So we were really like fax friends. Very often I would make difficult queries and ask for an answer within one hour. It says a lot for the discipline of the Chinese that they always kept to such tight schedules. We first met in late September of 1993 in Beijing and on 2 October signed the historic Agreement for this expedition.

From a height of 3354 metres with temperatures down to 0^{0}C, we drove to Kashgar where the temperature was well above 30^{0}C. Although, we reached Kashgar well past midnight, it was a wonderful feeling to be in this exotic ancient city. Kashgar played an important role during the early part of the century. It was a place where both the northern and the southern silk routes met. It was the hub of political activities of earlier times. Famous for its centuries old Sunday Bazar, even today it bustles with traders thronging with their various merchandise to the bazar. The atmosphere takes you

FACING PAGE: Sunday Bazaar, a popular feature of Kashgar, Central Asia

back a thousand years and you feel as if time has stood still here. It has a population of 2,80,000, predominantly Uigurs and Muslims.

We stayed in Chini Bagh Hotel, recently built on what used to be the garden of the British Consulate. Now only the residence of the Consul-general along with his office exists at the back of the hotel. This Consulate was set up in 1882 by Sir Younghusband with George McCartney as its first incumbent who stayed here for almost twenty-one years. It has a very exotic history and is mentioned by all the explorers and travellers in their accounts. Eric Shipton who was the Consul-General twice here, met me in Delhi in 1976 with his wife Diana. His stories about Central Asia filled me with a desire to visit this exotic region.

The Consulate had a gorgeous and charmingly laid out garden. I learnt that lady McCartney had taken a lot of personal interest and had imported over fifteen varieties of exotic plants including fruit trees from the UK. I could still see an over-hundred-year-old elm tree. I am sure it would have been planted with loving hands by the gracious Lady herself.

At Kashgar we were joined by Michael Haggiag a well-known British film and television script writer and director. His joining us made our film team much stronger. His company, Global Arts, London, is now one of the co-producers of our film.

From Kashgar we followed the lower silk route and reached Yarkand after a drive of five hours. We stayed in an old caravanserai, with a few modern touches here and there. I am afraid even this is not going to be there for long as a large modern hotel is being constructed next to it.

The night bazaar of Yarkand is held in the market square, which has a picture hall, a disco and shops on three sides with loudspeakers blaring at a high volume. Another common sight throughout Xinjiang are the billiard tables on the roadside. People play this game with high stakes and go on playing till early hours. Yarkand has old ties with India and the Gurdial Sarai and the Kashmir Kucha still exist here. It took us a long time to find these sarais.

Gan Gau, the Dry Ditch – this dangerous stretch is also one of the most charming areas between Kashgar and Turfan

From Yarkand the expedition moved to Khotan, a very large oasis which is famous for its jade, carpets and silk. Khotan was a very rich Empire and was the principal supplier of precious stones for almost 2,000 years. The white and black jade came from the river Karakash. We visited some of the mining areas and also the factory where exquisite carvings of jade are done. We also visited the famous carpet factory.

Khotan has a very long and rich history. Buddhist monk Fa-Hien has left vivid accounts of the Kingdom of Khotan when he passed through it in the late 4th century on his way to India. The other Chinese monk Huien-Tsang visited Khotan in the 7th century on his return from India. Marco Polo also travelled through this Kingdom in 1274 AD. Our stay in Khotan was a delightful one. Every evening we visited the night bazar where we interacted with the local people to understand their customs.

The night bazars are a unique feature of this area. The pavements would be swept, tables would be set up and the most mouth-watering dishes would be available at the instant restaurants. What was amazing was that there were concealed electric connections, and multi coloured bulbs, refrigerators and even disco lights would be connected.

Although we were not supposed to go beyond Khotan on the Southern silk route, the authorities were kind enough and special permission was granted to visit Keriya which lies eastward further into the Taklamakan desert. Keriya derives its name from River Keriya. It was an interesting drive along the desert for almost three hours. We were met by the Hakim of Keriya who took us around his office and residence.

The drive to Keriya was very unusual. Just picture in the mind's eye a harsh, sandy desert on your left and a yellow carpet below: the Taklamakan and the Gobi desert respectively. Gobi has small pebbles and between them a small yellow grass called 'Camel's Grass' grows and carpets the whole area.

The approach to Keriya is announced by willow trees. Four deep lines of trees on either side, creates an avenue, and driving through is like entering a meadow. What is remarkable is that good tapping of the oasis water has made Keriya a green area. There is a steady population increase as a result and now there are over 100,000, people up by twenty per cent from the 80,000 of a few years ago.

We wanted to go further but were informed that there had been a nuclear test explosion by the Chinese 150 kms away and it was therefore not safe for travel.

The expedition then took the route back to Yarkand by-passing Kashgar and passing through Aksu, Kucha, Kurla and then reaching Turfan.

Turfan principally is an agricultural oasis famous for its almost 200 varieties of grapes. It has 6,700 hectares of vineyards, not including those scattered in family, government and school yards. The trip to this wonderland oasis is fascinating for not only does Turfan have bold and rugged beauty but it also possesses the charm of delicate nature – willows, clear streams, stone bridges,

Donkey carts were still the most common and favourite mode of transport in this region

terraced fields and farm cottages on the slopes. Walking in the grape corridors of the valley is a delight. You can pluck a bunch of grapes anywhere and wash it in nearby spring water and eat. However, when we were there they had not fully ripened. Another fruit that had just started coming into the market was water melon.

Turfan is one of Xinjiang's fascinating open cities, famous for its hot weather with temperatures soaring up to 48^{0}C, and an annual rainfall of 16mm. Lake Aydinkel, 60 kms to the south of the city is the lowest place in China and the 2nd lowest in the world at 154.43 meters below sea level. It was an important town on the central route of the Old Silk Road. On the way back to Turfan from Goachang, are the Astana-Karakhoja Tombs of the 3rd–4th century where the corpses have been mummified by the extremely dry desert weather.

The Flaming Mountains, the Bazikelik – Thousand Buddha caves, the Emin Minaret and the ancient city of Jiaohe are also

At the Centre Point of the Asian continent, near Urmuchi

well worth a visit. Another fascinating aspect of Turfan is its *Karez*, an irrigation system of wells, connected underground by channels laboriously dug in regular descending lines from snow-mountains to the desert areas. Almost 1,000 *Karez* were dug over centuries and still play an important role in the irrigation system of the region.

We visited the ancient city of Goachang, an impressive city built in 1st century BC. The Chinese monk Huien-Tsang taught in this city for several months. From Turfan the expedition moved to Urumchi which is the capital of Xinjiang region.

Today Urumchi is like any other modern city having five star hotels and educational institutions. Urumchi is a very wide tree-lined city with open water channels. The city has well over 100 mosques. We visited the Academy of Sciences which controls the activities in the scientific field in this region. A three-hour drive took us to Heaven Lake. It is at the foot of the Mount Bogda, east of Northern Tian Shan mountains where one finds Kazakh families grazing herds of sheep, horses, cattle and even the double-hump camels. Heaven Lake is situated at 1982 metres above sea level, and the slopes of the surrounding hills are covered with tall pines and spruces. Blue skies, white clouds, snow-capped peaks and evergreen forests are all reflected in the limpid waters of the lake.

Close to Urumchi is another interesting spot which has recently been discovered by the Academy of Sciences. This is the Centre Point of the Asia Continent. Although the drive was long we were able to see the Centre Point which is at the base of the South Mountains where a large reserve of gold has also been discovered recently. In the vicinity a gold refining factory was under construction.

In Urumchi, we were joined by four Italians, film maker Sergio Scapagnini, and doctors Giovanni and Polo and Umberto, who was elected to the European Parliament three days before he joined us. They were very pleasant company.

The next important place where our caravan halted was Dunhuang. This is an old cultural city, having many ancient and interesting attractions spread across a vast desert, the Crescent Moon spring, Yangguan Pass and Yumen Pass. Mogao Grottoes, a treasure trove of Indian and Chinese art styles, are located between Sanwei and Mingshe mountains. Over a 1,600 metre expanse of sheer cliff are spread one thousand grottoes which, with twisting corridors, facades and tall towers have for centuries provided a solemn, sacred place for Buddhist pilgrims. We were lucky to be here at this time as these caves with beautiful sculptures and murals are going to be closed to public shortly and the replicas from the caves will be displayed in the newly constructed Dunhuang Museum aided by Japan and United Nations. The first printed manuscript in the world, the Diamond Sutra, was also discovered in these caves along with innumerable other manuscripts.

Lhasa, Tibet – The Forbidden City. A beautiful reflection of the Potala Palace

Dr Kulbhushan Warikoo from the lovely land of Kashmir felt that the natural beauty of Central Asia was almost like that of his home state. Every evening, Warikoo and other members of the expedition would have discussions and debates with local scholars. Harish Rawat, my rope mate on the Everest climb, grandson of the famous travellers Kishen Singh and Nain Singh and P. Wangdus, a Buddhist Scholar whose forefathers ran to the caravans in the good old days added to the content of the discussions with their personal knowledge. The other important area of study that we had undertaken was on Herbal medicine which included Ayurvedic, Chinese and Tibetans. This study was effectively conducted by Dr Rajesh Dogra who was also the deputy leader of the expedition.

From Dunhuang the expedition was again divided into two groups. Akhil took the route via Golmud to Lhasa which is a difficult route over high passes but I was confident that under Engineers of Mahindra & Mahindra, Gavin and Nazir there would not be any break down. This was the first time that any expedition was permitted to traverse this route.

The other group with three members and myself flew to Xian, an ancient Asian City served intermittently as the capital of eleven dynasties spanning a period of over 1000 years. It was also the starting point of the Silk Road. We visited the Huien-Tsang temple where he spent nineteen years translating the Sanskrit scriptures of seventy-five sets of over 1300 volumes which he carried from India. The discovery in 1974 of the Qin Dynasty (221-206 BC) terracotta army of 6,000 soldiers rocked the archaeological world. We were very impressed to see this terracotta army museum. This museum has been made at the site where the terracotta army was discovered.

To go to Lhasa we had to go to Chengdu, the capital of Sichuan province, the home of the panda and famous also for the largest sitting Buddha, which is 71 metres high, carved out of a cliff. I found Chengdu to be a delightful place.

We flew to Lhasa on the 4th of July early in the morning. It was a fascinating flight and a wonderful feeling to be in Lhasa. The city of Lhasa is 90 kms from the airport and the drive takes you through breathtaking scenery with roads lined at places with rows of poplar trees and the drive for the most part is along the river. I was now actually in the city which is called 'roof of the world.' When I looked at Potala Place (Dalai Lama's residence), I realised that it was mightier than I had imagined. My visit to the Potala Place on a wheelchair was by no means any less difficult than climbing the world's highest mountain, as hundreds of steps had to be negotiated. But going up these steps was an extremely spiritual experience – we felt as if the entire team was climbing up for an audience with God.

We were in time to witness the festivities in the monasteries to celebrate the 60th birthday of the Dalai Lama on 6th July. Visiting the market place was an experience. People were in a festive mood with whole families on the streets, attired in colourful clothes. However, we did sense some tension in the air. Joy was mixed with sorrow that the Dalai Lama was not present. There was presence of large contingents of police; said to be there for ensuring no violence erupted anywhere.

The moment the local people recognised the Indian Caravan, they clustered around us like bees and offered us the honey of their love and affection. There were three brothers, tiny tots, between the ages of three and six who were singing an ancient song. Goutam was so fascinated by them that he determined to make them into instant singing stars and he filmed them for almost 20 minutes.

Lhasa has been called the forbidden city, the forgotten city, and so many other cities. To us it was a place where we rediscovered our inner selves. We were overwhelmed by the mighty and the graceful monasteries all around us. We were fortunate to attend the assembly of the Rinpoche of Drepung Monastery. As we looked around and saw the monasteries perched perilously on the cliffs, in fact almost carved out of the mountainsides, it struck me that man's understanding of the service of the Lord was essentially the same: whether at the Jain temples erected in the middle of nowhere in the desert sands of Rajasthan or Tibetan monasteries blending in their harshness, starkness and beauty with the Himalayan mountains.

Along the way, we visited a monastery at Shaloo where the Lamas were taught to fly. Further along the drive across the roof of the world, we passed through Xigatse and Gyantse, both historical cities with beautiful monasteries. Then we crossed over to Nepal across the Friendship Bridge.

The mind now has peace and little or no restlessness. But I know that it is so only till yet another face of Mt. Everest presents itself to the mind!

After spending two delightfully relaxed days at Kathmandu, where the Prime Minister of Nepal received us over tea, the team returned to Delhi via Lumbini – Lord Buddha's birthplace.

The Central Asia Cultural Expedition has been yet one more caravan like many others before whether it be of explorers, scholars, merchants, monks or the humble traveller – all have come and gone, only the Silk Route remains forever.

A Long-Cherished Dream Fulfilled

Sometimes, just when you think you have reached the highest peak of success – an unforeseen event in life suddenly brings you crashing down from your pedestal. Then again, just as you hit the rock bottom rung of despair, life once again challenges you to rise, believe in yourself, dare to dream the impossible – and have the courage and conviction to make your dreams come true! My life has been an amazing roller-coaster journey of spectacular success, followed by devastation and despair; of long struggle and agony, when I couldn't see any light at the end of a long, dark tunnel; of healing and hope, of learning to laugh and live a full life again; and of ultimate triumph over tragedy. It has been a journey that has taught me much – but most of all it has taught me about the strength and resilience of the human spirit and its ability to conquer the ultimate summit – the summit of the mind.

FACING PAGE: Team ISIC (L to R) Chitra Kataria, Chief of Rehabilitation Services; Dr AK Mukherjee, Director General; Sugandh Ahluwalia, Chief Strategy Officer; Dr HS Chhabra, Medical Director; KV Uthaman, Chief Administrative Officer and Major Ahluwalia

My story begins in 1965. I was part of India's first successful team to climb Mt. Everest. I still remember that heady feeling of joy as I stood on the top of the world. Little did I know that life was just preparing me to face bigger hurdles. Three months after having stood atop Mt. Everest on 29 May 1965, I was severely wounded in the Indo-Pak war on the fateful evening of 30 Sep. 1965. I had suffered a devastating spinal cord injury and was paralysed from my waist down. I was just twenty-six years old and I thought my life had ended.

In those days, spinal cord injury management was non-existent in India. No one could even tell the difference between quadriplegia and paraplegia let alone, its treatment! The general perception back then was to keep the patient on maximum bed rest with minimal movement of any limbs – exactly opposite of what was actually the recommended treatment! There was no attempt to rehabilitate a person, or to care for a patient's emotional well-being. I was moved from one hospital to another as doctors were baffled by the extent of my injury.

I was fortunate to have the support of my family. My brother Somi who was in the Army got posted to Delhi. Above all my mother was always there to encourage me and keep my spirits high so that I could face any challenges – medical or otherwise. Later my youngest brother Kuljit Singh also joined me in Delhi after leaving his merchant navy job.

In April 1966, the then President of India, Dr S. Radhakrishnan, conferred the award of Padma Shri and on 8 July 1966, he conferred the Arjuna Award.

After struggling for two and a half years in various hospitals, I was finally sent for treatment to Stoke Mandeville Hospital in UK, with the help of friends and the government of India. This hospital in Aylesbury had been specially designed to cater to World War II patients. I reached Stoke Mandeville Hospital on 9th July 1967 for a five month rehabilitation course and was admitted to ward 5X under the care and charge of Sister Grace. I arrived broken in body but not in spirit. I was determined to rebuild my life against all odds. My Therapy Programme would begin at 7:30 am and continue till 5:00 pm under the Physiotherapist Robbie. Pre-lunch session comprised Therapy and Swimming on alternate days and training in Handicrafts and Typing. Post-lunch session started with Archery followed by Parallel Bar exercises and sports like Ping-Pong or Volley Ball.

The 1967 Paraplegic Games began in Stoke Mandeville Hospital. The participants who had been disabled in war bore no grudge to the nationals of their erstwhile enemy country. India had not entered a team for this tournament. These games aimed at uniting paralysed men and women from all parts of the world in an international sports movement and promote understanding amongst nations. The restoration of Self Confidence was the most important element in my rehabilitation through the methods adopted at the hospital.

It was a life changing experience for me! The outstanding rehab facilities, the extraordinary skill of doctors and compassionate nursing care soon began their healing effect on my body and spirit. For the first time I dared to hope, to look forward to a day when I could once again live a meaningful life and enjoy the simple pleasures of life. Over the years, I visited Stoke Mandeville Hospital many times for my check-ups. Every visit reinforced my conviction that India desperately needed a centre like this and I became obsessed with the idea of setting up a similar institute in India. Sir Ludwig Guttman, the Founder Chairman of Stoke Mandeville Hospital inspired me to follow my dream, while Dr Walsh, his successor and my physician, motivated and helped me design and establish my dream project.

The spinal-injured need to be rehabilitated, both physically and mentally and trained to acquire a skill to become gainfully employed. We need to enable those with spinal injuries to live a joyful, meaningful life. We also need to bring about critical awareness among the general public of the grave situation of the spinal-injured in India. Rehabilitation involves restoring the patient's self-esteem and imparting personal, social and vocational independence.

My dream was to build a Hi-Tech Holistic Care Centre that would offer the world's most advanced medical care to patients, that would be at the cutting edge of medical and surgical technology, that would play a leading role in path-breaking medical research and treatment, that would set the standards in teaching and training a new generation of specialists – an institute where the mind, body and spirit would be nurtured with compassion.

A hospital of this nature would require enormous funding and the support of the medical fraternity. Therefore, I thought it would be best to get the government entrusted to establish such a comprehensive hospital and rehab centre. A detailed project report was made and submitted to the health department of the Delhi Government who would then examine and forward the same to the Union Health Ministry. I kept following the progress of this project. After much persuasion and meetings we got the project through the Delhi Government which was recommended to the Ministry of Health, Government of India. My team and I lobbied for this project at every conceivable level. It finally reached the office of the Secretary, Health Ministry for final approval. This took almost two years when I was finally called for a meeting with the Secretary. The Secretary was kind enough to appreciate the need for such a comprehensive rehabilitation centre on the pattern of Stoke Mandeville Hospital but felt that the government would not be able to muster the required funds. It was a major disappointment for me as I had started believing that this project would be taken up by the government and my meeting would definitely yield positive results. It was like setting out to climb Everest but failing to reach the summit. But Everest had taught me that when the going gets tough, the tough get tougher. They don't give up on their dreams; they just redouble their efforts.

After having discussion among friends and well-wishers it was felt that resubmitting the project to the government will not be a viable solution. The only other course was to set up an NGO. I felt that to start this mega project I should seek the blessings of our Prime Minister Smt Indira Gandhi. This thought started consuming me and imparted enough courage in me to personally meet our mountain-lover Prime Minister. I sought a direct audience with her and she most readily agreed to meet me during a cultural show that was to be put up by a North Eastern Troupe. I was overjoyed at

Mrs Indira Gandhi with author's family and friends

her positive response and was simply thrilled when she asked me to be seated by her side during that cultural show which was being held in the garden of her residence. She had been totally engrossed in watching the feats of the troupe and never so much as even looked towards me, leave alone exchange a single word. As soon as the show got over, she turned her compete undivided attention to me and asked me as to what had prompted me to meet her. I urged her to become Patron-in-Chief of the Indian Spinal Injuries Centre as that would be the biggest blessing in giving a concrete shape to my dream project. Briefly I told her what the project was and how important it was for India as such a centre did not exist in our country. Mrs Indira Gandhi readily agreed to lend her name to the Institute as its Patron-in-Chief, provided I were to give her a commitment that no politician would be elected or nominated to the Board of Directors and that the Institution would function exclusively as a Voluntary Organisation and not succumb to the pressures of the Ministries. I gave her my unstinting commitment to abide by these conditions.

The Indian Spinal Injuries Centre, with Mrs Indira Gandhi as its Patron-in-Chief, was thus born. Her affiliation yielded handsome dividends in setting up this institute where we are striving towards assisting the spinal-injured persons in conquering the summits of their minds and enabling them to live life with hope.

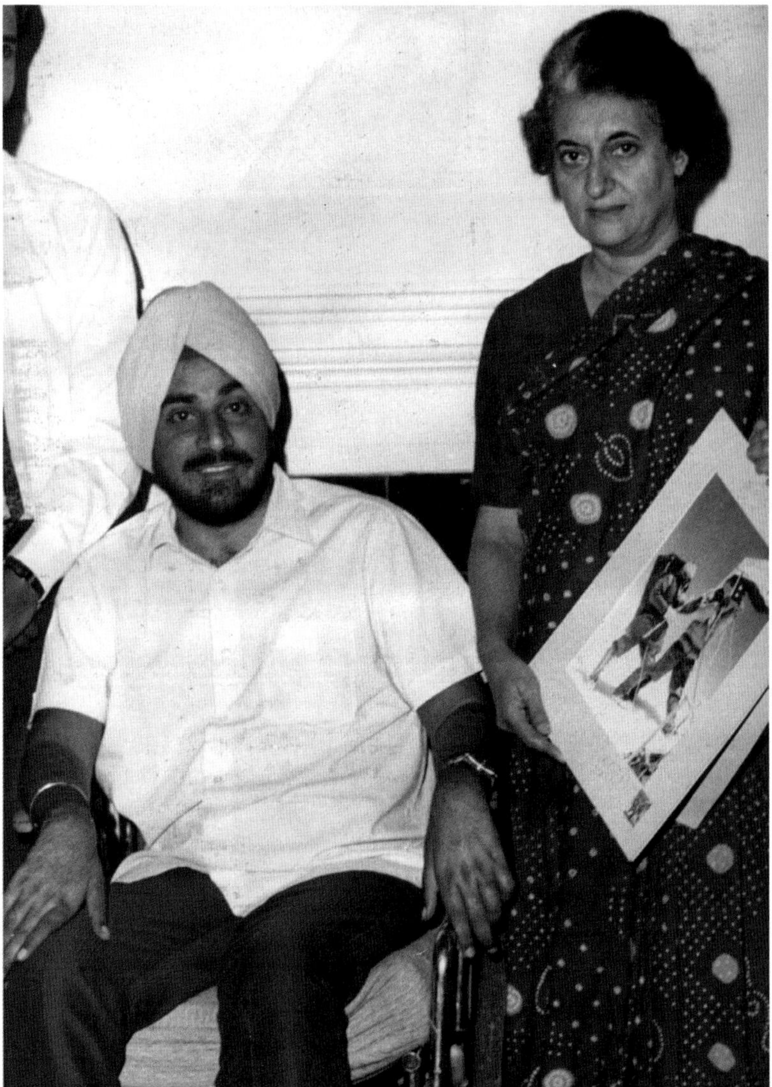

Prime Minister, Rajiv Gandhi with the model of the hospital along with Architect, Gautam Shah, Minister of State for Foreign Affairs of Italy, Sen. G. Bonalumi and HC Sarin the first Chairman, Indian Spinal Injuries Centre.

The Centre was registered on 25 February 1983 as a society, by its seven founding members – HC Sarin, LN Jhunjhunwala, Virender Singh, Dr Kalyan Singh Sachdev, Bishan Singh Bedi, Manjit Singh and myself. The centre was to run on no-profit basis for promotion, development and stimulation of research and scientific exchange of technical and medical knowledge. Our next priority was to get an appropriate logo designed. We were lucky to get the services of a very senior artist, Srivastava who designed our logo. The letters ISIC form a graphic of a person on a wheelchair in motion and ready to lead a full life. It reflects the philosophy of the institute that life goes on, full of hope and joy.

Later Shri Rajiv Gandhi, the then Prime Minister, appointed me as a founder member of the Indira Gandhi Memorial Trust, that was formed after the most tragic and untimely demise of Smt Indira Gandhi.

FACING PAGE: Mrs Indira Gandhi and author

I am deeply indebted to my mentor, guide and Founder Chairman of ISIC, HC Sarin, who had held the prestigious office of the President of Indian Mountaineering Foundation for twenty-two long years while he was the Defence Secretary and India's Ambassador to Nepal. In fact, it was HC Sarin who had organised my rehabilitation in Stoke Mandeville Hospital. He fulfilled his commitment given to Dr Walsh, Director Stoke Mandeville Hospital that he would help me find a job, because as per the prevalent rules I could no longer serve in the Army.

Besides HC Sarin, Dr Kalyan Singh Sachdev, Dr AK Mukherjee, Air Marshal AS Chahal, Gen AM Sethna, Vikram Kapur, GC Baweja and the Arch Bishops Angella Fernandez and Vincent M Concessao supported my endeavour from the inception to the fulfilment stage. All these great individuals helped me with an utterly selfless and missionary zeal in their respective fields of expertise and remained involved in all multifarious activities with utmost devotion and dedication, as board members of the hospital.

My relentless efforts resulted in obtaining the formal sanction of the Ministry of Health for applying for allocation of land by the DDA. We appointed Joseph Allenstein as the Architect and based on his detailed plan, we managed to get fifteen acres of land in Vasant Kunj, allocated to the Indian Spinal Injuries Centre in August 1985. Manjit Singh and I planted over 3000 saplings at our residences as a nursery for the subsequent landscaping of the proposed building. 11.02 acres of litigation free land was taken over by the ISIC on10th November 1986 at Vasant Kunj.

For preparing a detailed architecture plan, Joseph Allenstein recommended Gautam Shah, who was a practising architect in the USA and hoping to come to India. In order to have a clear understanding of the nature of the project particularly suitable to persons with disabilities I took Gautam Shah to visit almost ten centres in USA but the designs made were not acceptable to us. So finally we decided upon the age-old Indian house design which is also followed in all the houses in Central Asia. First you lay out a courtyard and then build everything around that. We followed the same principle. The advantage of this design is that every room is extremely well lit with sunlight from morning till evening.

Gautam Shah prepared a detailed plan of the Hospital and made the presentation of the same to the Board Members, who appreciated the design. On 30th March 1989, the Prime Minister Rajiv Gandhi laid the foundation stone of the Indian Spinal Injuries Centre. The Foundation stone laying ceremony was attended by Sen. G. Bonalumi, Minister of State for Foreign Affairs of Italy Smt Rajendra Kumari Bajpai, Minister of State for Welfare, Government of India, and Romesh Bhandari, Lt Governor of Delhi. In his inauguration speech Rajiv Gandhi, highlighted the fact that few injuries inflict such pain and suffering as those of the spine and complimented the Indian Spinal Injuries Centre for focusing attention on the treatment of spinal injuries. The Architect made the presentation of the plan through the model to the Prime Minister. Rajiv Gandhi had spent a great deal of time in examining the model of the centre during the foundation stone laying ceremony.

Regarding funds I felt that the corporate houses would be one option to raise funds. Another option would be various types of grants from the government for a project of this nature. My efforts to involve corporate and industrial houses in donating funds did not yield any result. However, in some areas we were lucky to have a good breakthrough with the help of friends like Virendra, Sergio and my brother Somi for funding from Italy and my visit to Rome where I was invited to give a talk on adventure tourism. It was sponsored by Air India. The possible funding from Italy would be through the Department of Co-operation in the Ministry of Foreign Affairs. The file for approving the Italian grant was however stuck in the Italian Government offices. Fortunately during that period the Italian Prime Minister was visiting India and with a great deal of effort I managed to get an appointment to meet him. It was during this one minute meeting of mine with the Italian Prime Minister, Giulio Andreotti, while he was leaving for

ICICI Bank

Breezy

the airport, that he told me that he fully understood my project and asked me to meet him in Rome in the next fifteen days where he would have the concerned officials and give his final decision. I left for Rome and took the help of Sergio Scapagnini and met the Prime Minister, who was extremely kind and announced his decision that ten million dollars would be sanctioned as a co-operation project for the ISIC – this was the largest co-operation project for any country given by the Government of Italy. For me it was a matter of great joy as by then I had experienced how difficult it was to raise funds for projects such as ours.

The construction plan of ISIC catered for a 150-bed hospital with the housing area confined to less than one-third of the total area. ISIC was to have fifty beds for spinal injury patients and the rest for neuro, urology, plastic surgery and orthopaedic patients. An auditorium with a seating capacity of 250, sports/recreation complex, solar heated hydrotherapy pool and a conference room with seating capacity of sixty were included in the construction plan.

PGS. 270-271: A panoramic view of ISIC

FACING PAGE: Author and Don Verze, president, AISPO and Chairman, San Raffaele Hospital, Italy

Bishan Singh Bedi, legendary cricketer and author at the ISIC Sports Day, 2009

For construction of the building, I managed to solicit a contribution of ₹ 2.5 crores from the Welfare Ministry, the National Committee for Forty Years of Independence and ₹ 25 lakhs as an advance from the Lottery Fund from the Lt Governor of Delhi. I also managed to obtain the clearance of Delhi Urban Arts Commission for the conceptual design of ISIC.

Free OPD consultations were started in December 1991 for poor patients. The President of AISPO & San Raffaele Hospital, Don Verze visited ISIC from 16th to 18th November 1992. At this stage I was also able to obtain an interest-free loan of rupees three crores from the National Defence Fund of the Ministry of Defence for construction work.

Doctor members of the board of Directors and myself, made concerted efforts to persuade eminent orthopaedics and spine surgeons to become part of the ISIC medical team. We also scouted for a team of young enthusiastic spine specialists who wished to enhance their specialisation in the field of spinal injuries. This initiative resulted in Dr HS Chhabra, our present Chief of Spine and the Medial Director joining our medical team. Today he is a well-known name in spine surgeries not only in India but worldwide. Likewise, we recruited a most enterprising, competent and dedicated Physiotherapist, Chitra Kataria who now heads our internationally recognised Rehabilitation Centre and the Institute of Rehabilitation Sciences.

In October 1994, we set up a committee to evolve Medical & Rehabilitation policy of the ISIC under the chairmanship of Dr AK Mukherjee, who later became Director General and board member of the ISIC. Dr Mukherjee apart from being the Director General Health Services, Government of India, had held important positions such as Medical Advisor to World Health Organization (WHO) and Chairman, Rehabilitation Co-ordination, India.

On 18th May 1995 I was asked to assume the charge of Chairman of ISIC as HC Sarin wanted to be relieved of his responsibilities. Soon after my taking over as the Chairman of ISIC, we organised

Atal Bihari Vajpayee, former Prime Minister of India and author

a Training Workshop under the aegis of International Medical Society of Paraplegia in October 1995. Sixty-five participants from eleven countries attended this workshop. In December1997, Mrs Vatsala Khurana and Mrs Bholi Ahluwalia were nominated to the General Body and the Board of ISIC.

Balwant Singh Ramoowalia, Union Minister of Welfare inaugurated the Intensive Care Unit of ISIC on 7 May 1997. US Ambassador HE Richard F Celiste presided over a seminar held at ISIC on 23 March 1998. We had managed to obtain government sanction for completing the remaining construction and government sponsorship of thirty beds for the poor.

On 1 Aug 2000, Dr CP Thakur, Minister for Health, Government of India, inaugurated the ISIC-Escorts Heart Command Centre and Research Unit. International Spine and Spinal Injuries Conference (ISSICON) was held at ISIC from 27-

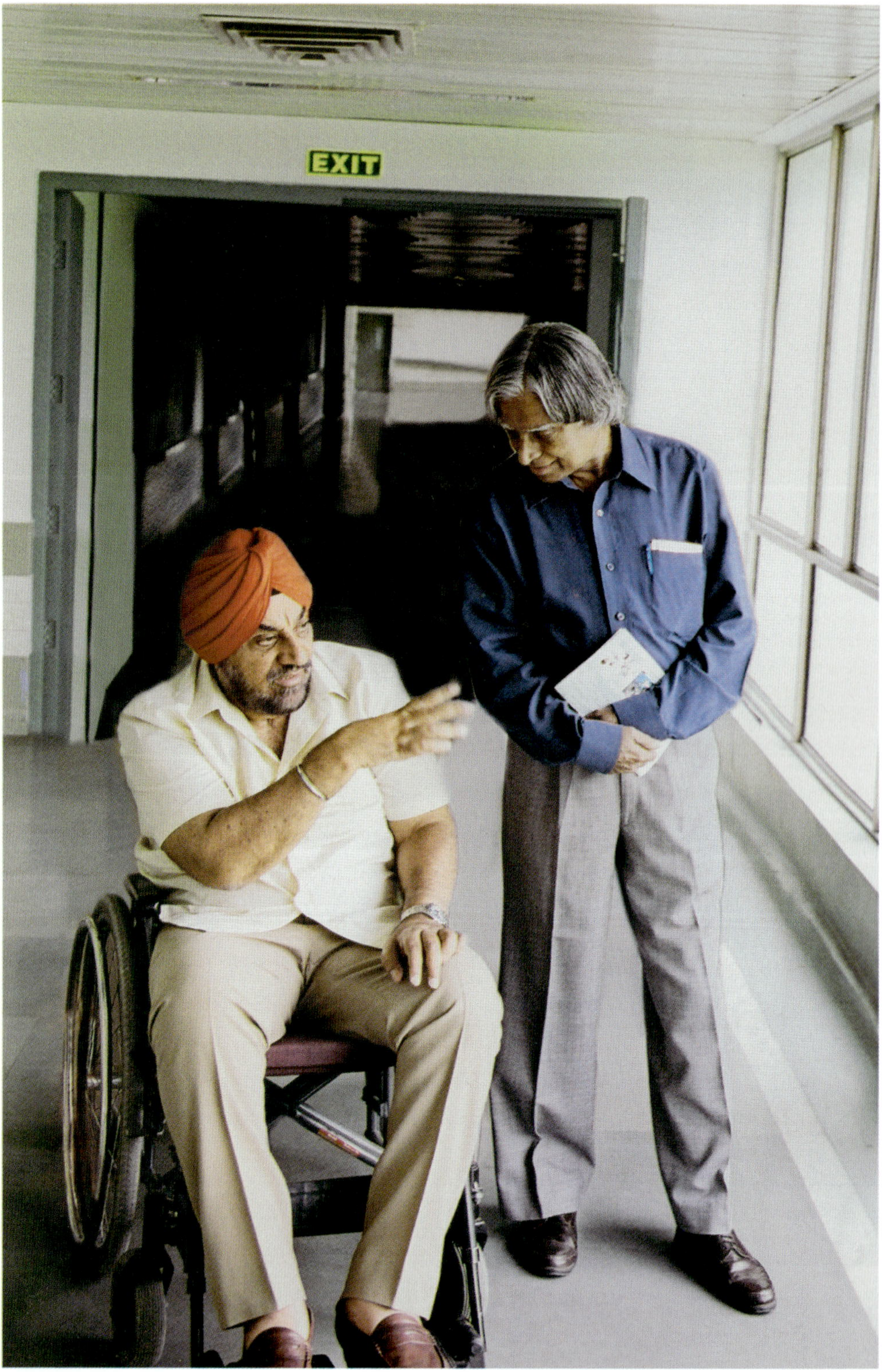
EXIT

29 October 2000, during which six eminent specialists from US and Europe gave presentations.

The main complex of ISIC was inaugurated by Lamberto Dini, Minister of External Affairs, Italy on 12 November 2000. New facilities like the Blood Storage Centre, Emergency Services, Urology, ISIC Door Step Health Clinic, Neurology and Plastic Surgery were started in 2002-2003 and Solar Heating System for the Hydrotherapy pool was installed. An International Spine and Spinal Injuries Conference was organised by ISIC in November 2002. I along with Dr HS Chhabra made a presentation in Naples, Italy in August 2003 to highlight the substantial impact the Indo-Italian cooperation had made in the hitherto neglected area of spinal injuries. This was followed by a similar presentation made in Beijing from 15-20 October 2003. In October 2004, I attended the International Spinal Cord Society's Annual International

FACING PAGE: Dr APJ Abdul Kalam, former President of India and author

Interacting with a patient at the Rehab department of ISIC

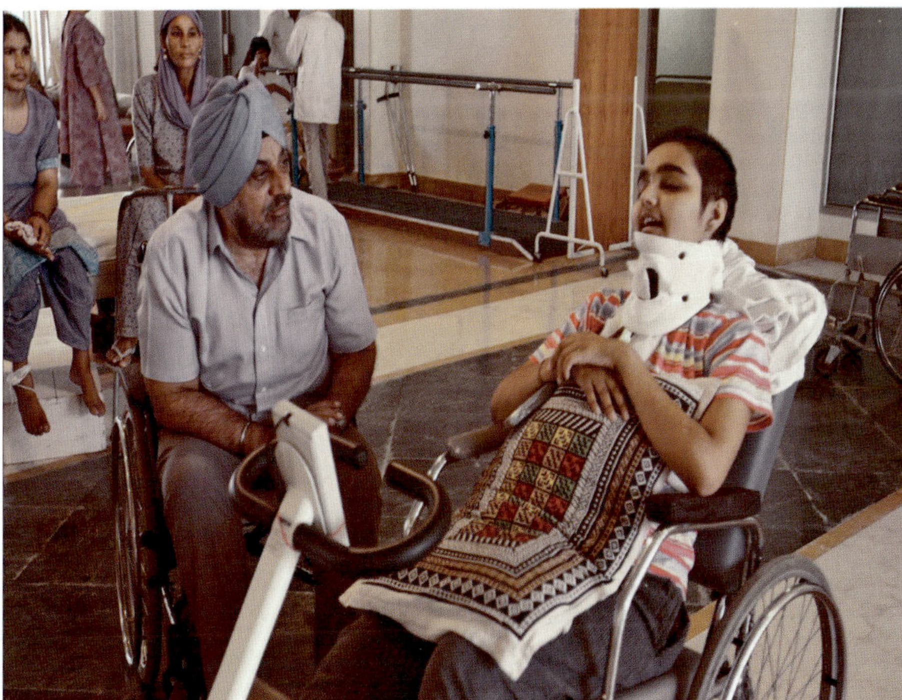

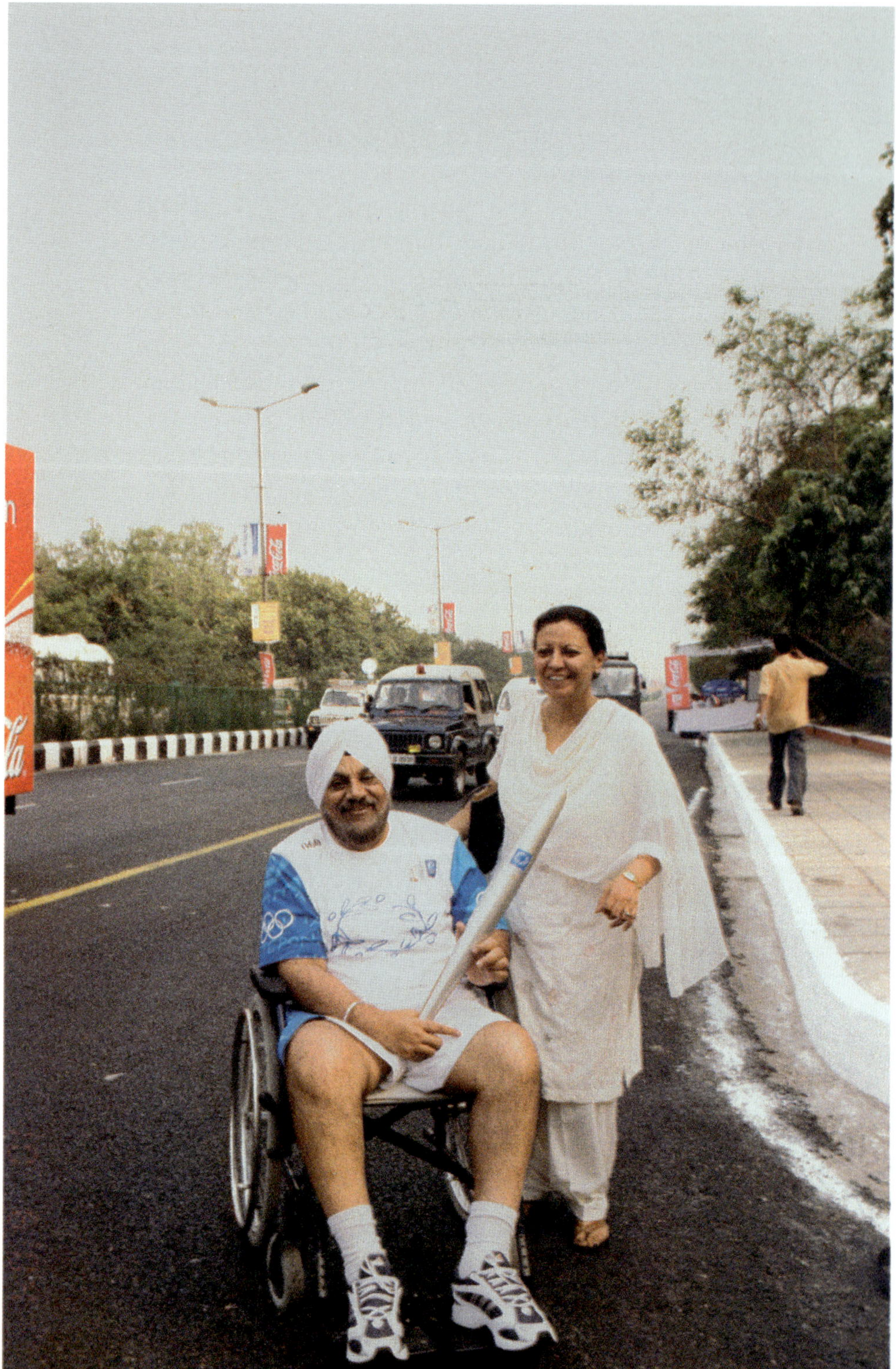

Conference at Athens, Greece and managed to get the ISIC bid to hold ISSICON 2010, accepted.

In 2004 ISIC Institute of Rehabilitation Sciences started under the IP University affiliation where we offer Masters Degree programs like MPT Sports, MPT Neurology, MPT Musculo-Skeletal, MPT Cardio-Pulmonary, MPT Neurology. It is also the first institute in the country to start Masters in Prosthetics and Orthotics.

My wife, Bholi, has over the years, rendered unstinting support and dedicated herself to the fulfilment of my dream project. She has been my pillar of strength in giving a concrete shape to my dream and vision. She has made an invaluable contribution in conceptualising the interiors of the building. It is largely her penchant for an elegant, sober décor and her sharp eye for detail that has given ISIC a most enviable ambience. The floor, walls, roofs, doors and windows have all been designed and furnished with Bholi's painstaking efforts. Her involvement in designing uniforms for the staff, along with her designer friend Hashi Ghosh, the running of the hospital shop, 'Namche Bazar' – named after Namche Bazar located on the way to Mt. Everest in the Solo Khumbu Region, all bear testimony to the devotion and dedication with which Bholi continues to oversee the functioning of these vital services along with her team of workers. The profits generated in Namche Bazar are utilised for the treatment of poor patients. This role is also being performed by Bholi in her capacity as Chairperson of the ISIC Welfare Committee. Our daughter, Sugandh, who has done her Masters in Health & Social Sciences from Oxford, UK, has dedicated herself to further refining the services of ISIC and to focus her expertise in evolving strategies for improving the quality of hospital services.

The philosophy of ISIC is to reach out to the lives of spinal-injured patients, both urban and rural, and bring a new dimension into their lives. ISIC believes that successful rehabilitation involves not only the body, but also the mind and spirit i.e. it must involve

FACING PAGE: Bholi and author as Torch Bearer for India, Greece Olympics, 2004

PG. 280 ABOVE: Members of 1965 Everest Expedition with Prime Minister Narendra Modi

PG. 280 BELOW: Celebrating 50 glorious years of the First Indian Ascent of Mt. Everest at Indian Spinal Injuries Centre. (L to R) Dr HS Chhabra, Col HS Chauhan, Mrs Chauhan, Mrs Mridula Kumar, Major HPS Ahluwalia, Mrs Mulk Raj, Col N Kumar, Mrs Bholi Ahluwalia, Mrs Pushpa Kohli, Capt MS Kohli, Brig. Mulk Raj and Dr A K Mukjerjee

PG. 281 ABOVE: HH Sri Sri Ravi Shankar and author

PG. 281 BELOW: His Holiness the Dalai Lama and author

CELEBRATING
50
GLORIOUS YEARS OF THE
FIRST INDIAN ASCENT
OF MT. EVEREST
MAY 29, 1965

physical, psychological as well as sociological rehabilitation. We have paid attention to every detail – the view from every room and ward, the noise pollution levels, the creation of completely barrier-free and wheelchair-friendly facilities. Our aim is to restore mobility and encourage patients to look after their own needs and live as independently as possible.

Today, the Indian Spinal Injuries Centre is a landmark healthcare institute at par with the best in the world. We provide

Playing Table Tennis

Somi with family (L to R) Sonu, Gina, Dolly, Arhaan, Somi, Tanya and Raj

comprehensive medical care of the highest international standards and conduct some of the most advanced surgeries performed anywhere in the world. We have revolutionised the diagnosis, treatment and rehabilitation of patients with spinal cord injuries. For me, personally, it is the fulfilment of a long-cherished dream.

The Summit Within

To the question 'Why climb a mountain?' the famous mountaineer Mallory is supposed to have answered, 'Because it is there.' A good answer, but I wonder if it is quite complete or wholly satisfying.

The physical conquest of a mountain is, I think, only part of the achievement. More than that it is a sense of fulfilment, of satisfaction of that deep urge within every man which impels him to rise above his environment. It is part of the eternal quest for adventure, the passion for exploring the hazardous and the unknown. The experience is not only physical, it is also intensely emotional and even spiritual.

American mountaineers have called climbing 'nine-tenths hell, one-tenth beauty.' I am inclined to endorse this graphic description. Consider a typical climb, especially at the higher altitudes and within a short distance of the summit. You are sharing a rope with another climber. You firm in and he cuts the steps ahead in hard ice. Then he belays you and you proceed inching your way up. The climb is grim. You strain every nerve as you take another step. I am reminded of an interesting episode about Norton, the famous mountaineer, while he was climbing Everest with Somervell. He recalled, 'I had to cross a patch of snow lying thinly over some sloping rocks. It was

FACING PAGE: Rongbuk Monastery, against the North Face of Mount Everest in the background

neither steep nor difficult, and not to be compared to the ground I had just left, yet suddenly I felt that I could not face it without help, and I shouted to Somervell to come and throw me the end of the rope. Here again I remember the difficulty I had in making my voice carry perhaps 100 yards. Somervell gave me the required aid, and I could see the surprise he felt at my needing it in such a place.'

Breathing is very hard and as you gasp for breath, you curse yourself inwardly and wonder why you ever undertook the ascent. These are moments when you feel like turning back and dwell on the sheer relief of going downhill. But almost at once you snap out of this momentary mood. There is something in you that does not let you give up the struggle. And you go on. Just another fifty feet, you think, or perhaps another hundred feet. The slope leads on and on and you ask yourself, 'Is there no end?' You look up at your partner and he looks at you, and each seems to draw inspiration from the other. You feel all is not lost yet and keep plodding on. And then, suddenly a shape emerges in dim outline which becomes clearer as you approach it. What joy to find yourself at last on the summit! Was it not worth all the effort and the agony of the climb?

Once on the top you look around you. Other silvery peaks appear through the clouds. If you are lucky, you may find the sun shining on them and turning them into so many jewelled necklaces around the mountain. Below you are vast valleys, sloping far away in the distance as far as the eye can reach. It is an uplifting, ennobling experience. Carried away by all the beauty and the glory of the panorama surrounding you, you bow down and make your obeisance to whichever god you worship.

I left on Everest a picture of Guru Nanak, and Rawat a picture of goddess Durga. Phu Dorji, who accompanied us, offered the mountain a relic of Buddha. Some years earlier Edmund Hillary buried a cross under a cairn in the snow. These offerings are not symbols of conquest but of trust and reverence. Climbing a mountain peak is loving it and constantly wondering if it will let you come nearer and closer. When at length you reach the peak, you are overwhelmed by a deep sense of joy and thankfulness. It is a joy which lasts a lifetime.

The experience changes you completely. The man who has been to the mountains is never the same again. He gains immensely from the mountains. He becomes conscious of his own smallness and loneliness in the immeasurable universe. As I come to the end of this narrative, much of which has been concerned with my mountaineering activities and my climb to the summit of Everest, I cannot help remarking about that other summit – the summit of the mind – no less formidable and none the easier to reach.

Each man carries within himself his own mountain, which he must climb to attain a fuller knowledge of himself. The mind has its mountains and cliffs, fearful, sheer, unfathomed. The physical act of climbing a mountain has a kinship with the ascent of that inward, spiritual mountain which every man has to climb sometime or the other. The kinship is shown most clearly from the effects. Whether the mountain you climb is physical or spiritual, the climb will change you. It will teach you much about yourself and about the world.

In my case the physical feat of scaling Everest was followed, soon after, by the supreme need to get over, as far as possible, the severe handicap of the injury I sustained in war. This involved an unusual effort at adjusting myself to the new conditions of life imposed by my disability. I am thankful that the effort has been largely successful and, consistent with my physical state, I am both active and contented.

I venture to think that my experience as an Everest climber has provided much of the inspiration to face life's ordeals resolutely. If climbing the mountain was a worthwhile achievement, would it be an exaggeration to describe the conquest of the 'internal' summit as something higher than Everest?

100

Glossary

Avalanche	A large mass of snow and ice sliding down a mountain slope.
Belay	Securing of a rope by hitching it over a projection or passing it around the body.
Chimney	A steep, narrow cleft in a wall of rock or ice.
Col	A pass or the low point of a ridge.
Cornice	A projecting mass of snow or ice on the leeward side of a ridge.
Couloir	A gulley, usually in an up-and-down direction.
Crampons	Steel frames with projecting spikes that are attached to the soles of boots to prevent slipping on steep snow or ice.
Crevasse	a deep crevice or fissure in a glacier, caused by its downward movement.
Cwm	a hollow in a mountain; a deep ravine.
Eiderdown	Small soft feathers from the breast of the eider duck, a northern species used for quilting clothing.
Fixed rope	Rope attached to a mountainside, or against that which is used to tie climbers together.
Glacier	'River' of ice formed by accumulation or consolidation of snow.
Haversack	A canvas bag with a shoulder-strap to carry up to 20 lbs or so.
Ice-axe	A mountaineer's axe mainly used for cutting steps on ice and as a stout walking stick for keeping balance on snow and ice.

FACING PAGE: Admiring the exteriors of the caves in Dunhuang

Ice-fall	The steepest section of a glacier, usually taking the form of a widely jumbled mass of ice.
Karabiner (also Carbiner)	A metal snap ring, usually used in conjunction with a piton, through which a rope many be passed for greater security during difficult climbing.
Massif	A compact range or group of mountain heights.
Mitten	A kind of glove with thumb but no fingers. It is of three types, viz., eiderdown, woollen and wind-proof.
Moraine	Rock and debris carried down by a glacier, distinguished by their position as medial, lateral and terminal.
Nylon rope	A soft rope made of nylon material about three-fourths of an inch thick which has a breaking strength of about 3,000 lbs.
Piton	A metal spike designed to give support in steep climbing to hand, foot or rope. Pitons are made in varying sizes and shapes, some designed for use on ice, some for driving into cracks in rock.
Rappel	Roping down; the manoeuvre of letting oneself down a steep place by means of supplementary rope.
Rucksack	A bag slung by straps for both shoulders and resting on the back for carrying a climber's accessories.
Saddle	The low point of a ridge, a col.
Serac	A tower of ice, usually found on a glacier.
Sleeping bag	A type of quilt, very warm and light, filled with eiderdown or kapok material, fitted with a zip in the centre, joining the sides of the quilt.
Snow bridge	An arch of snow joining two sides of a crevasse.
Spur	Rib, or lateral projection of rock.
Traverse	The horizontal or diagonal crossing of a mountain-side; also the crossing of a peak or pass from one side to the other.